one bad day

by
steve rolston

book design by
keith wood with steve rolston

edited by
james lucas jones

Thanks to friends and family for their continued support. And much gratitude to J. Torres, Hubert Chan, and Sabina for helping get this thing done.

Published by Oni Press, Inc.
joe nozemack, publisher
jamie s. rich, editor in chief
ian shaughnessy, editorial intern

Oni Press, Inc.
6336 SE Milwaukie Ave, PMB 30
Portland, OR 97202

www.onipress.com
www.steverolston.com

First Edition: August 2003
ISBN 1929998-50-3

1 3 5 7 9 10 8 6 4 2

Printed in Canada

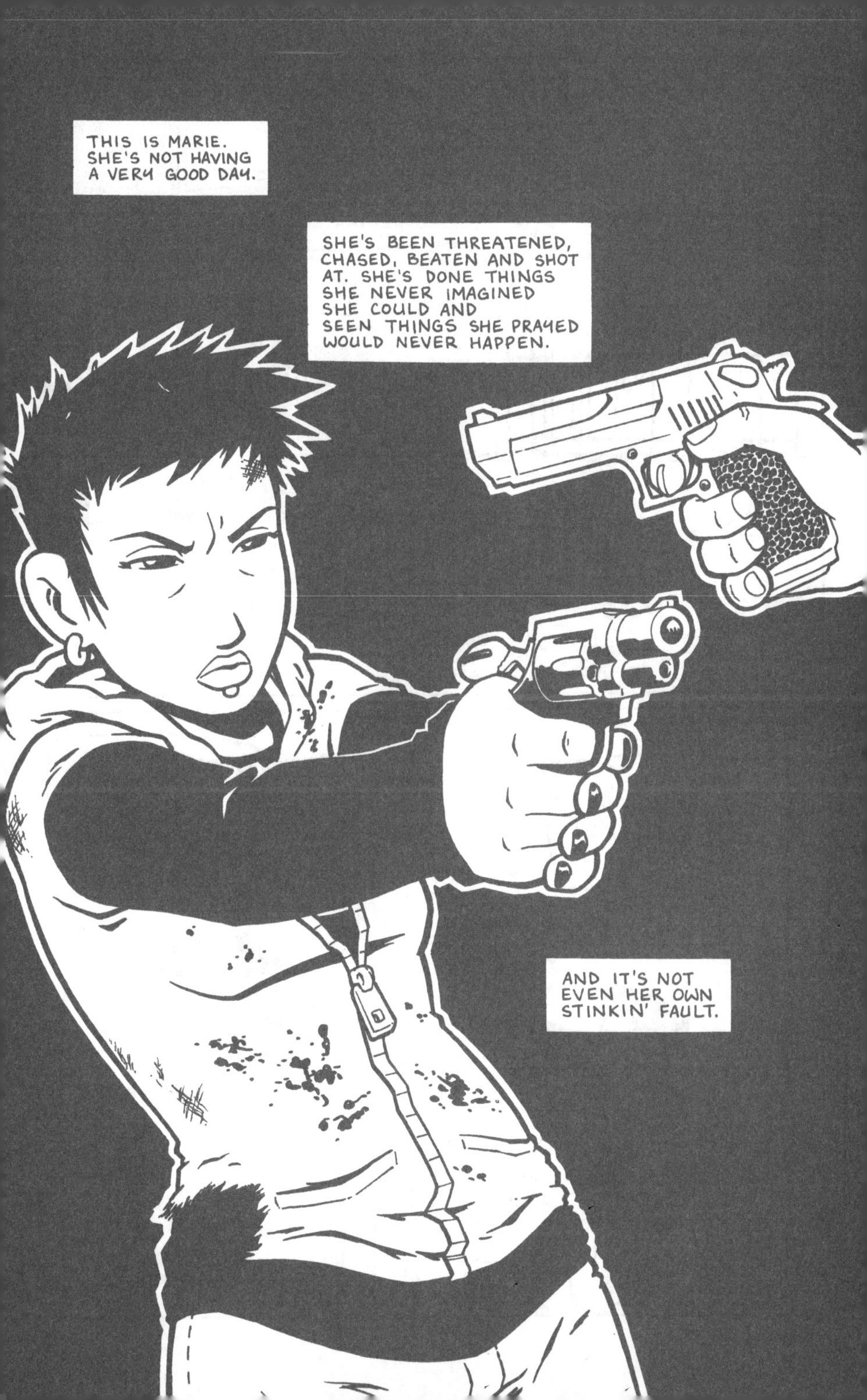
THIS IS MARIE.
SHE'S NOT HAVING
A VERY GOOD DAY.
SHE'S BEEN THREATENED,
CHASED, BEATEN AND SHOT
AT. SHE'S DONE THINGS
SHE NEVER IMAGINED
SHE COULD AND
SEEN THINGS SHE PRAYED
WOULD NEVER HAPPEN.
AND IT'S NOT
EVEN HER OWN
STINKIN' FAULT.

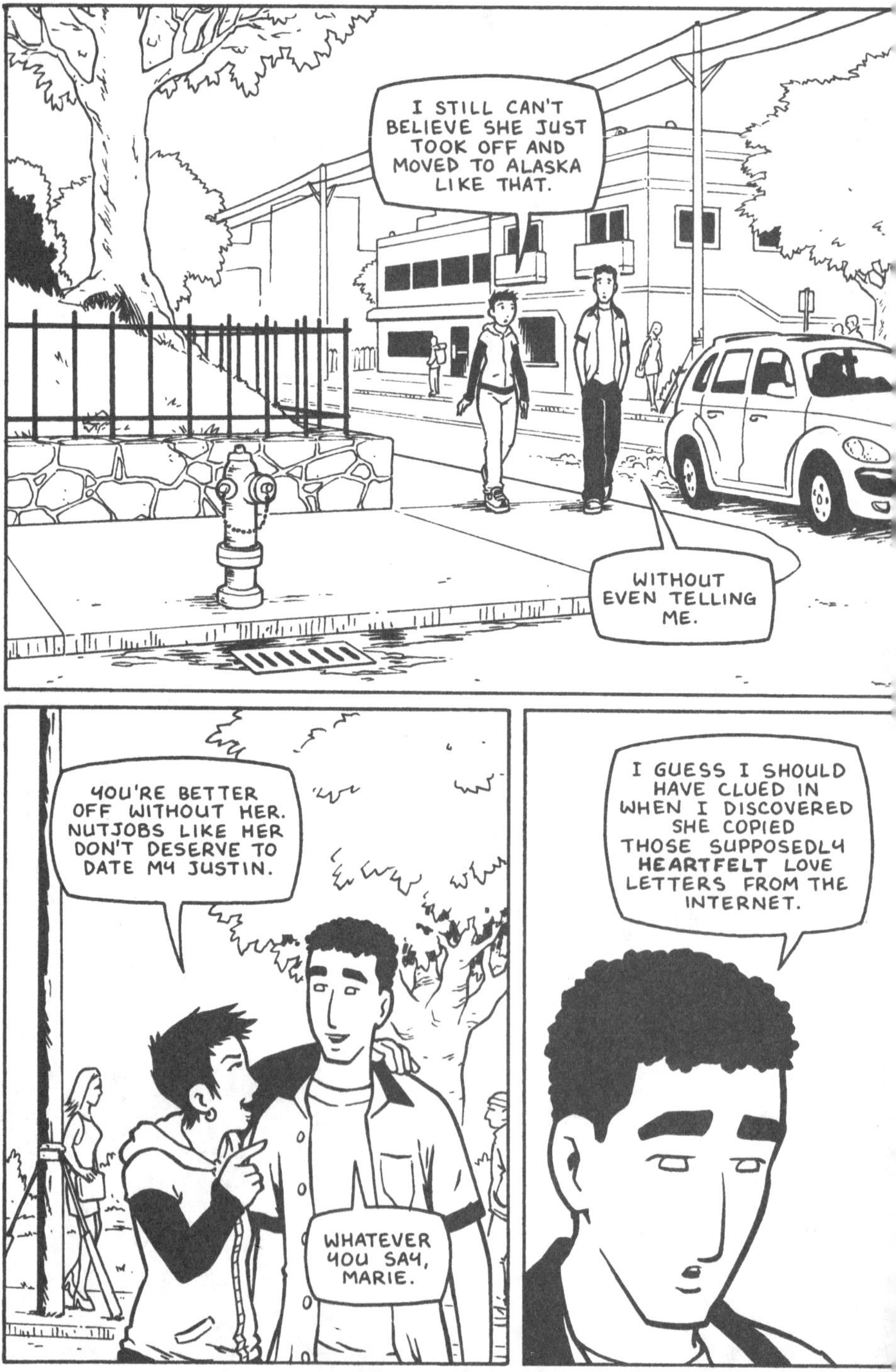
I STILL CAN'T BELIEVE SHE JUST TOOK OFF AND MOVED TO ALASKA LIKE THAT.
WITHOUT EVEN TELLING ME.
YOU'RE BETTER OFF WITHOUT HER. NUTJOBS LIKE HER DON'T DESERVE TO DATE MY JUSTIN.
WHATEVER YOU SAY, MARIE.
I GUESS I SHOULD HAVE CLUED IN WHEN I DISCOVERED SHE COPIED THOSE SUPPOSEDLY **HEARTFELT** LOVE LETTERS FROM THE INTERNET.

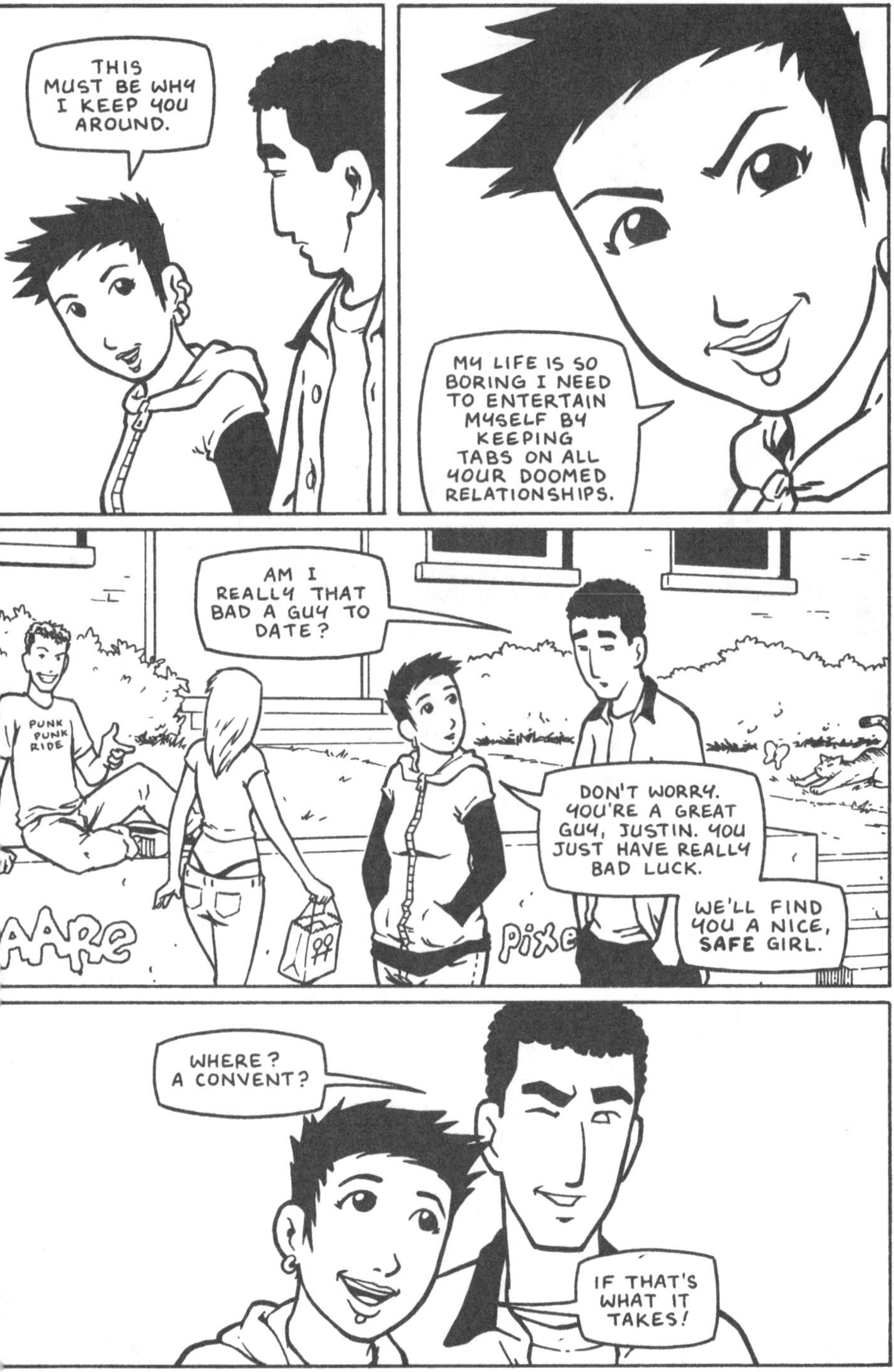
THIS MUST BE WHY I KEEP YOU AROUND.
MY LIFE IS SO BORING I NEED TO ENTERTAIN MYSELF BY KEEPING TABS ON ALL YOUR DOOMED RELATIONSHIPS.
AM I REALLY THAT BAD A GUY TO DATE?
PUNK PUNK RIDE
DON'T WORRY. YOU'RE A GREAT GUY, JUSTIN. YOU JUST HAVE REALLY BAD LUCK.
WE'LL FIND YOU A NICE, SAFE GIRL.
WHERE? A CONVENT?
IF THAT'S WHAT IT TAKES!

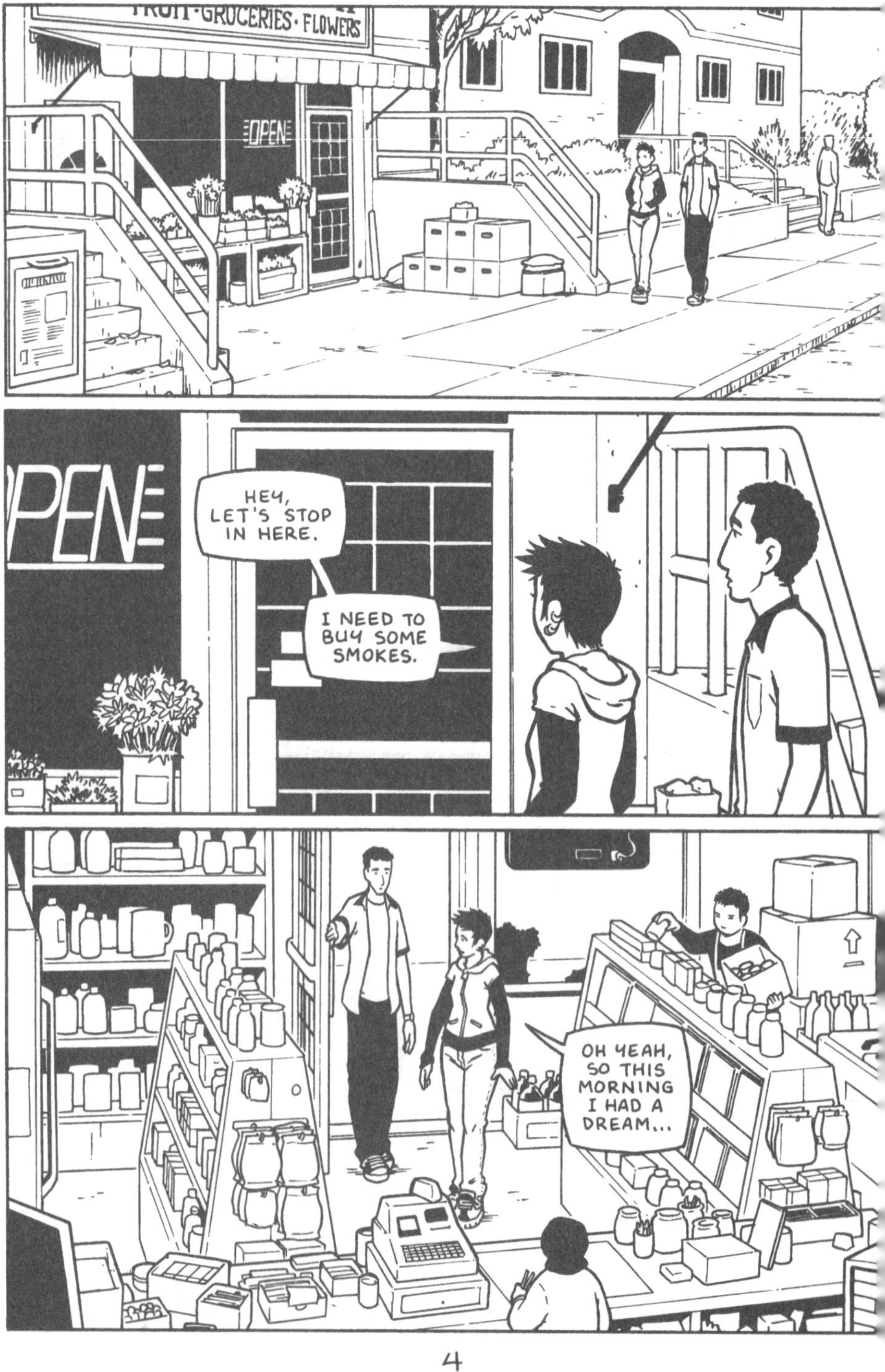
GROCERIES · FLOWERS
OPEN
HEY, LET'S STOP IN HERE.
I NEED TO BUY SOME SMOKES.
OH YEAH, SO THIS MORNING I HAD A DREAM...

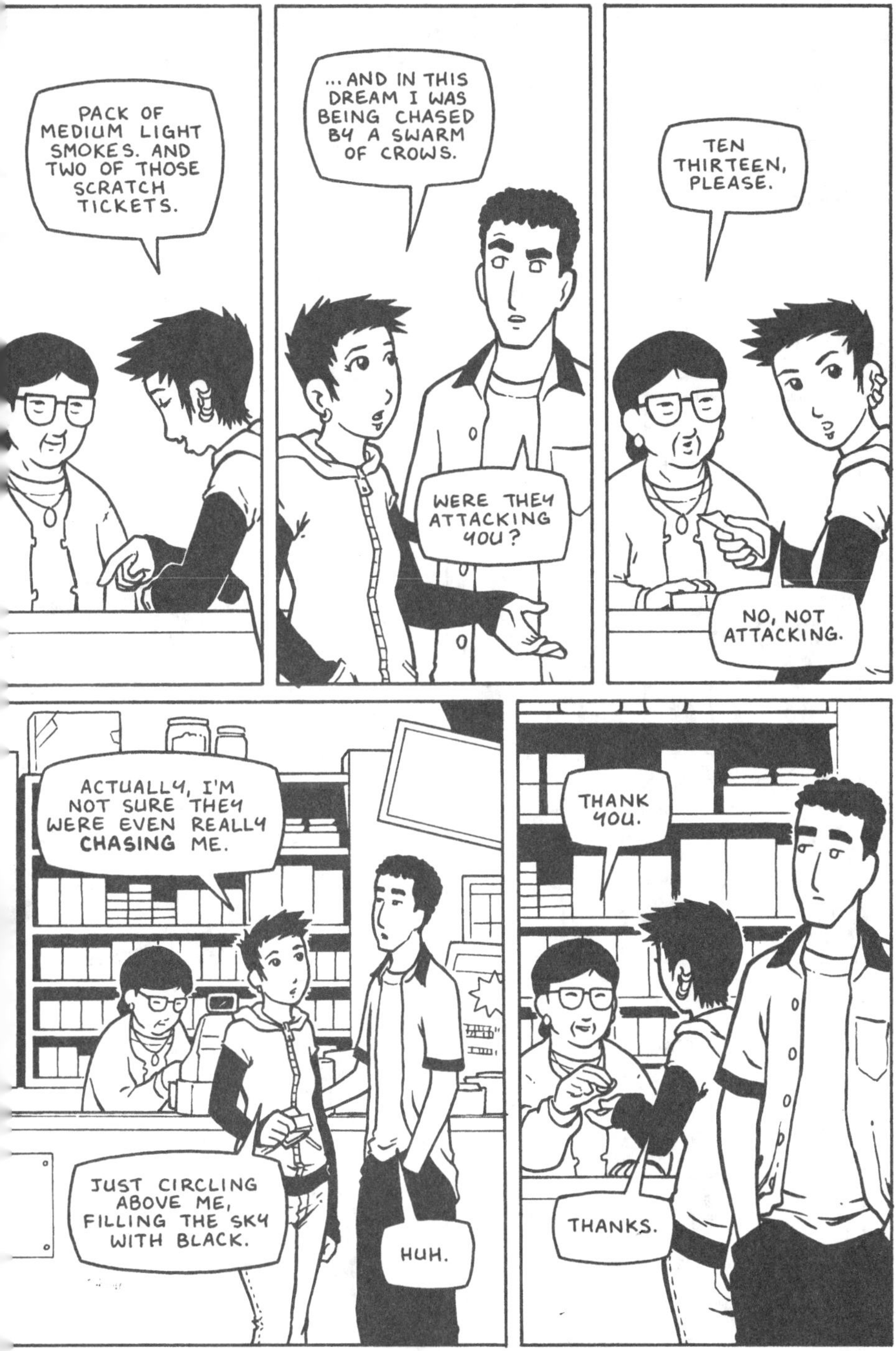
PACK OF MEDIUM LIGHT SMOKES. AND TWO OF THOSE SCRATCH TICKETS.
...AND IN THIS DREAM I WAS BEING CHASED BY A SWARM OF CROWS.
WERE THEY ATTACKING YOU?
TEN THIRTEEN, PLEASE.
NO, NOT ATTACKING.
ACTUALLY, I'M NOT SURE THEY WERE EVEN REALLY **CHASING** ME.
JUST CIRCLING ABOVE ME, FILLING THE SKY WITH BLACK.
HUH.
THANK YOU.
THANKS.

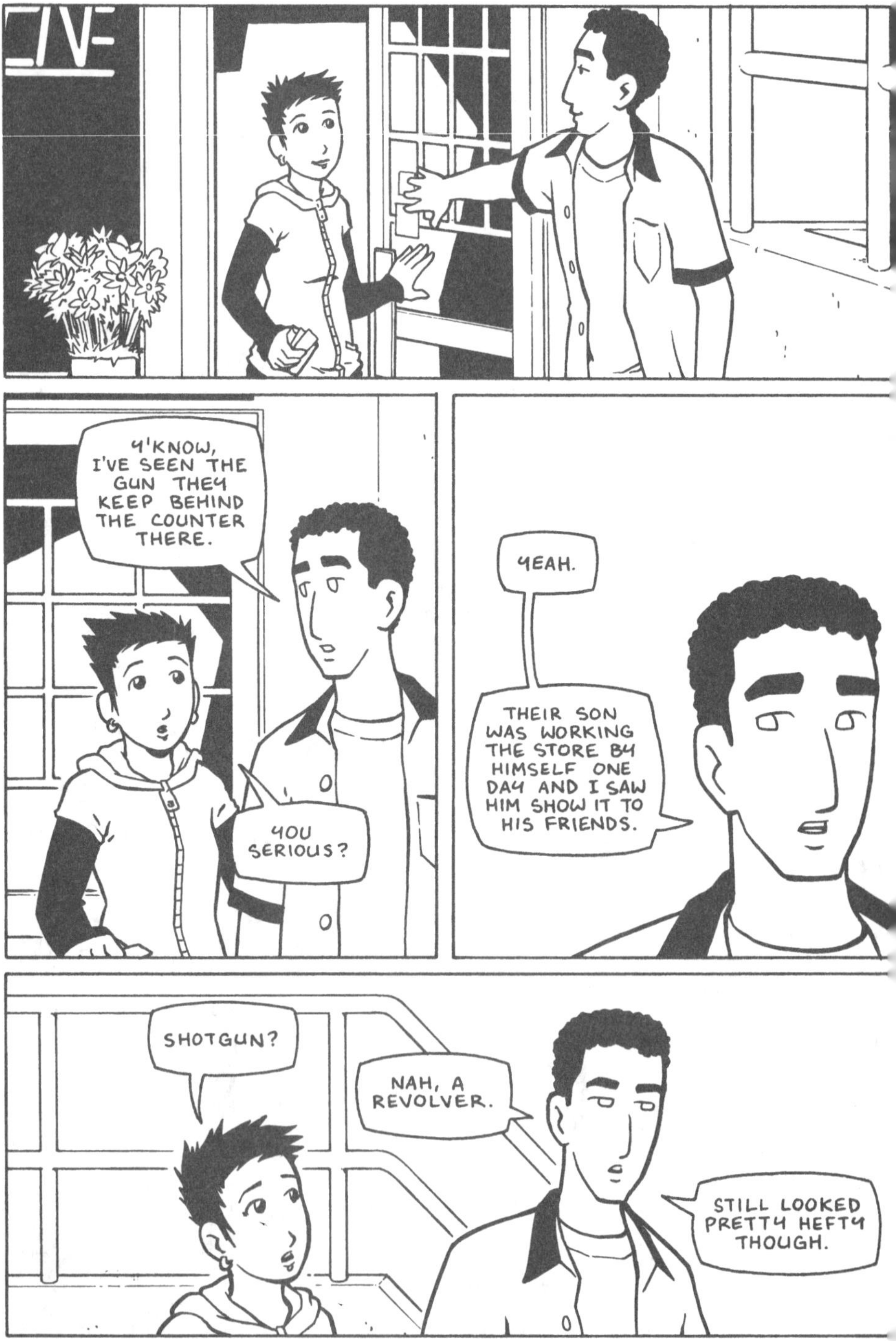
Y'KNOW, I'VE SEEN THE GUN THEY KEEP BEHIND THE COUNTER THERE.
YOU SERIOUS?
YEAH.
THEIR SON WAS WORKING THE STORE BY HIMSELF ONE DAY AND I SAW HIM SHOW IT TO HIS FRIENDS.
SHOTGUN?
NAH, A REVOLVER.
STILL LOOKED PRETTY HEFTY THOUGH.

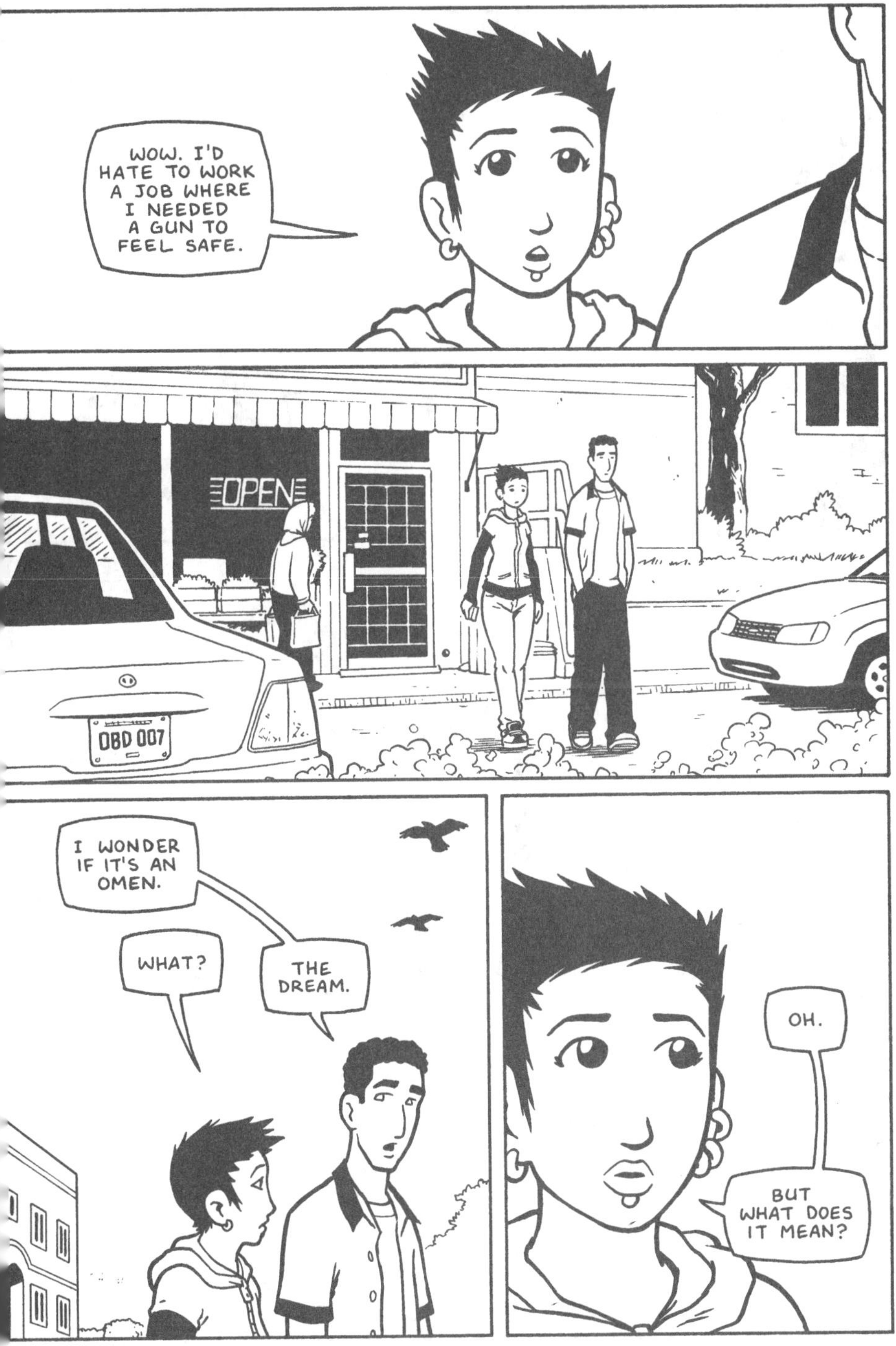
WOW. I'D HATE TO WORK A JOB WHERE I NEEDED A GUN TO FEEL SAFE.
OPEN
OBD 007
I WONDER IF IT'S AN OMEN.
WHAT?
THE DREAM.
OH.
BUT WHAT DOES IT MEAN?

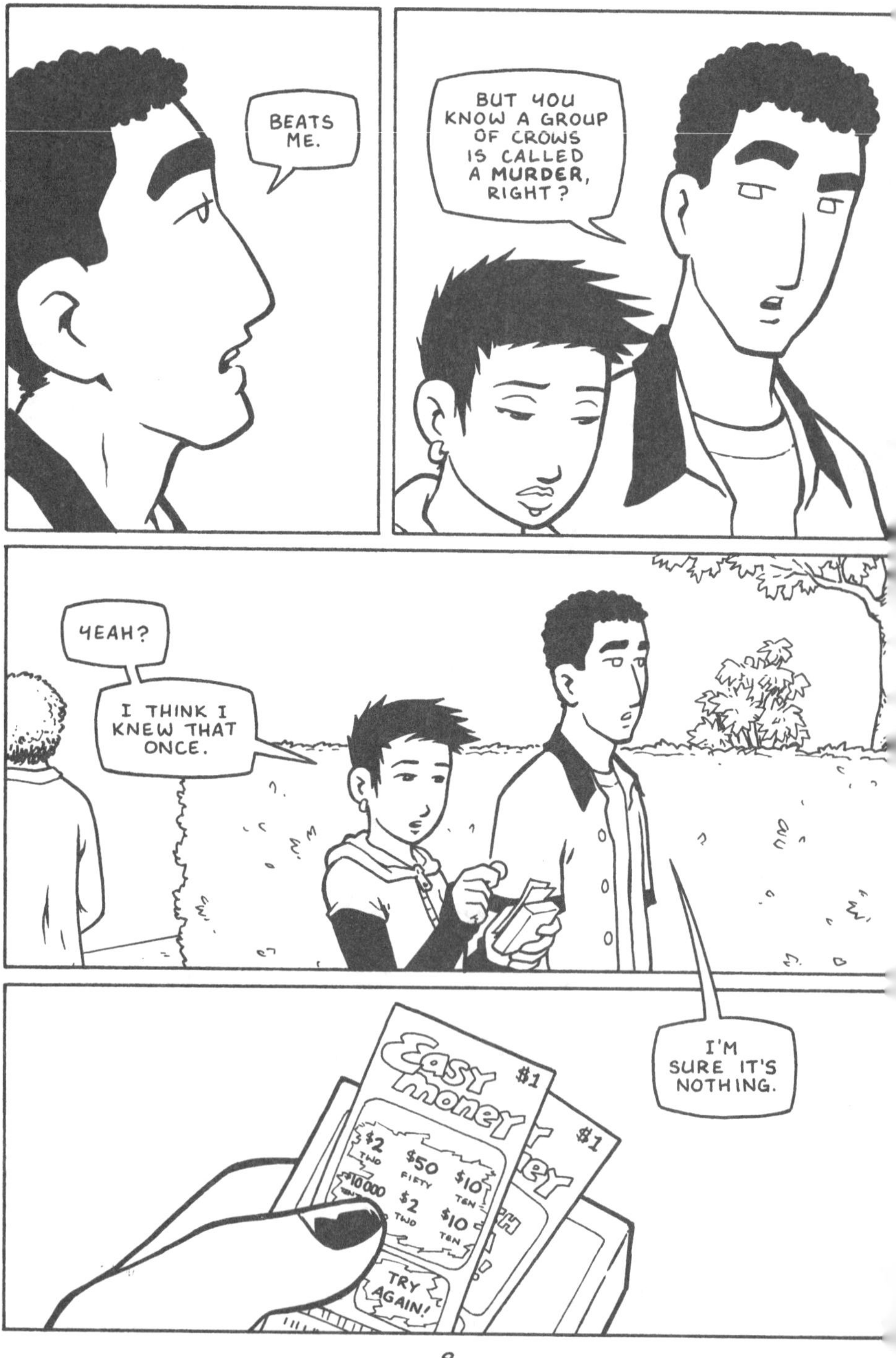
BEATS ME.
BUT YOU KNOW A GROUP OF CROWS IS CALLED A MURDER, RIGHT?
YEAH?
I THINK I KNEW THAT ONCE.
I'M SURE IT'S NOTHING.
Easy money
$1
$2 TWO
$50 FIFTY
$10 TEN
$2 TWO
$10 TEN
TRY AGAIN!

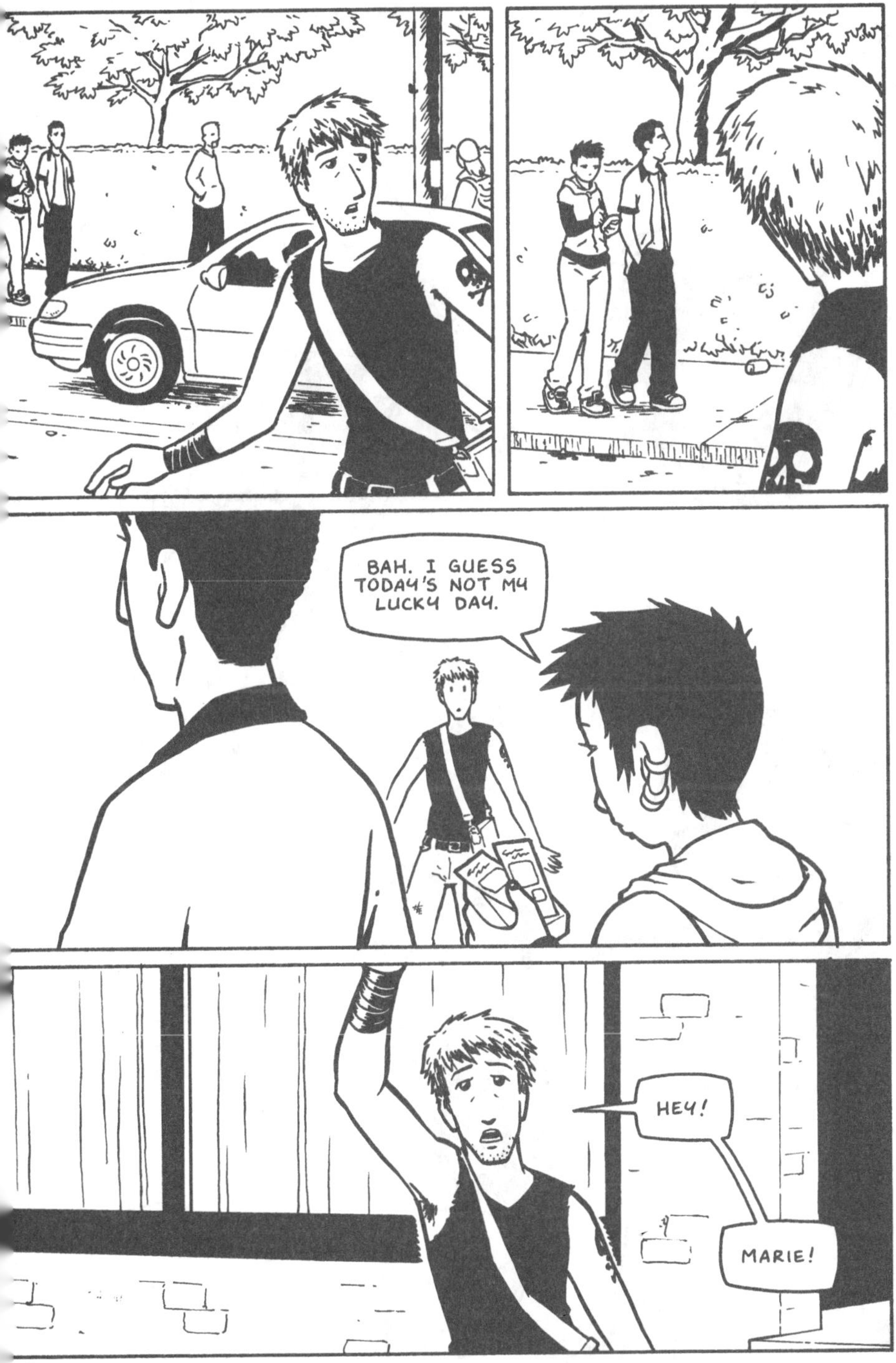
BAH. I GUESS TODAY'S NOT MY LUCKY DAY.
HEY!
MARIE!

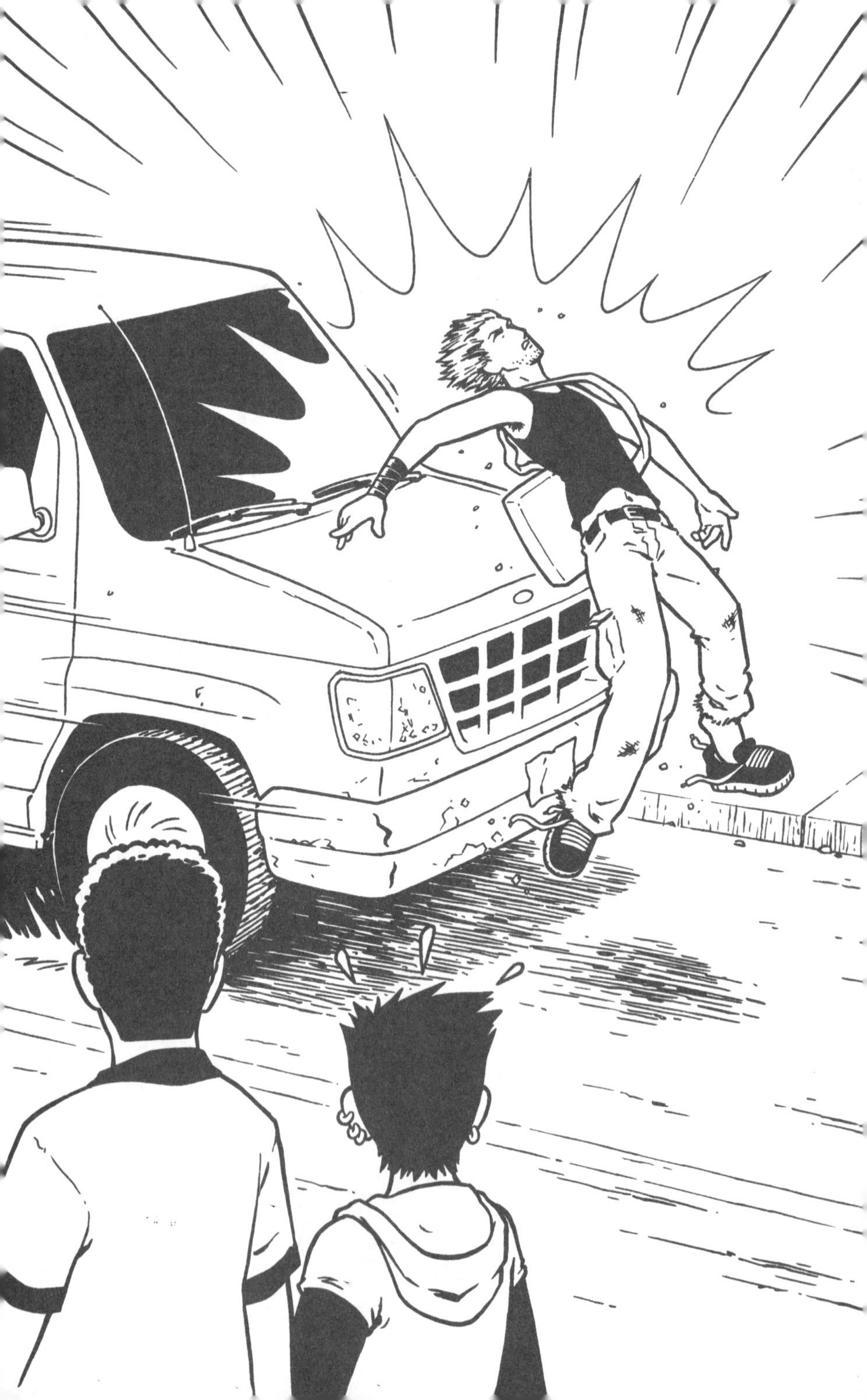

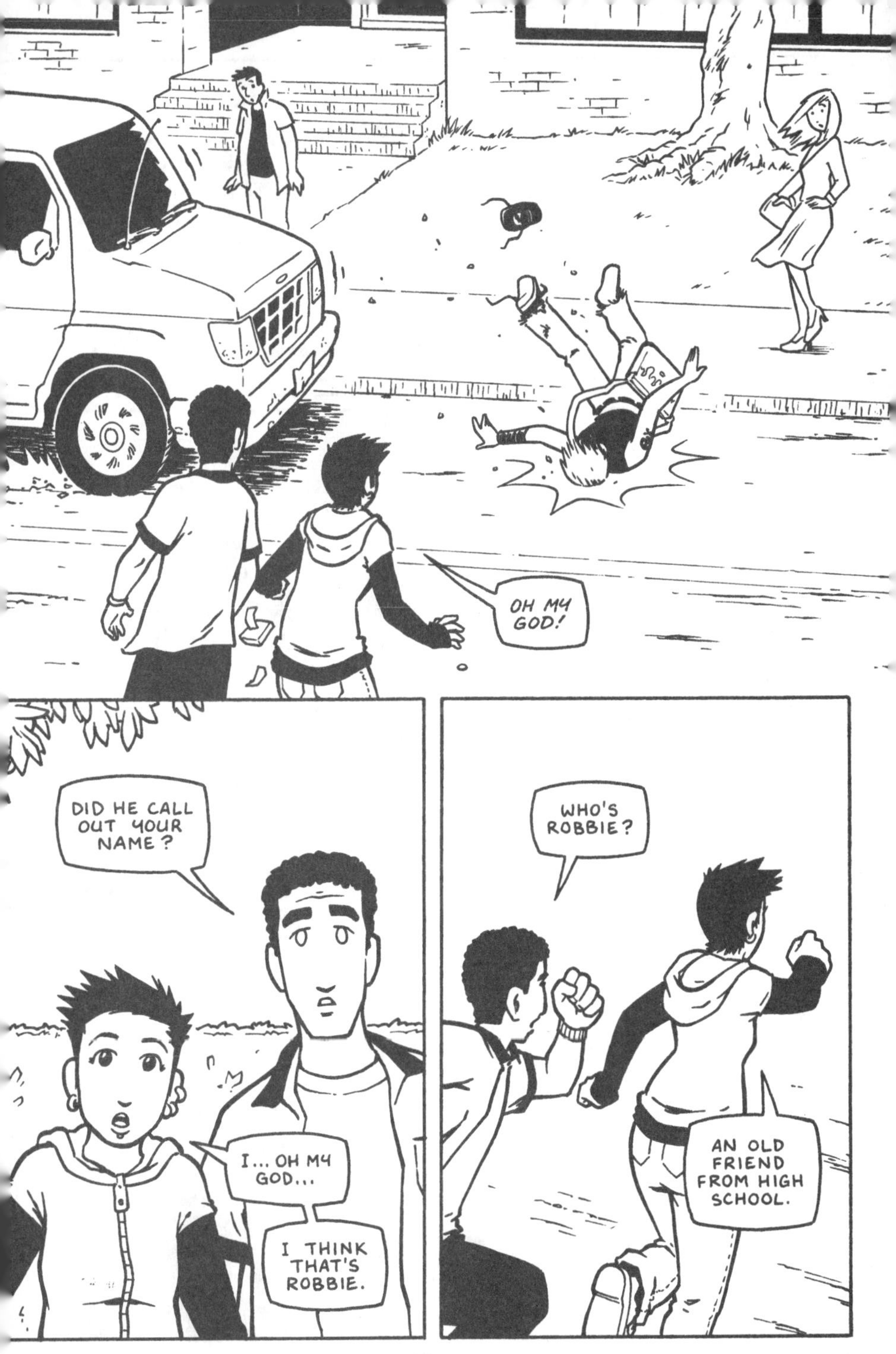
OH MY GOD!
DID HE CALL OUT YOUR NAME?
I... OH MY GOD...
I THINK THAT'S ROBBIE.
WHO'S ROBBIE?
AN OLD FRIEND FROM HIGH SCHOOL.

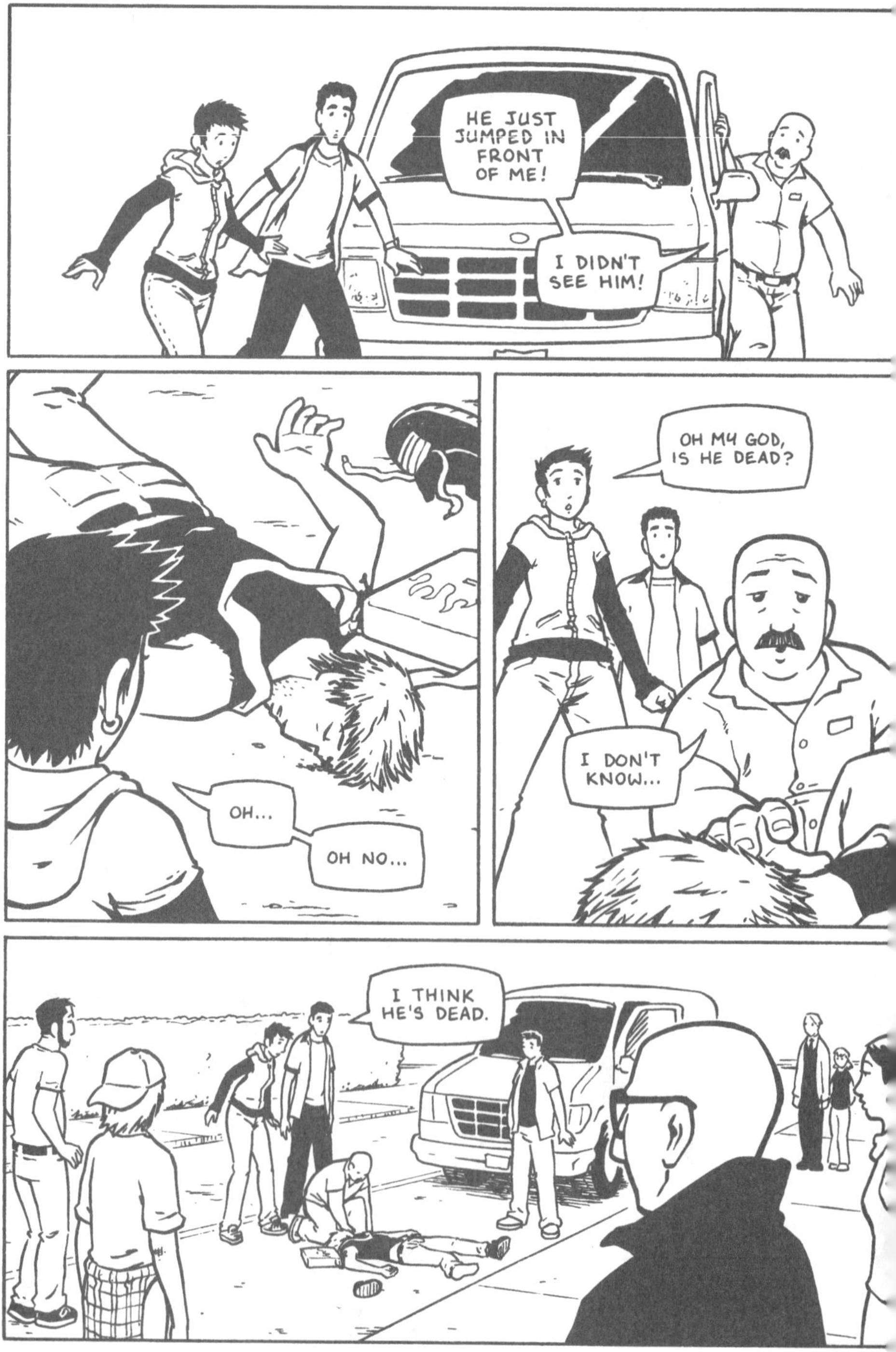
HE JUST JUMPED IN FRONT OF ME!
I DIDN'T SEE HIM!
OH...
OH NO...
OH MY GOD, IS HE DEAD?
I DON'T KNOW...
I THINK HE'S DEAD.

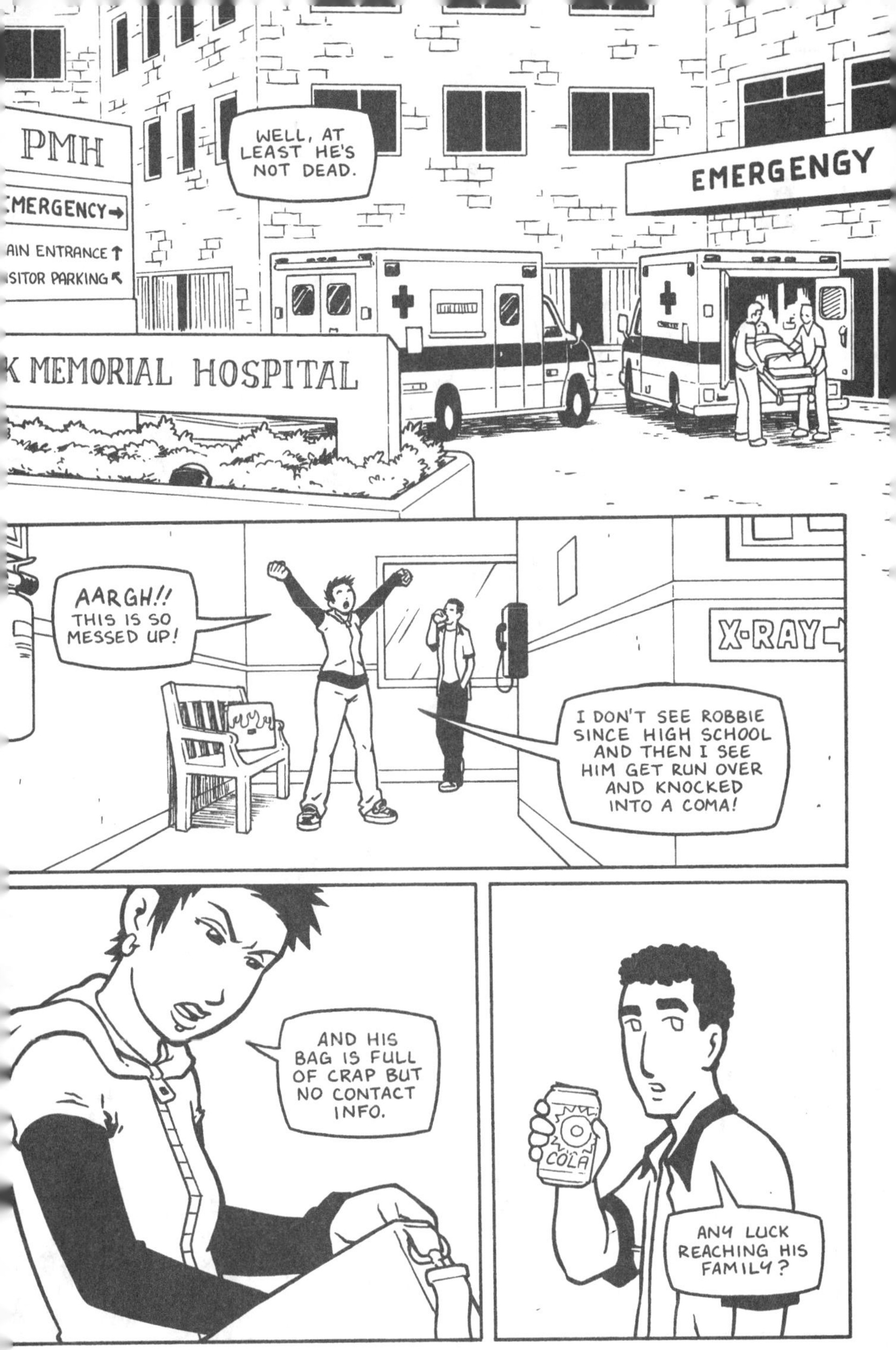
PMH
EMERGENCY
AIN ENTRANCE
SITOR PARKING
WELL, AT LEAST HE'S NOT DEAD.
EMERGENGY
K MEMORIAL HOSPITAL
AARGH!! THIS IS SO MESSED UP!
X-RAY
I DON'T SEE ROBBIE SINCE HIGH SCHOOL AND THEN I SEE HIM GET RUN OVER AND KNOCKED INTO A COMA!
AND HIS BAG IS FULL OF CRAP BUT NO CONTACT INFO.
COLA
ANY LUCK REACHING HIS FAMILY?

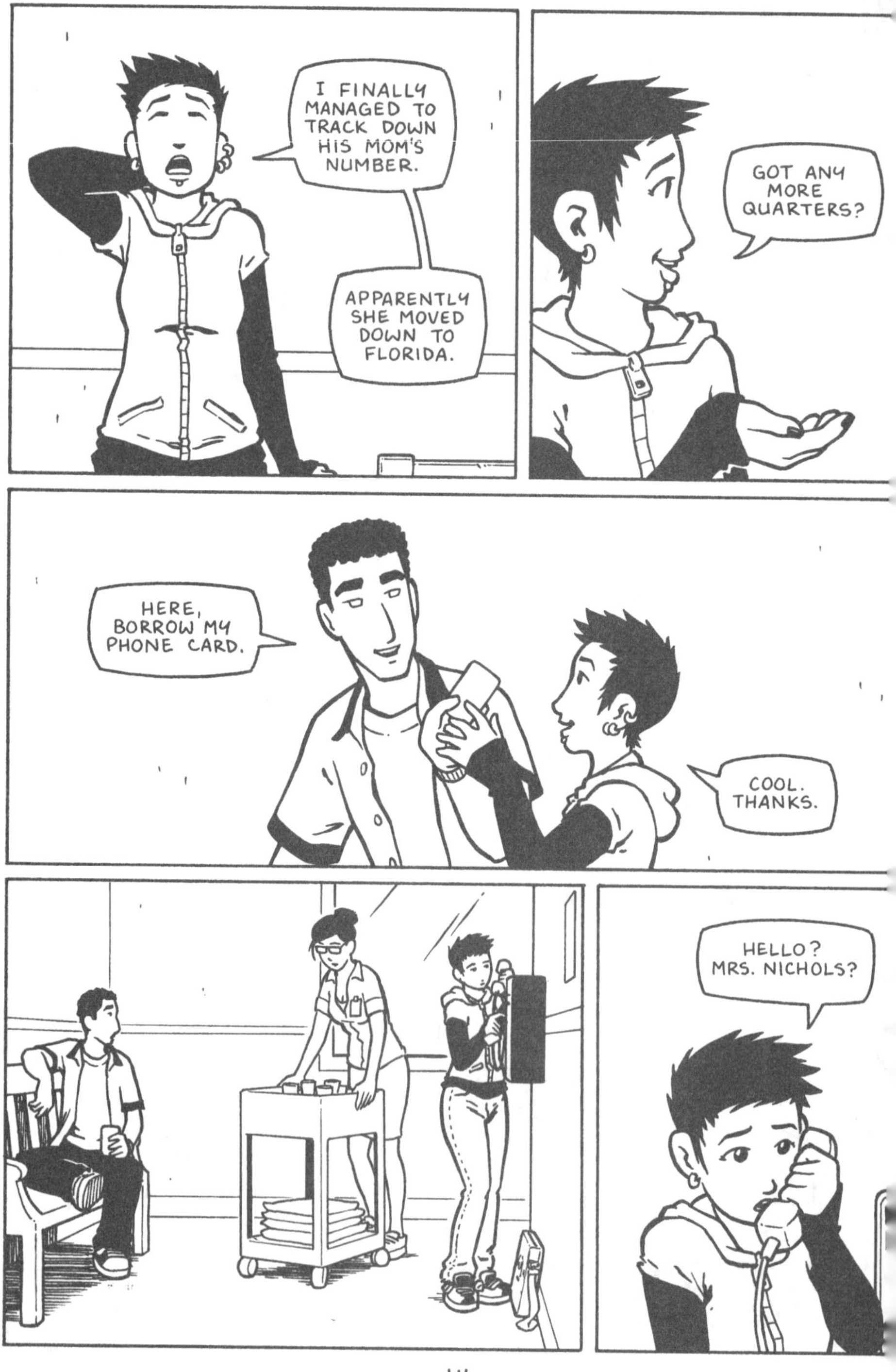
I FINALLY MANAGED TO TRACK DOWN HIS MOM'S NUMBER.
APPARENTLY SHE MOVED DOWN TO FLORIDA.
GOT ANY MORE QUARTERS?
HERE, BORROW MY PHONE CARD.
COOL. THANKS.
HELLO? MRS. NICHOLS?

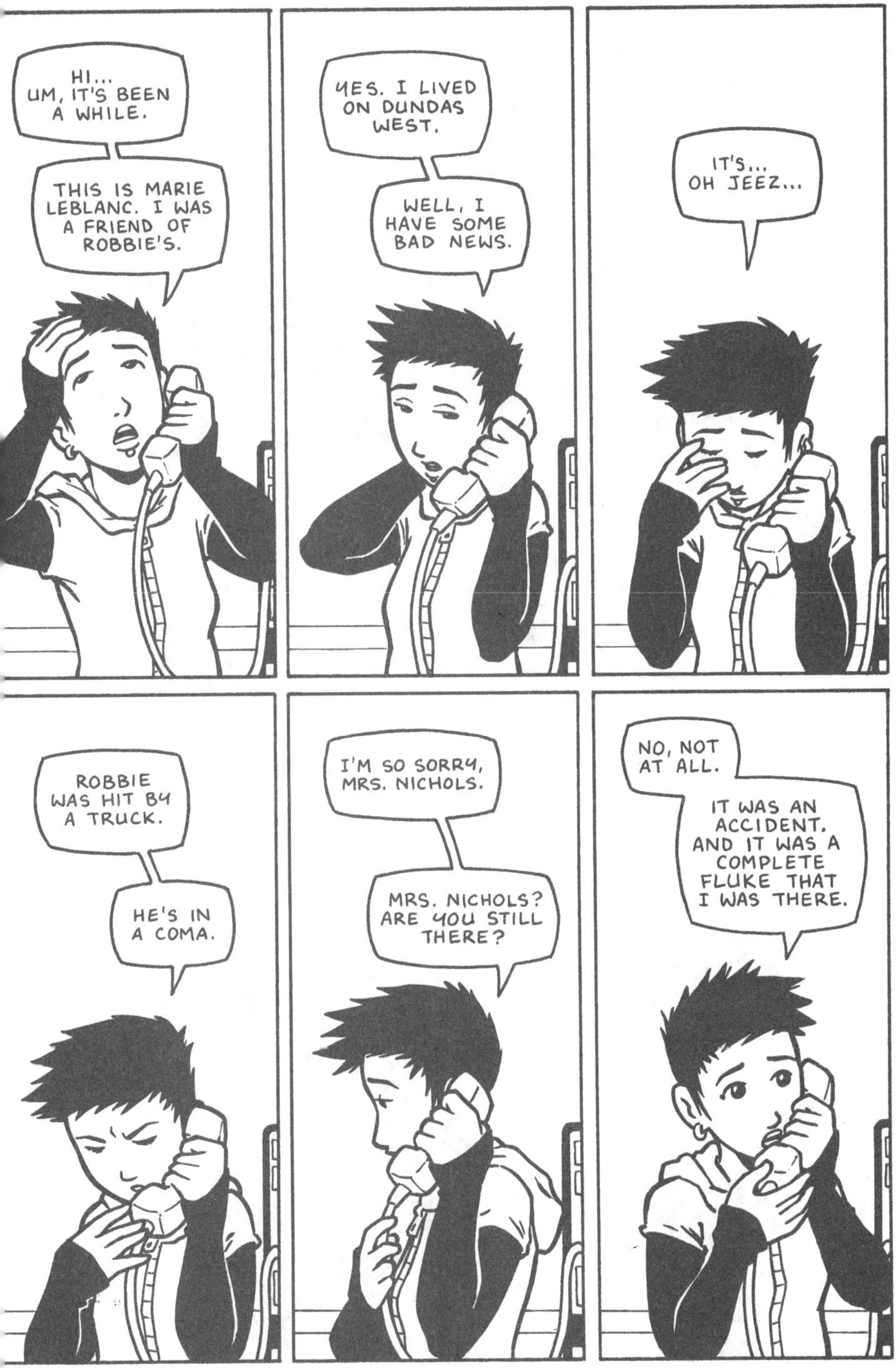
HI... UM, IT'S BEEN A WHILE.
THIS IS MARIE LEBLANC. I WAS A FRIEND OF ROBBIE'S.
YES. I LIVED ON DUNDAS WEST.
WELL, I HAVE SOME BAD NEWS.
IT'S... OH JEEZ...
ROBBIE WAS HIT BY A TRUCK.
HE'S IN A COMA.
I'M SO SORRY, MRS. NICHOLS.
MRS. NICHOLS? ARE YOU STILL THERE?
NO, NOT AT ALL.
IT WAS AN ACCIDENT. AND IT WAS A COMPLETE FLUKE THAT I WAS THERE.

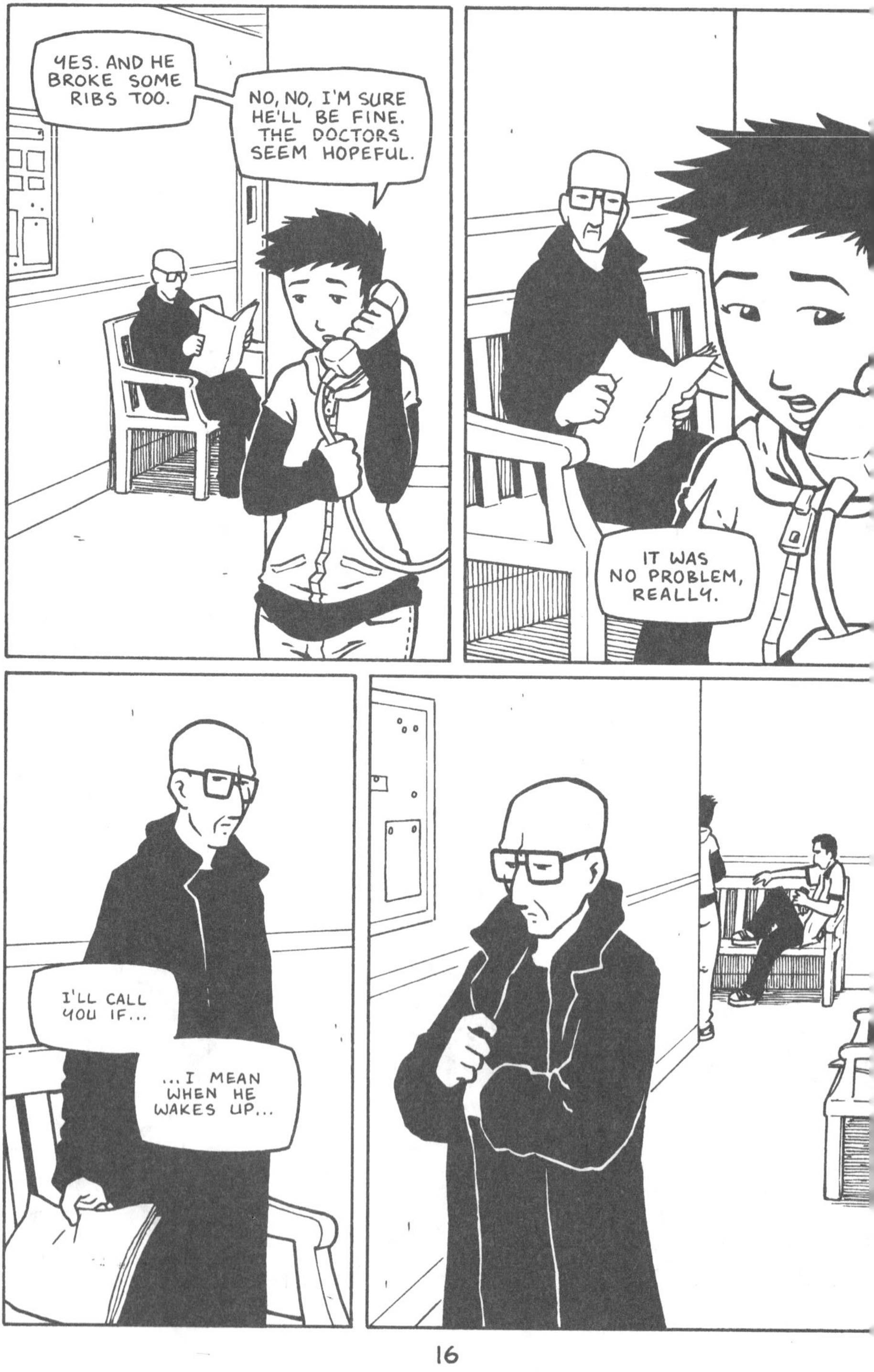
YES. AND HE BROKE SOME RIBS TOO.
NO, NO, I'M SURE HE'LL BE FINE. THE DOCTORS SEEM HOPEFUL.
IT WAS NO PROBLEM, REALLY.
I'LL CALL YOU IF...
...I MEAN WHEN HE WAKES UP...

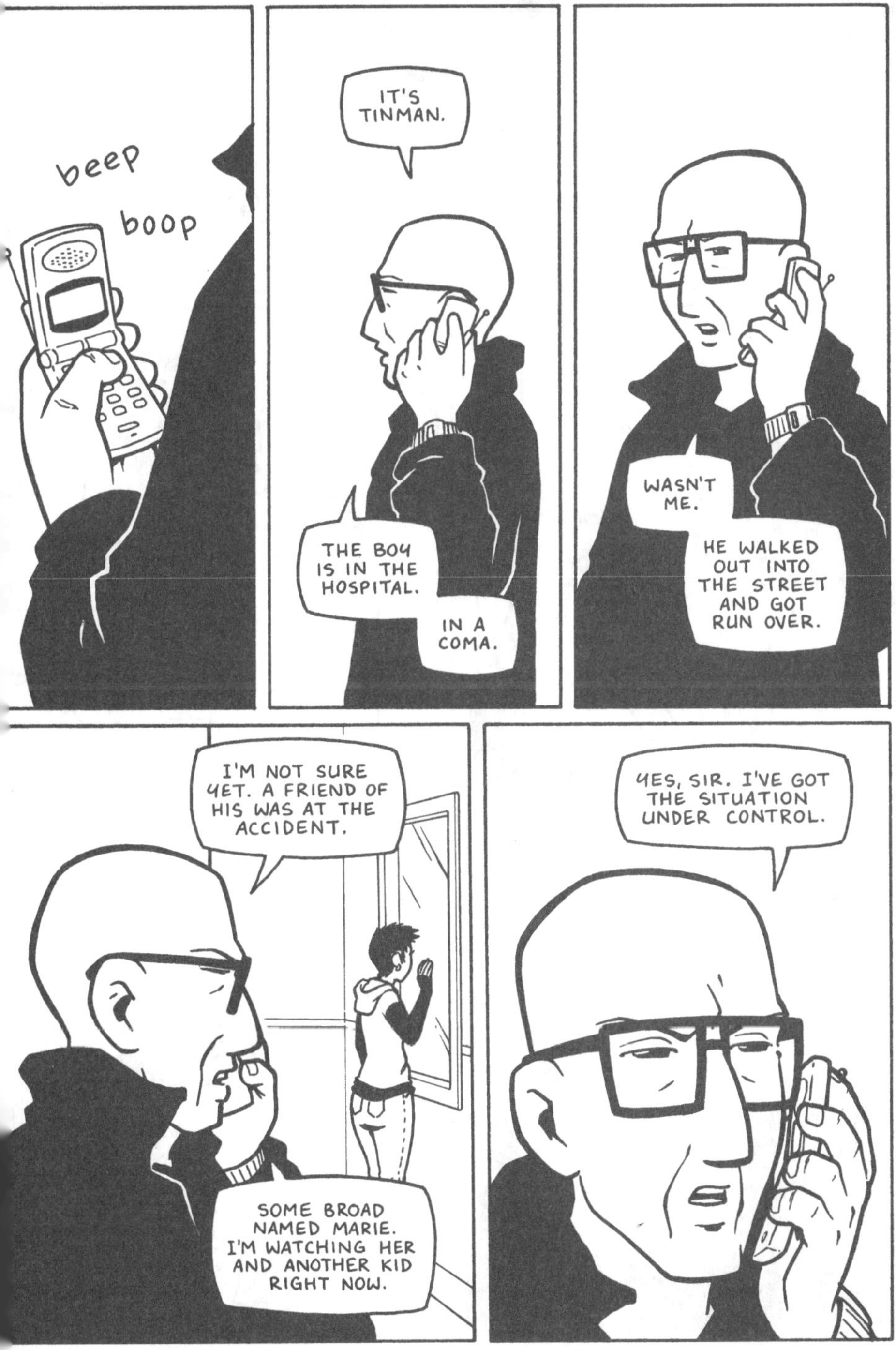
beep
boop
IT'S TINMAN.
THE BOY IS IN THE HOSPITAL.
IN A COMA.
WASN'T ME.
HE WALKED OUT INTO THE STREET AND GOT RUN OVER.
I'M NOT SURE YET. A FRIEND OF HIS WAS AT THE ACCIDENT.
SOME BROAD NAMED MARIE. I'M WATCHING HER AND ANOTHER KID RIGHT NOW.
YES, SIR. I'VE GOT THE SITUATION UNDER CONTROL.

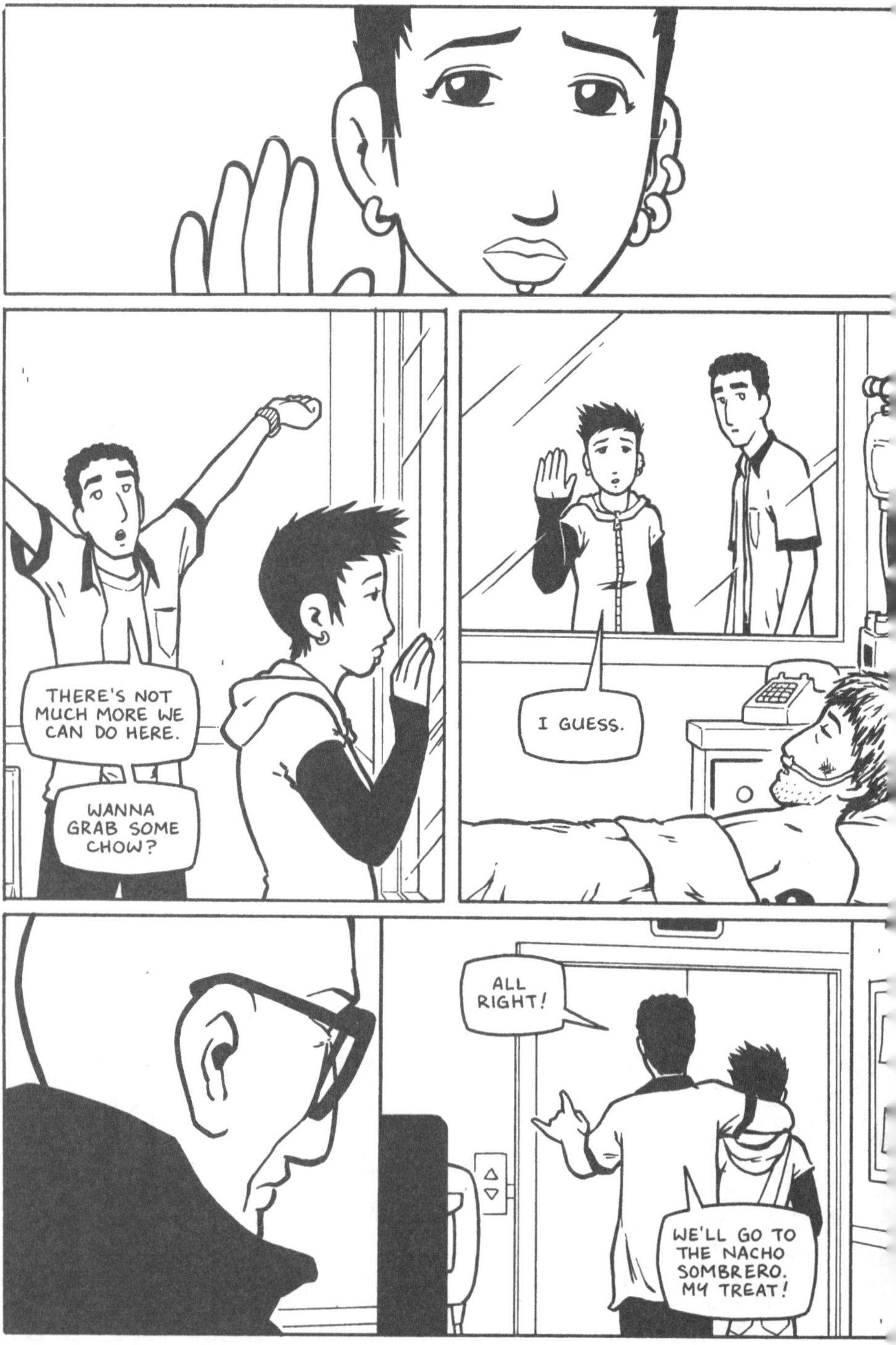
THERE'S NOT MUCH MORE WE CAN DO HERE.
WANNA GRAB SOME CHOW?
I GUESS.
ALL RIGHT!
WE'LL GO TO THE NACHO SOMBRERO. MY TREAT!

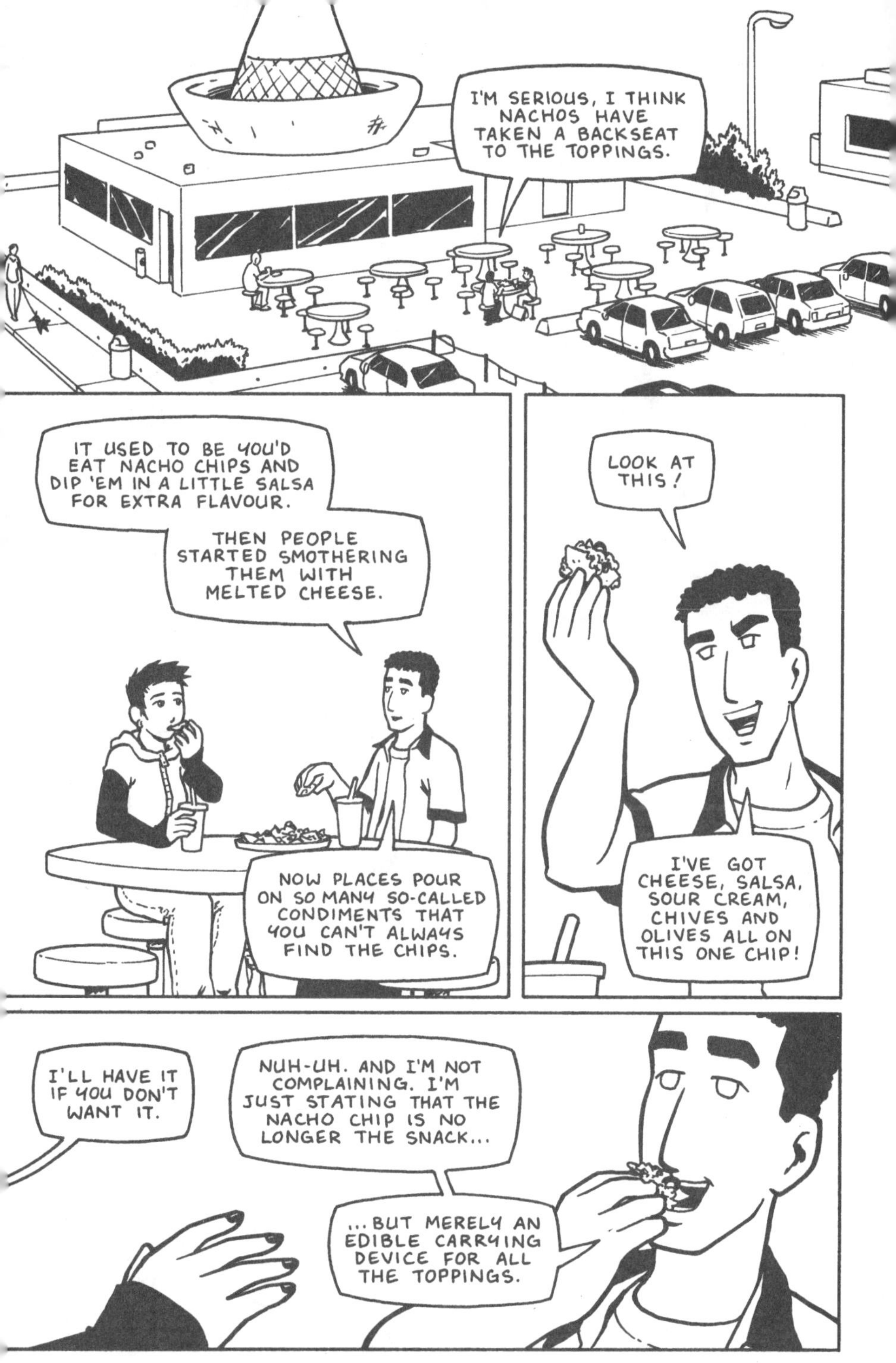

I'M SERIOUS, I THINK NACHOS HAVE TAKEN A BACKSEAT TO THE TOPPINGS.
IT USED TO BE YOU'D EAT NACHO CHIPS AND DIP 'EM IN A LITTLE SALSA FOR EXTRA FLAVOUR.
THEN PEOPLE STARTED SMOTHERING THEM WITH MELTED CHEESE.
NOW PLACES POUR ON SO MANY SO-CALLED CONDIMENTS THAT YOU CAN'T ALWAYS FIND THE CHIPS.
LOOK AT THIS!
I'VE GOT CHEESE, SALSA, SOUR CREAM, CHIVES AND OLIVES ALL ON THIS ONE CHIP!
I'LL HAVE IT IF YOU DON'T WANT IT.
NUH-UH. AND I'M NOT COMPLAINING. I'M JUST STATING THAT THE NACHO CHIP IS NO LONGER THE SNACK...
...BUT MERELY AN EDIBLE CARRYING DEVICE FOR ALL THE TOPPINGS.

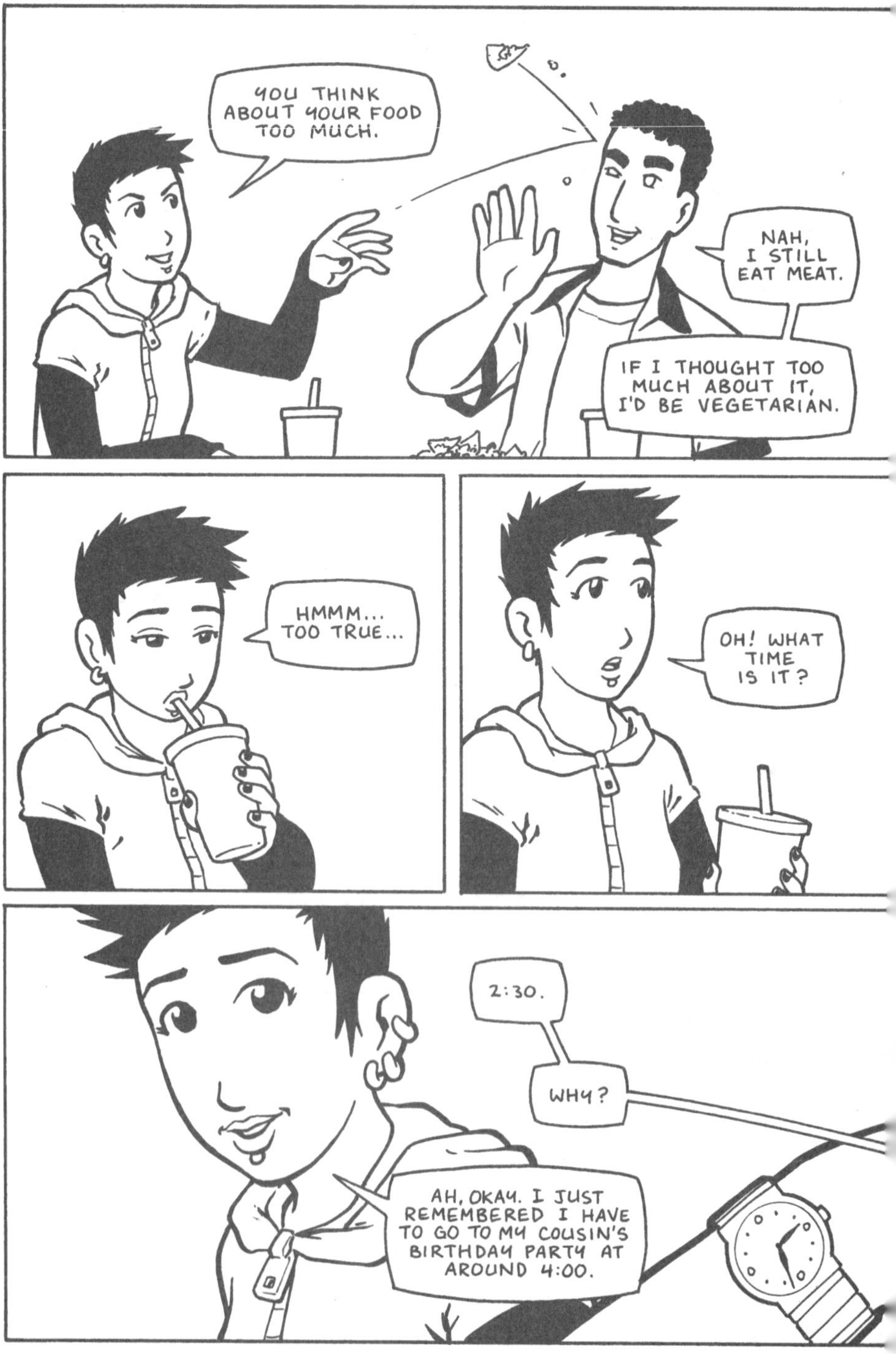
YOU THINK ABOUT YOUR FOOD TOO MUCH.
NAH, I STILL EAT MEAT.
IF I THOUGHT TOO MUCH ABOUT IT, I'D BE VEGETARIAN.
HMMM... TOO TRUE...
OH! WHAT TIME IS IT?
2:30.
WHY?
AH, OKAY. I JUST REMEMBERED I HAVE TO GO TO MY COUSIN'S BIRTHDAY PARTY AT AROUND 4:00.

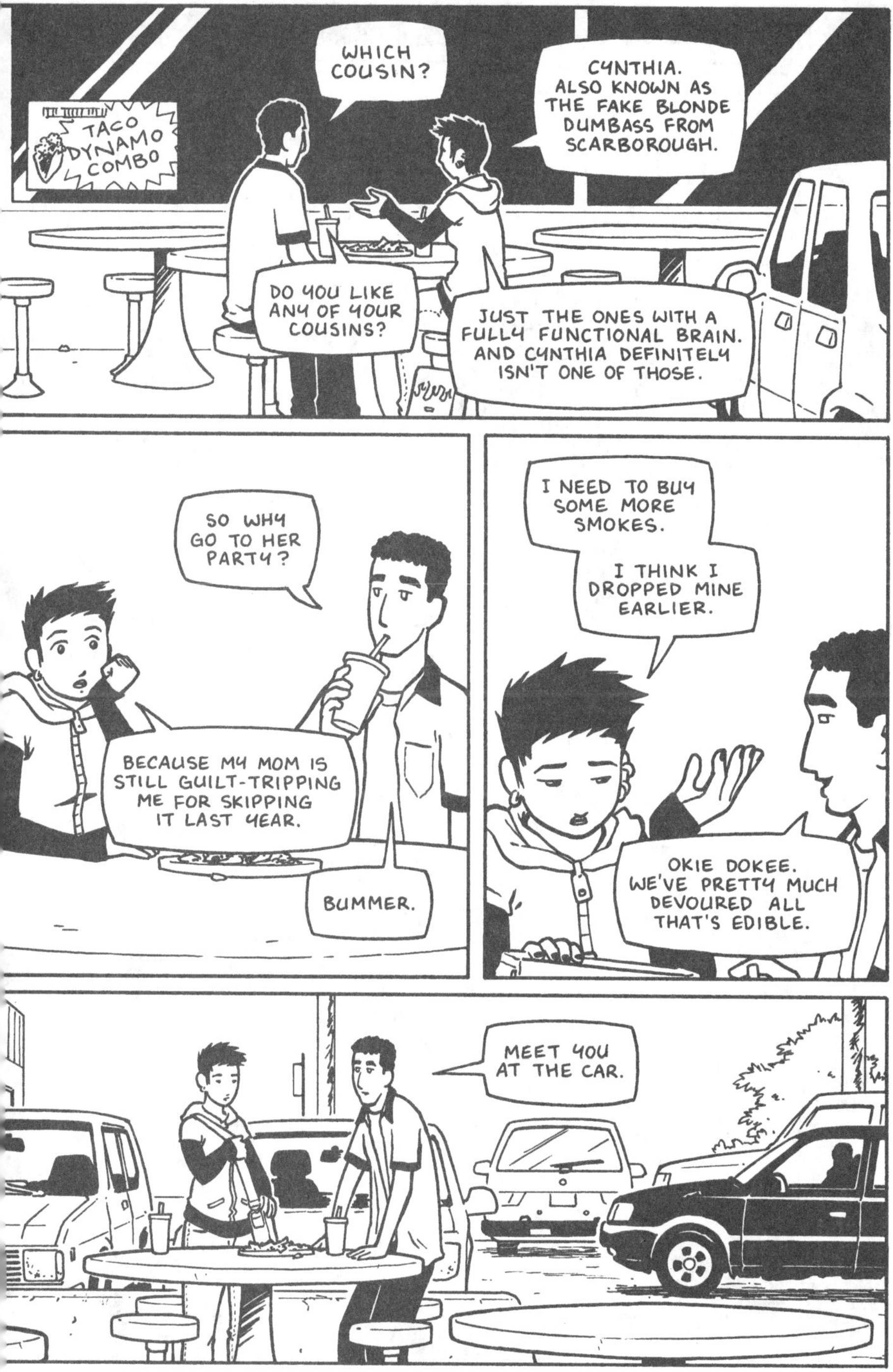
TACO DYNAMO COMBO
WHICH COUSIN?
CYNTHIA. ALSO KNOWN AS THE FAKE BLONDE DUMBASS FROM SCARBOROUGH.
DO YOU LIKE ANY OF YOUR COUSINS?
JUST THE ONES WITH A FULLY FUNCTIONAL BRAIN. AND CYNTHIA DEFINITELY ISN'T ONE OF THOSE.
SO WHY GO TO HER PARTY?
BECAUSE MY MOM IS STILL GUILT-TRIPPING ME FOR SKIPPING IT LAST YEAR.
BUMMER.
I NEED TO BUY SOME MORE SMOKES.
I THINK I DROPPED MINE EARLIER.
OKIE DOKEE. WE'VE PRETTY MUCH DEVOURED ALL THAT'S EDIBLE.
MEET YOU AT THE CAR.

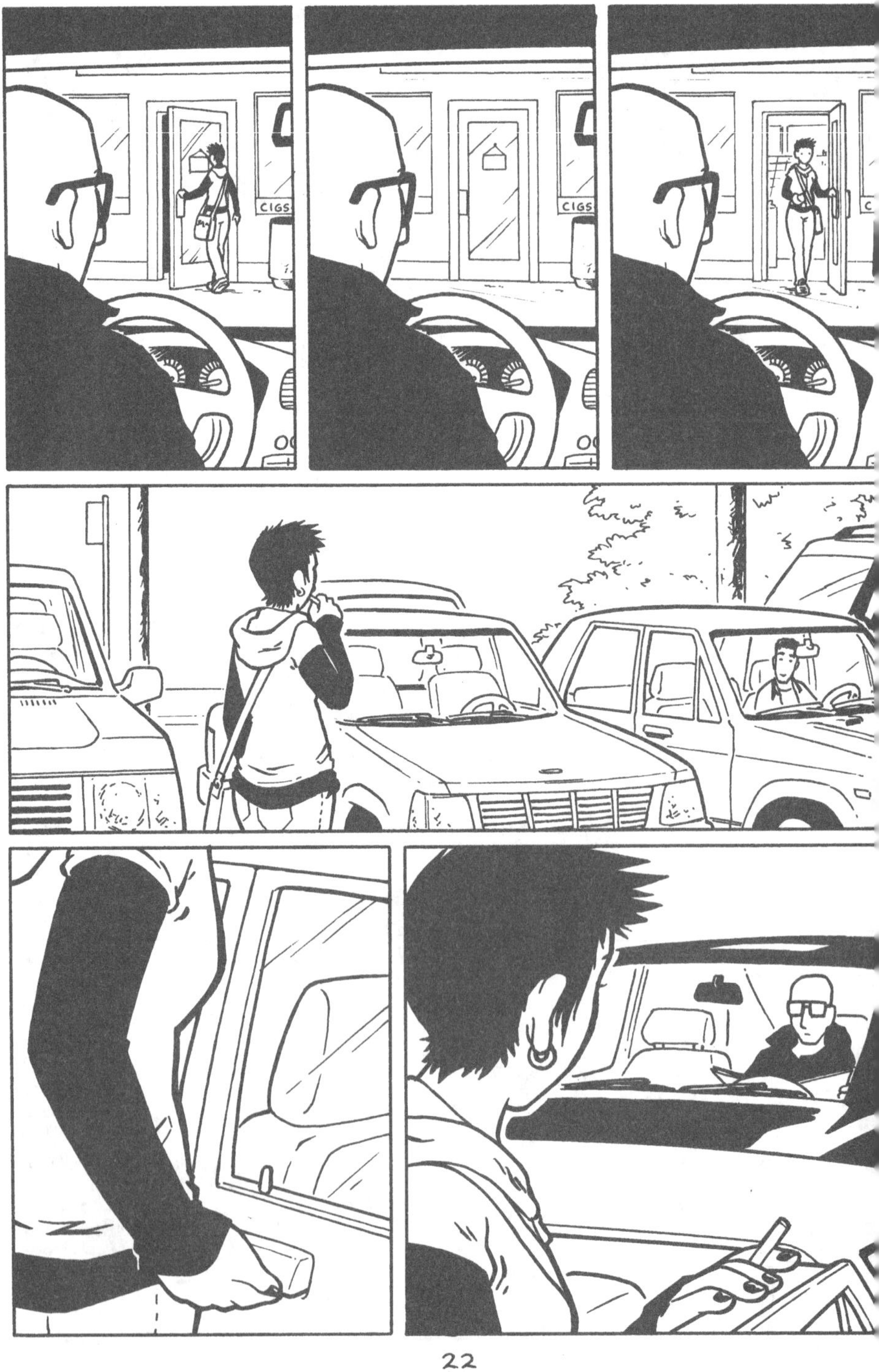
CIGS
CIGS

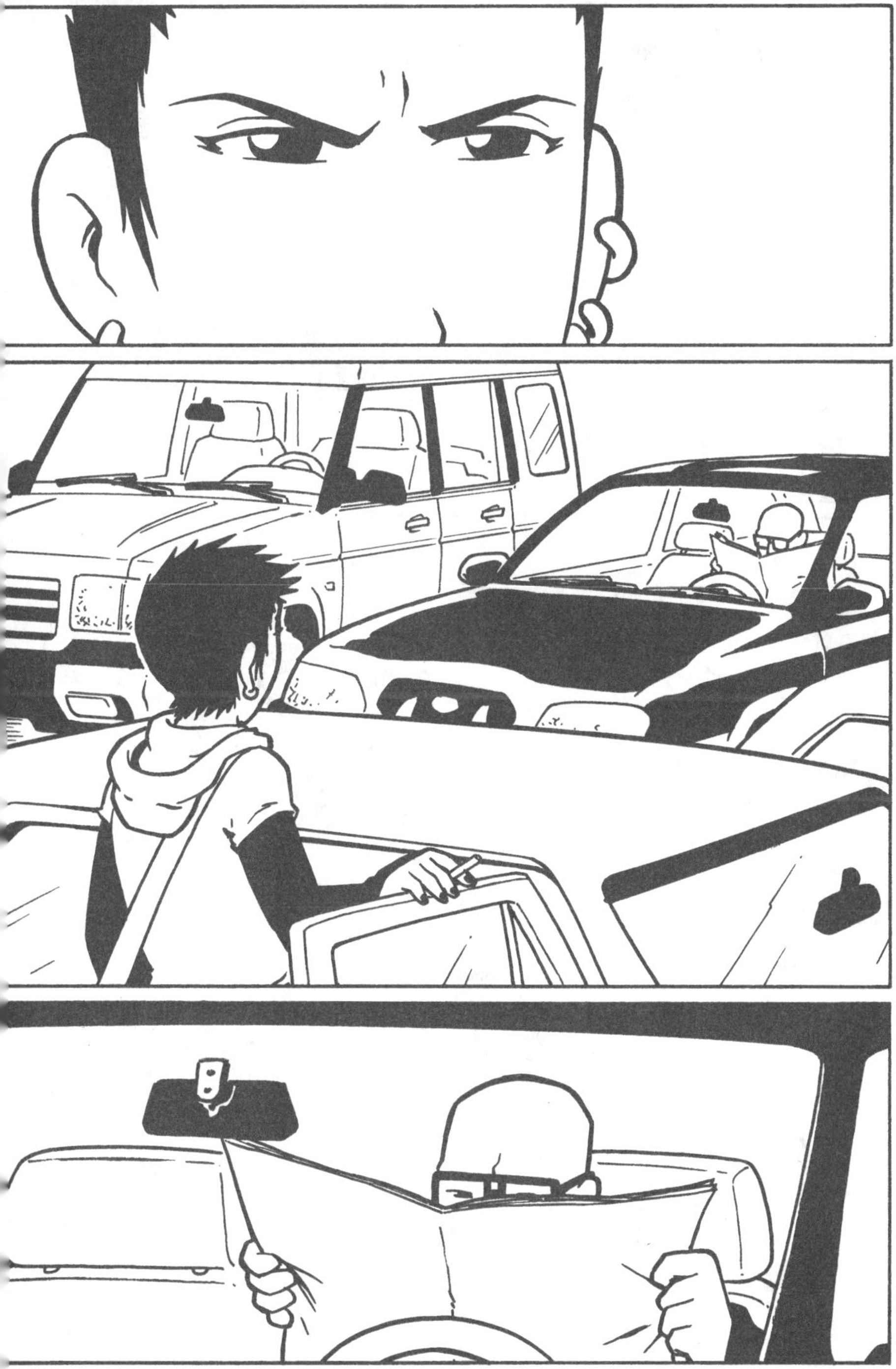

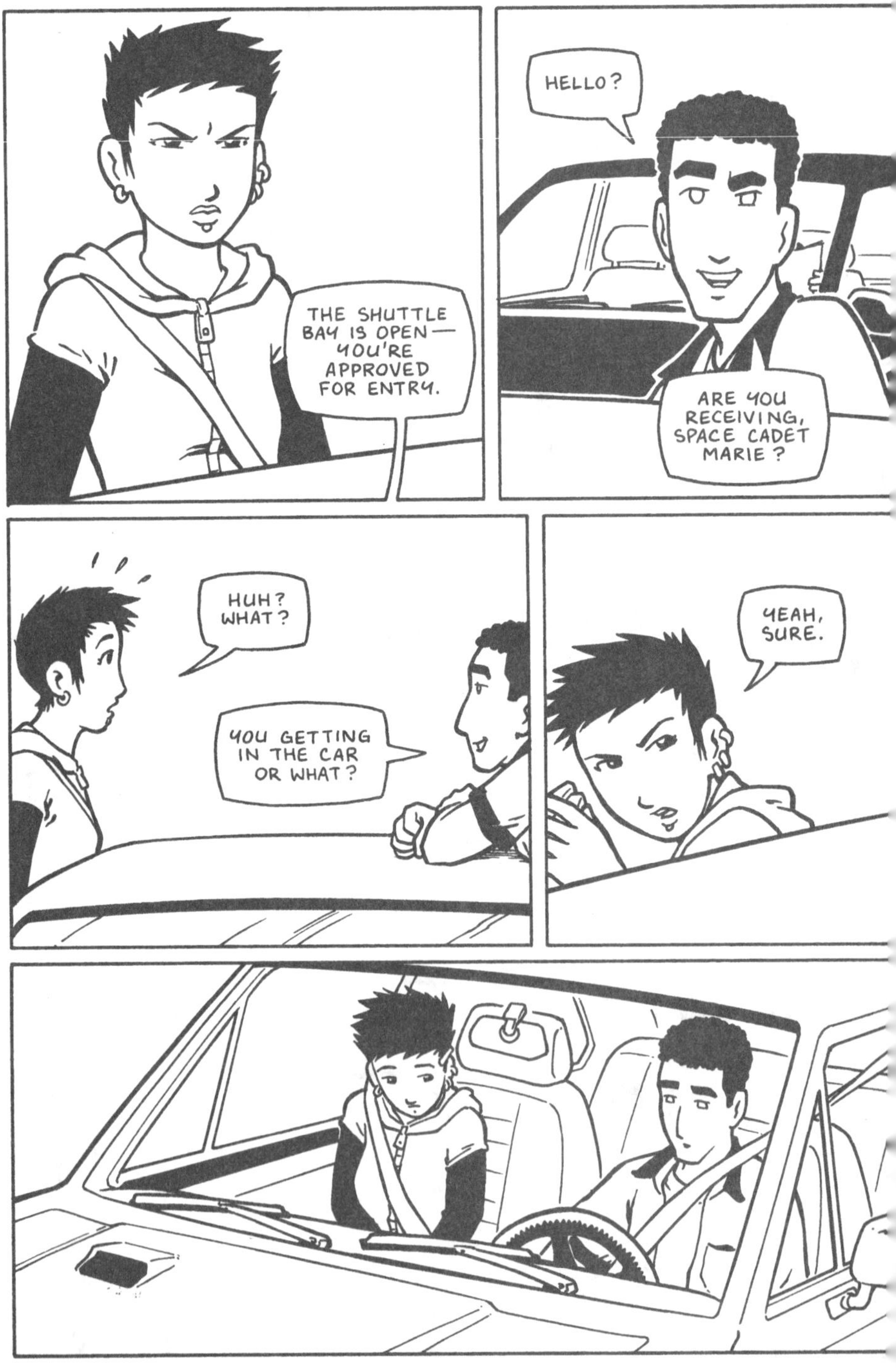
THE SHUTTLE BAY IS OPEN— YOU'RE APPROVED FOR ENTRY.
HELLO?
ARE YOU RECEIVING, SPACE CADET MARIE?
HUH? WHAT?
YOU GETTING IN THE CAR OR WHAT?
YEAH, SURE.

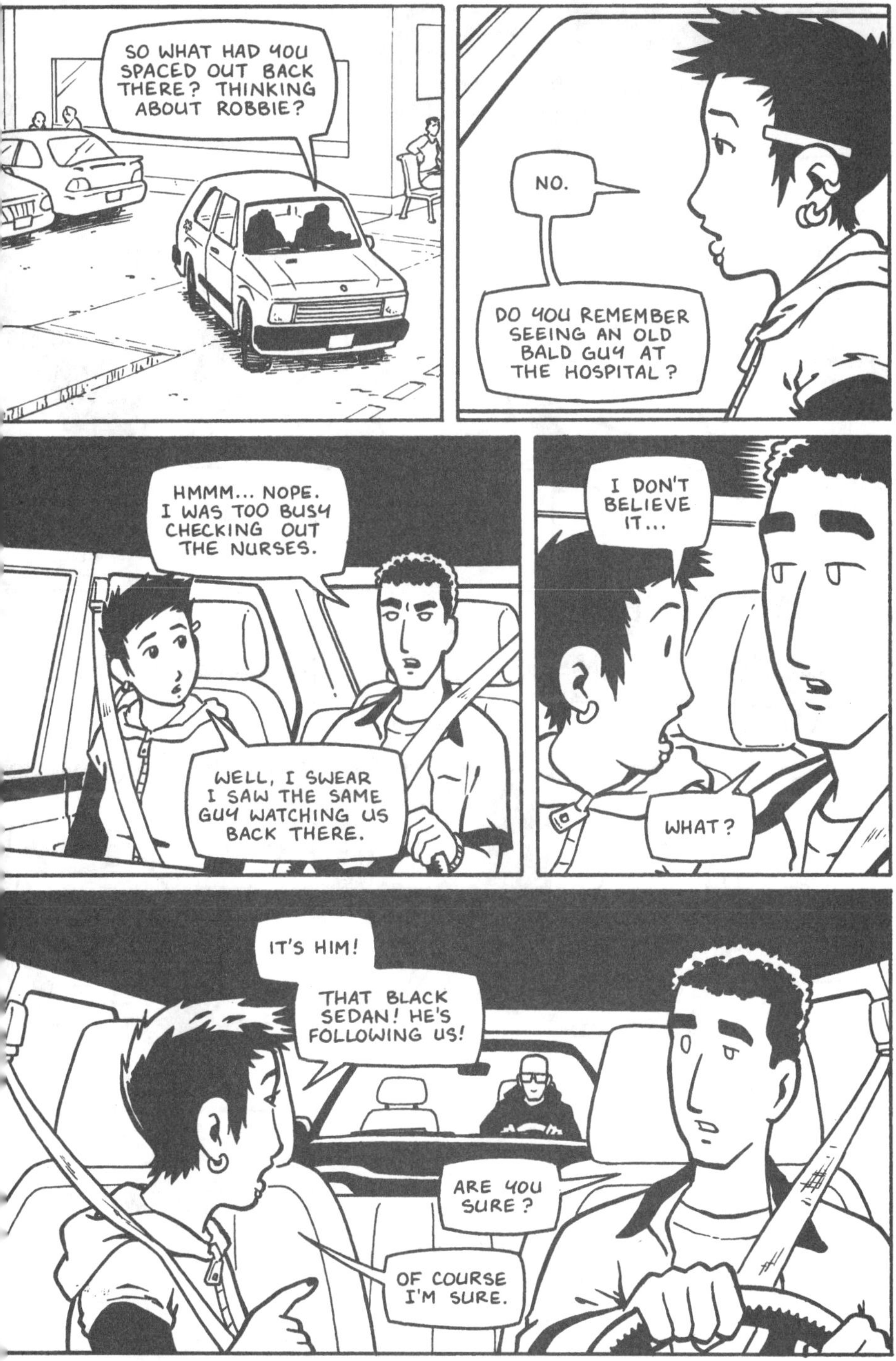
SO WHAT HAD YOU SPACED OUT BACK THERE? THINKING ABOUT ROBBIE?
NO.
DO YOU REMEMBER SEEING AN OLD BALD GUY AT THE HOSPITAL?
HMMM... NOPE. I WAS TOO BUSY CHECKING OUT THE NURSES.
WELL, I SWEAR I SAW THE SAME GUY WATCHING US BACK THERE.
I DON'T BELIEVE IT...
WHAT?
IT'S HIM!
THAT BLACK SEDAN! HE'S FOLLOWING US!
ARE YOU SURE?
OF COURSE I'M SURE.

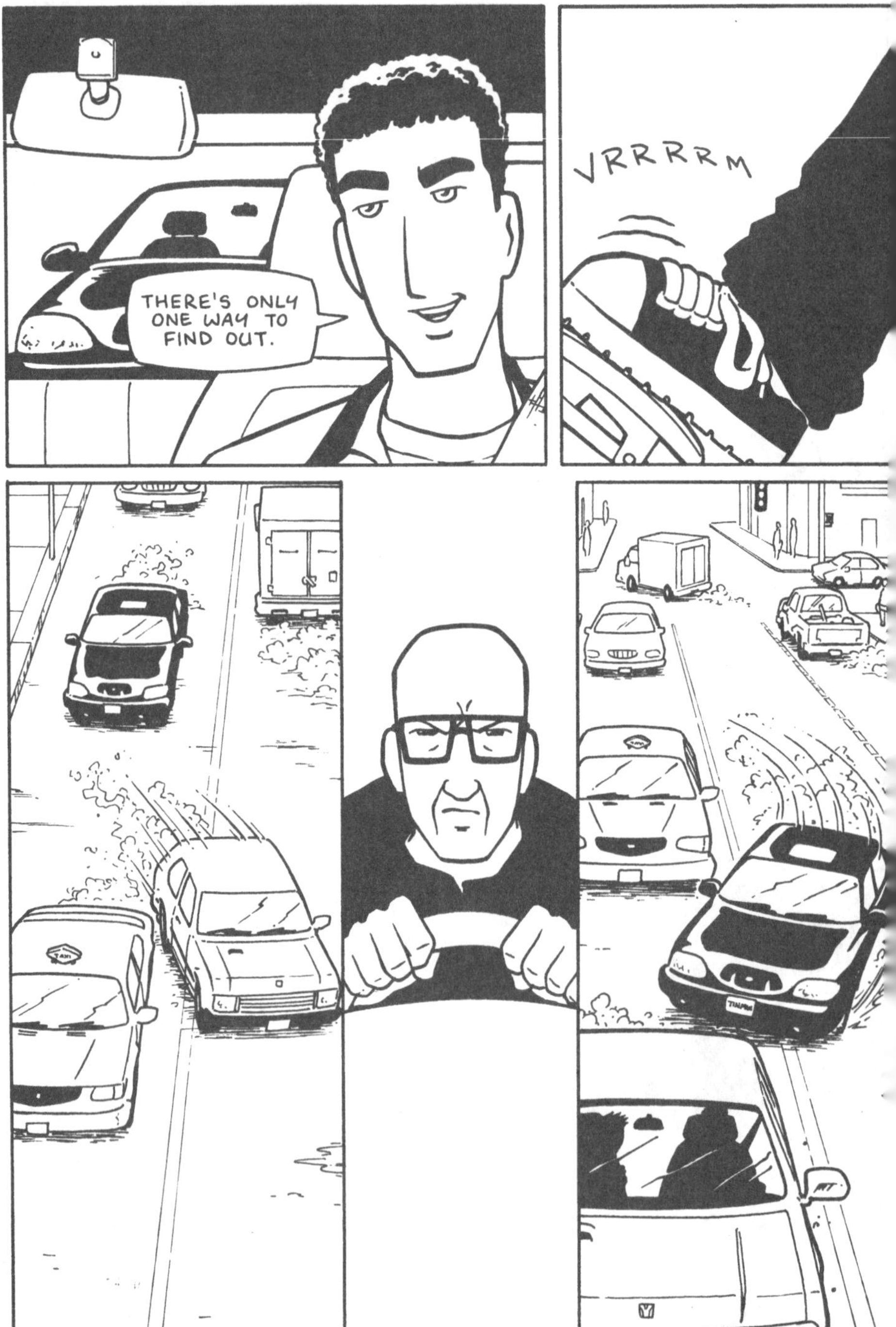
THERE'S ONLY ONE WAY TO FIND OUT.
VRRRRM

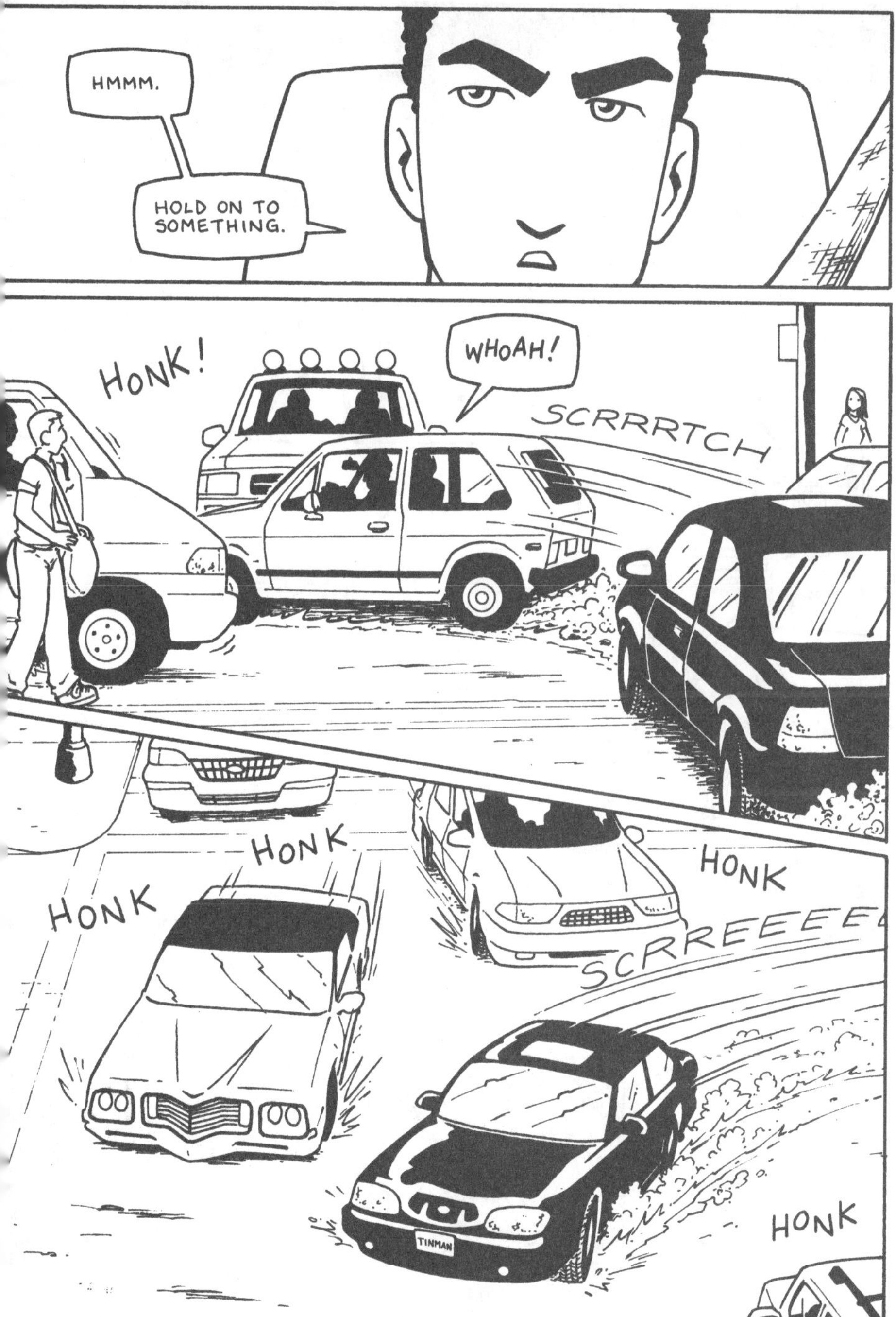
HMMM.
HOLD ON TO SOMETHING.
HONK!
WHOAH!
SCRRRTCH
HONK
HONK
HONK
SCRREEEEE
TINMAN
HONK

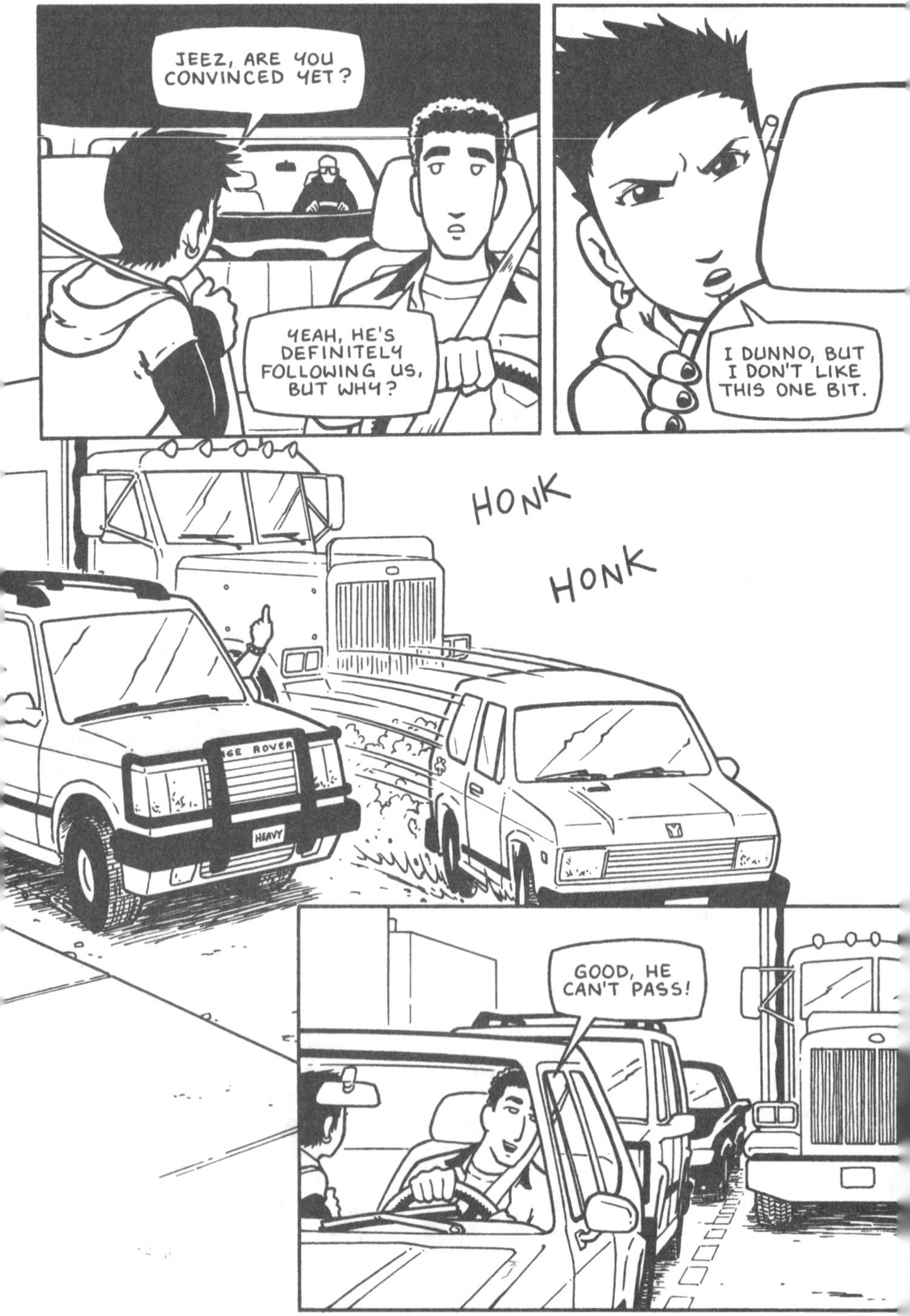
JEEZ, ARE YOU CONVINCED YET?
YEAH, HE'S DEFINITELY FOLLOWING US, BUT WHY?
I DUNNO, BUT I DON'T LIKE THIS ONE BIT.
HONK
HONK
HEAVY
GOOD, HE CAN'T PASS!

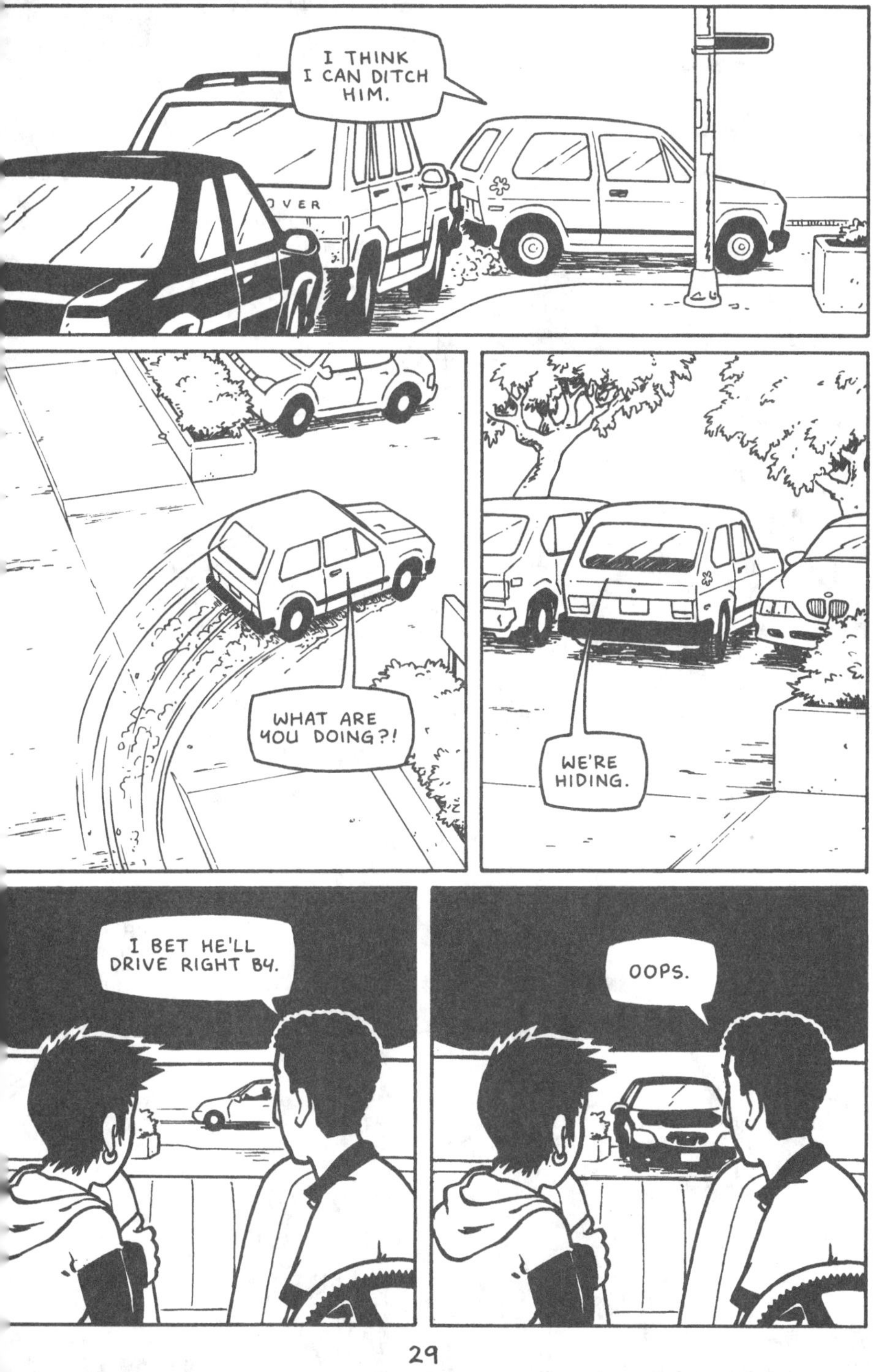
I THINK I CAN DITCH HIM.
OVER
WHAT ARE YOU DOING?!
WE'RE HIDING.
I BET HE'LL DRIVE RIGHT BY.
OOPS.

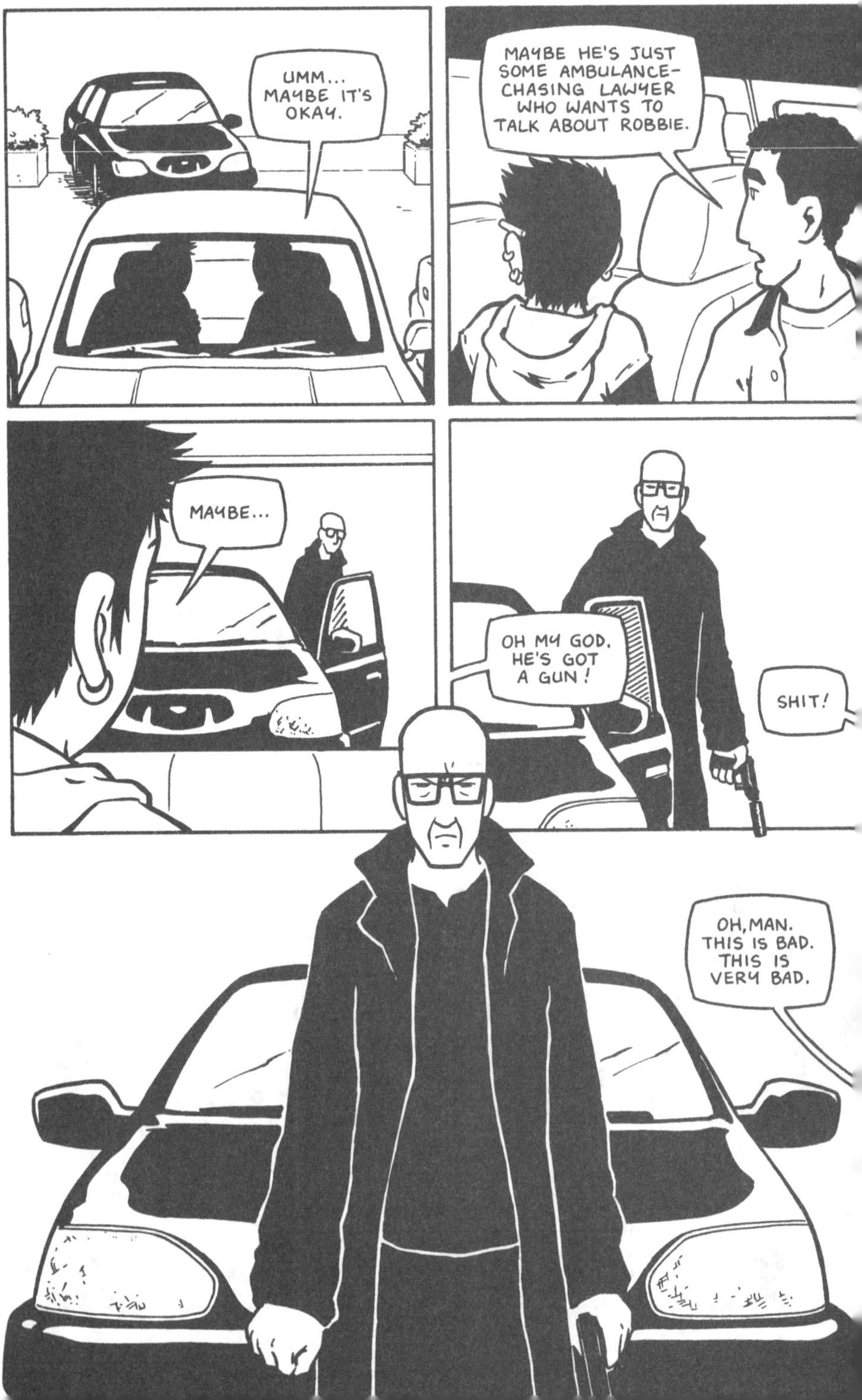
UMM... MAYBE IT'S OKAY.
MAYBE HE'S JUST SOME AMBULANCE-CHASING LAWYER WHO WANTS TO TALK ABOUT ROBBIE.
MAYBE...
OH MY GOD. HE'S GOT A GUN!
SHIT!
OH, MAN. THIS IS BAD. THIS IS VERY BAD.

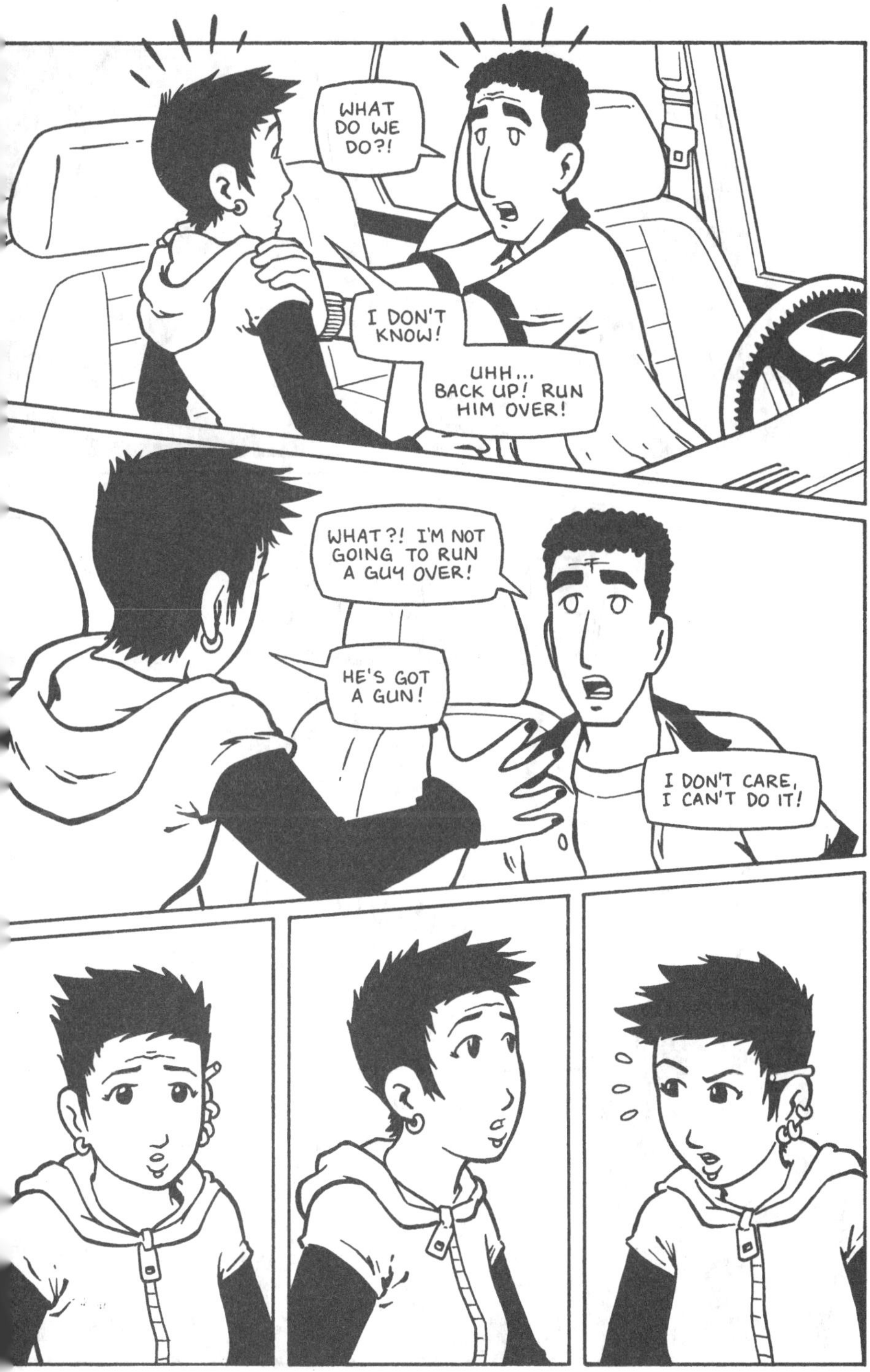
WHAT DO WE DO?!
I DON'T KNOW!
UHH... BACK UP! RUN HIM OVER!
WHAT?! I'M NOT GOING TO RUN A GUY OVER!
HE'S GOT A GUN!
I DON'T CARE, I CAN'T DO IT!

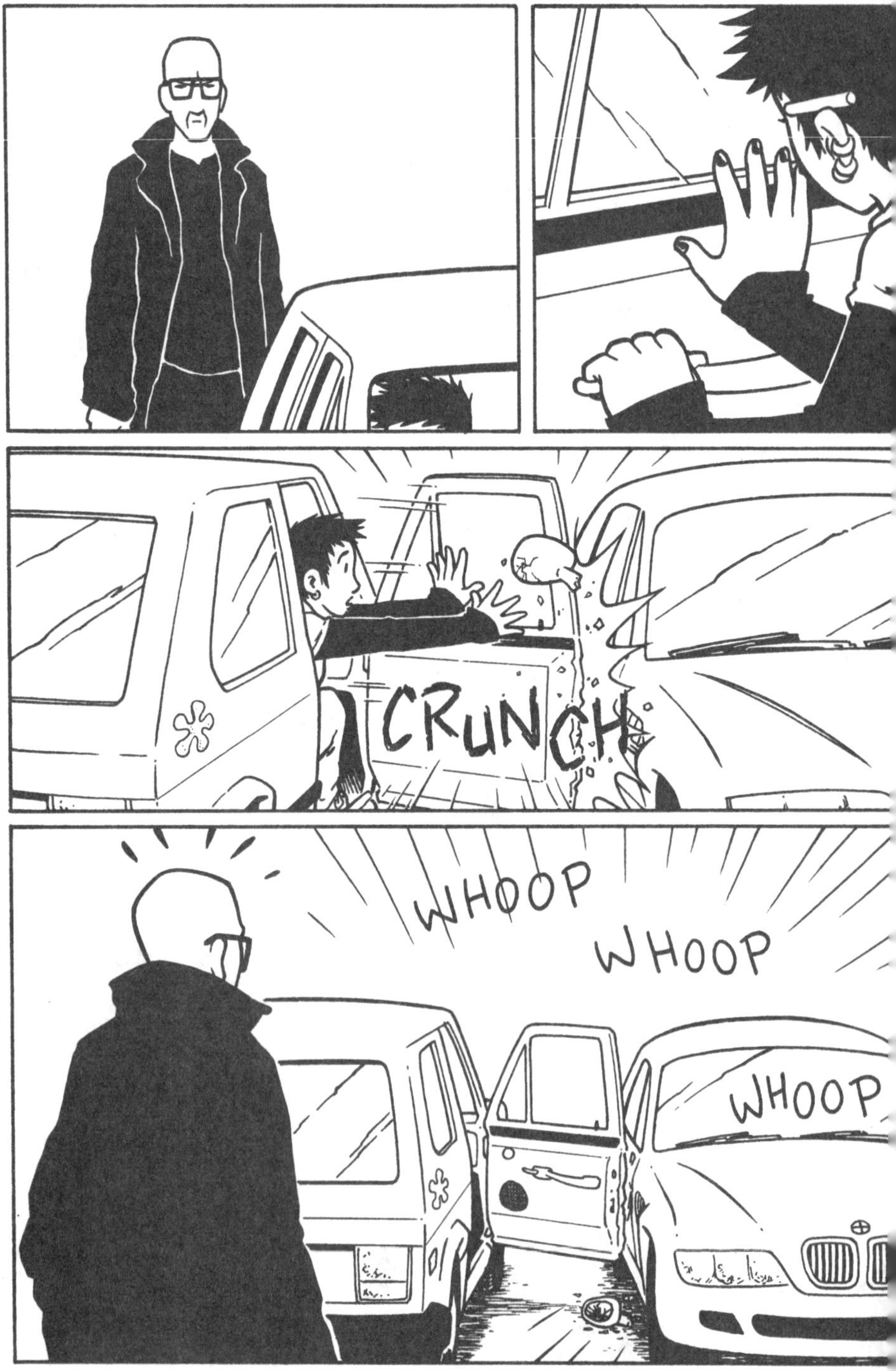
CRUNCH
WHOOP
WHOOP
WHOOP

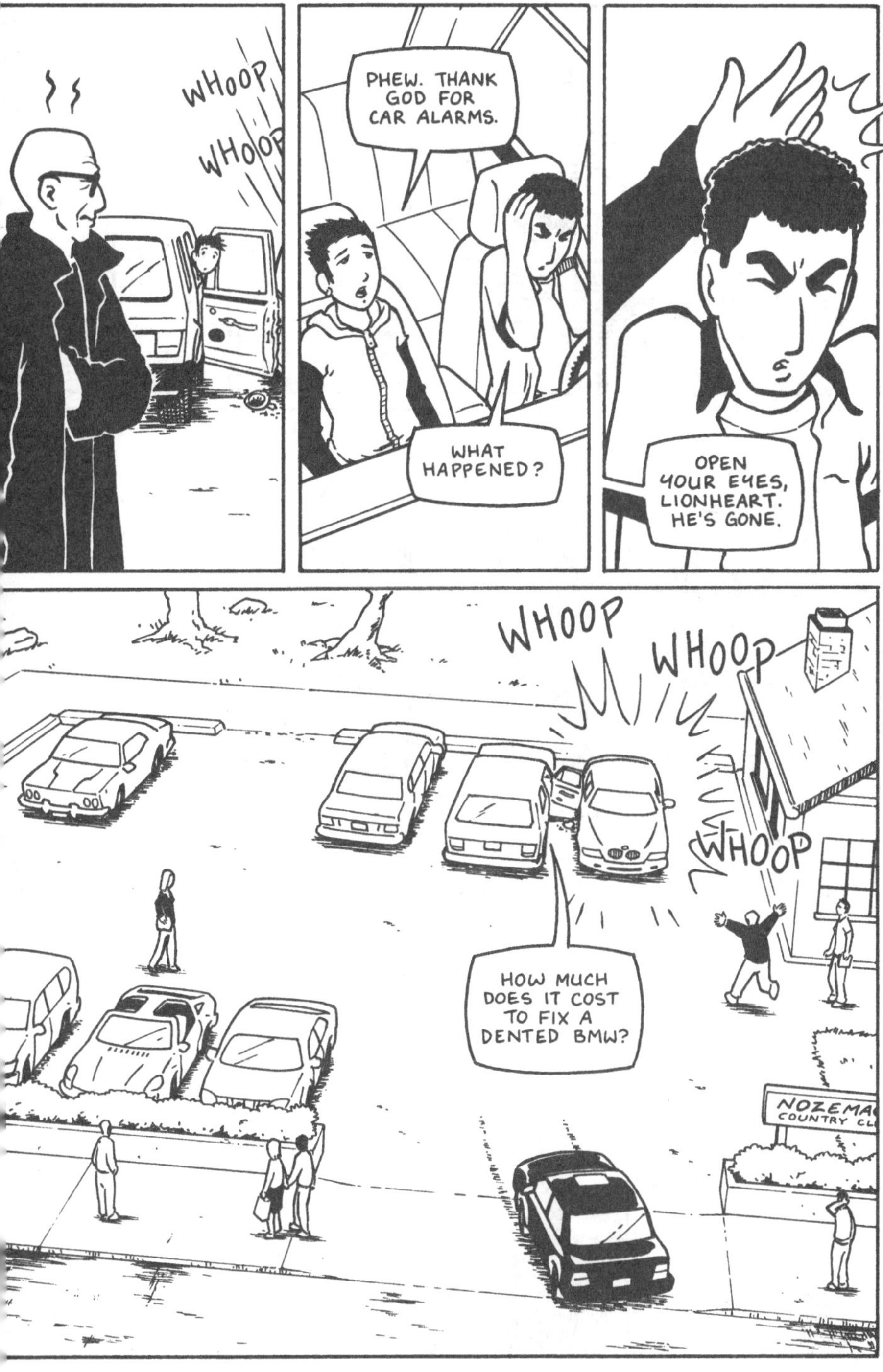
WHOOP
WHOOP
PHEW. THANK GOD FOR CAR ALARMS.
WHAT HAPPENED?
OPEN YOUR EYES, LIONHEART. HE'S GONE.
WHOOP
WHOOP
WHOOP
HOW MUCH DOES IT COST TO FIX A DENTED BMW?

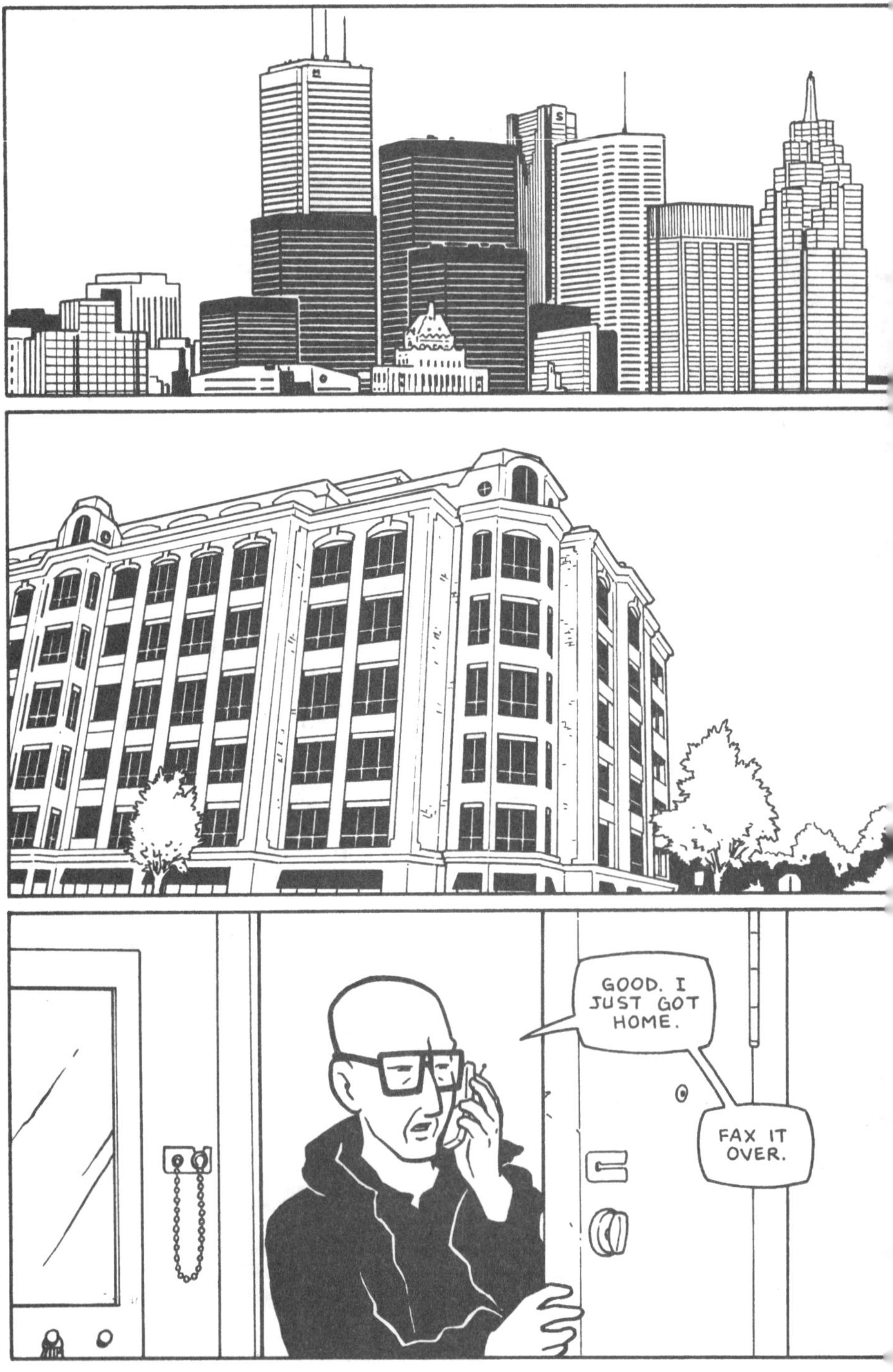
GOOD. I JUST GOT HOME.
FAX IT OVER.

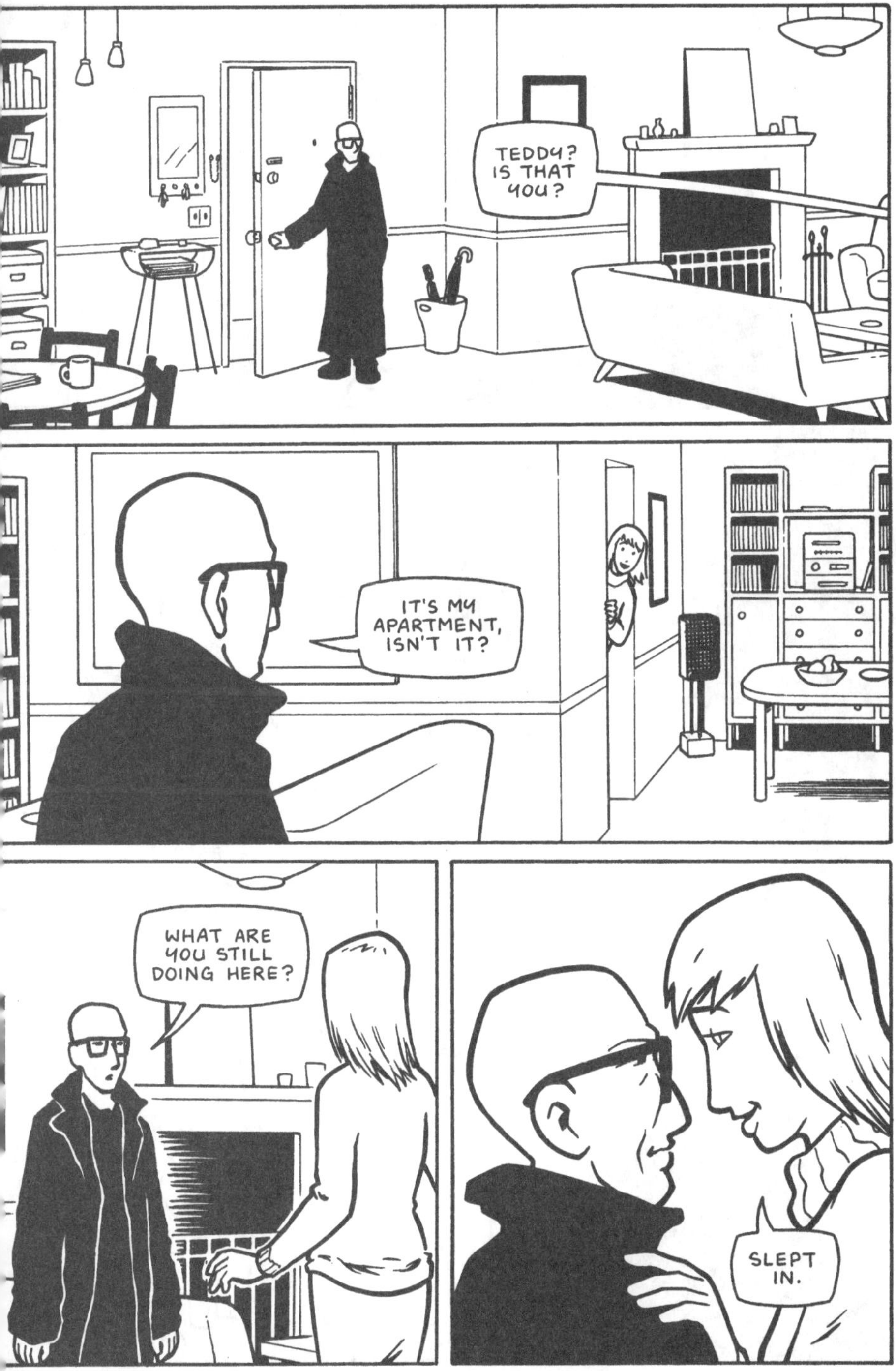
TEDDY? IS THAT YOU?
IT'S MY APARTMENT, ISN'T IT?
WHAT ARE YOU STILL DOING HERE?
SLEPT IN.

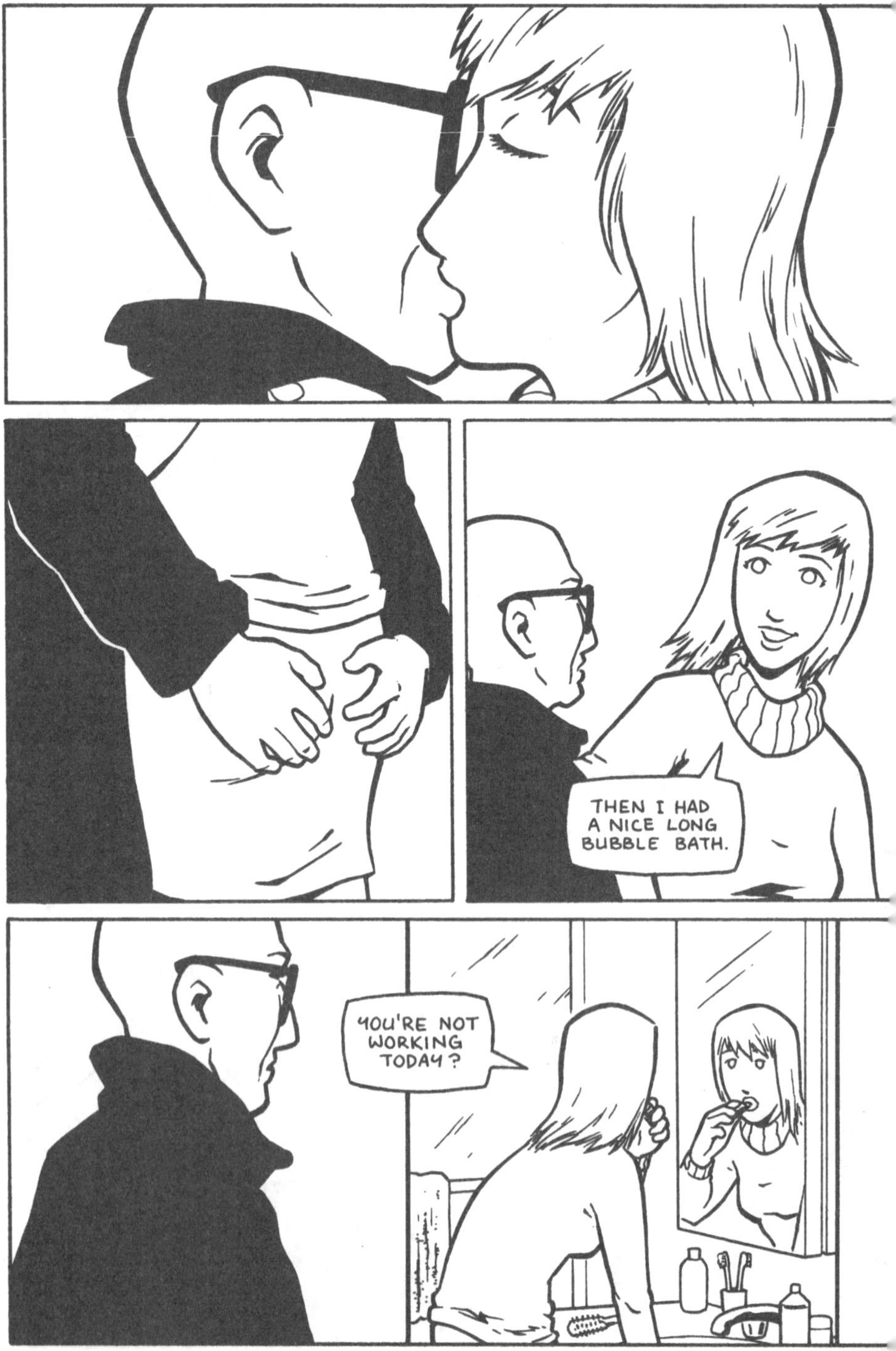
THEN I HAD A NICE LONG BUBBLE BATH.
YOU'RE NOT WORKING TODAY?

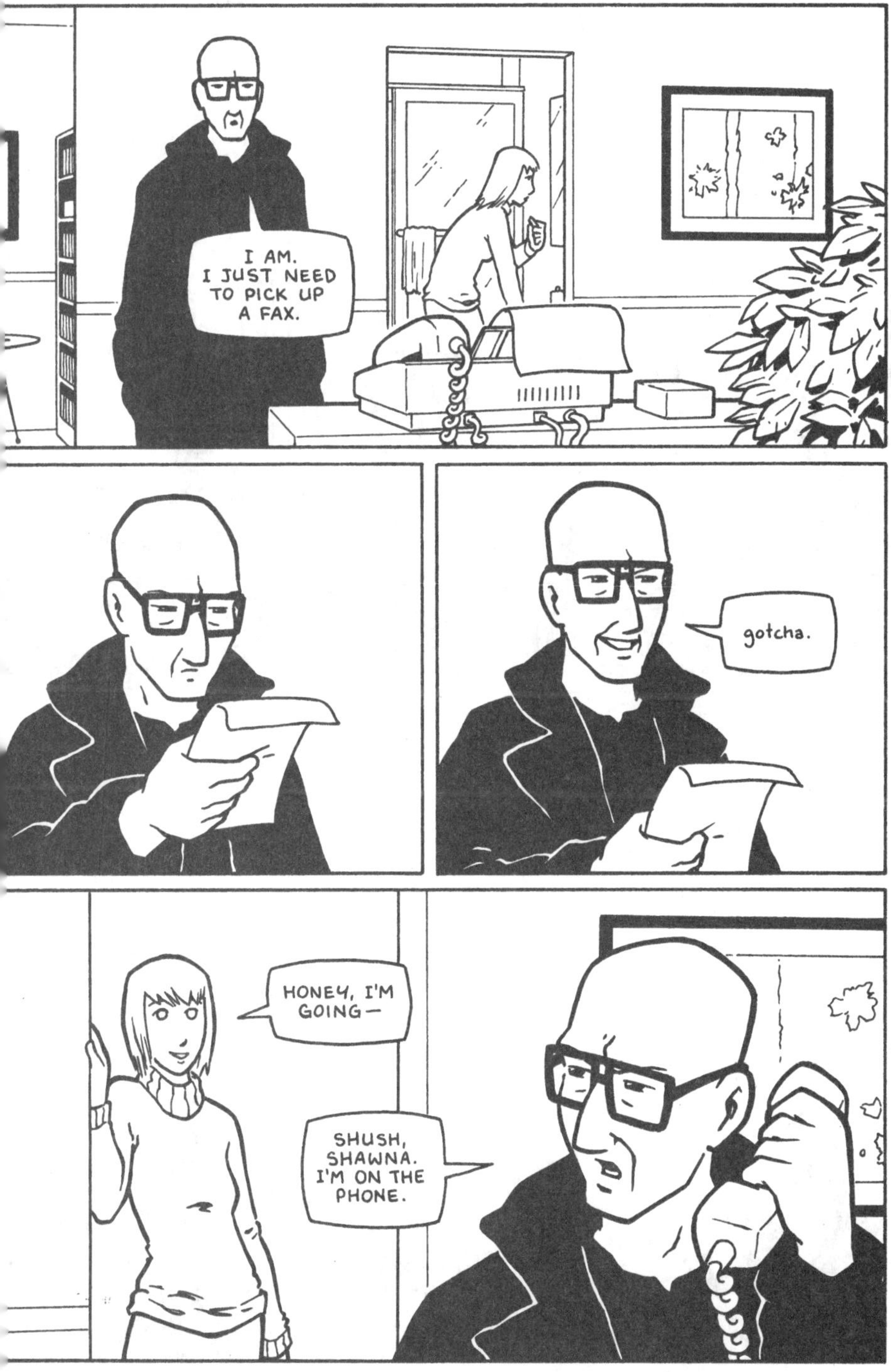
I AM. I JUST NEED TO PICK UP A FAX.
gotcha.
HONEY, I'M GOING—
SHUSH, SHAWNA. I'M ON THE PHONE.

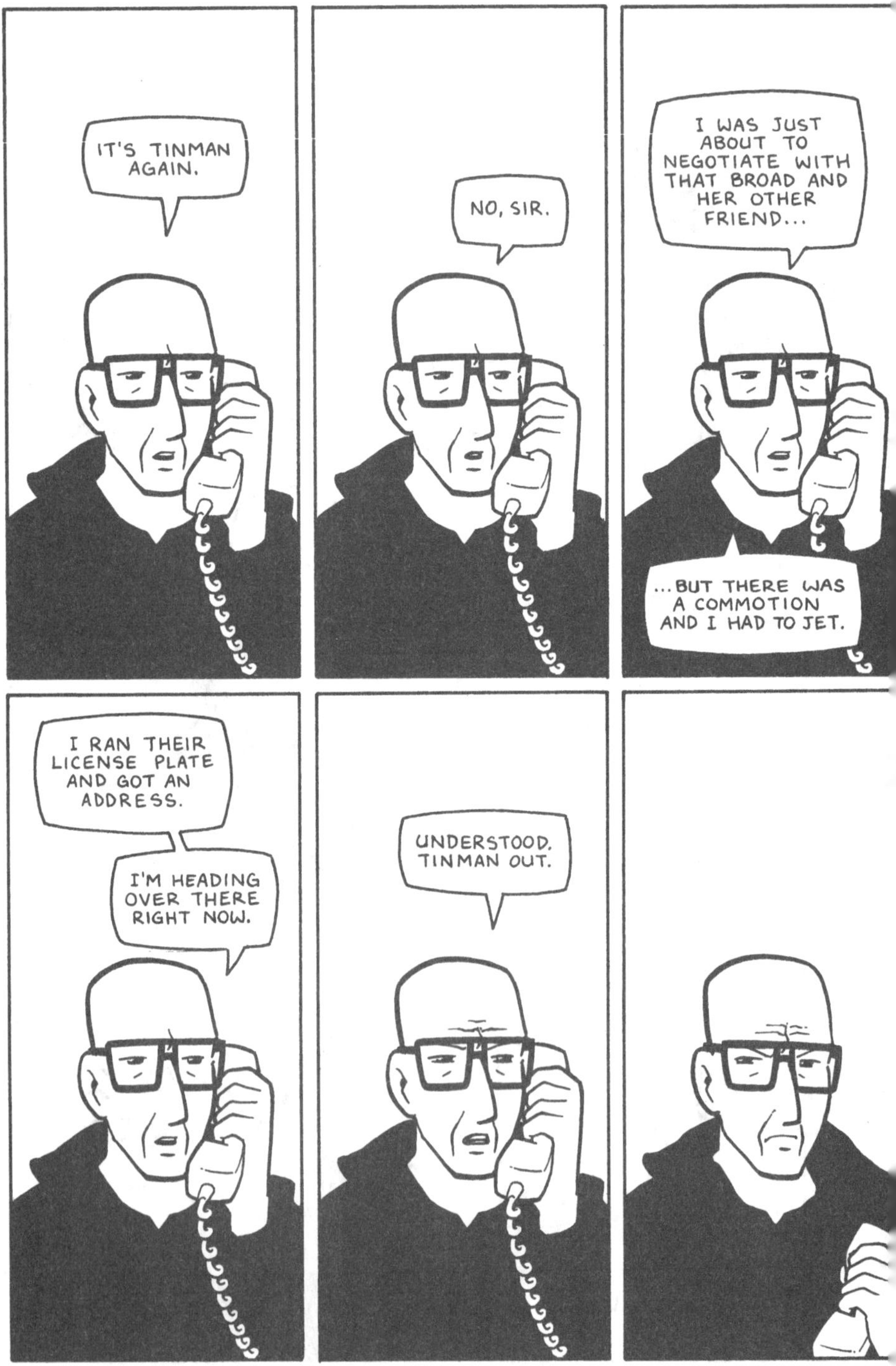
IT'S TINMAN AGAIN.
NO, SIR.
I WAS JUST ABOUT TO NEGOTIATE WITH THAT BROAD AND HER OTHER FRIEND...
...BUT THERE WAS A COMMOTION AND I HAD TO JET.
I RAN THEIR LICENSE PLATE AND GOT AN ADDRESS.
I'M HEADING OVER THERE RIGHT NOW.
UNDERSTOOD. TINMAN OUT.

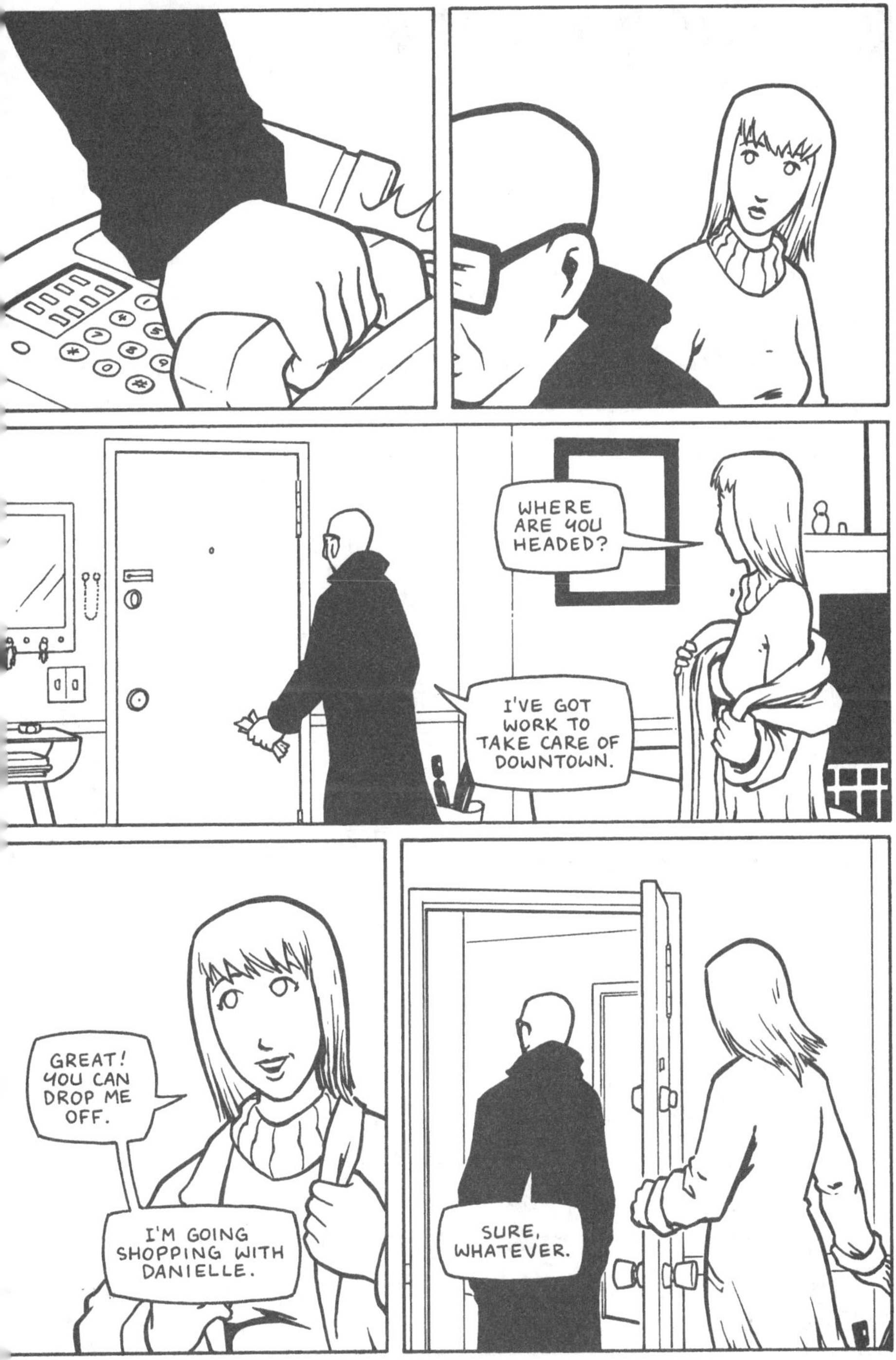
WHERE ARE YOU HEADED?
I'VE GOT WORK TO TAKE CARE OF DOWNTOWN.
GREAT! YOU CAN DROP ME OFF.
I'M GOING SHOPPING WITH DANIELLE.
SURE, WHATEVER.

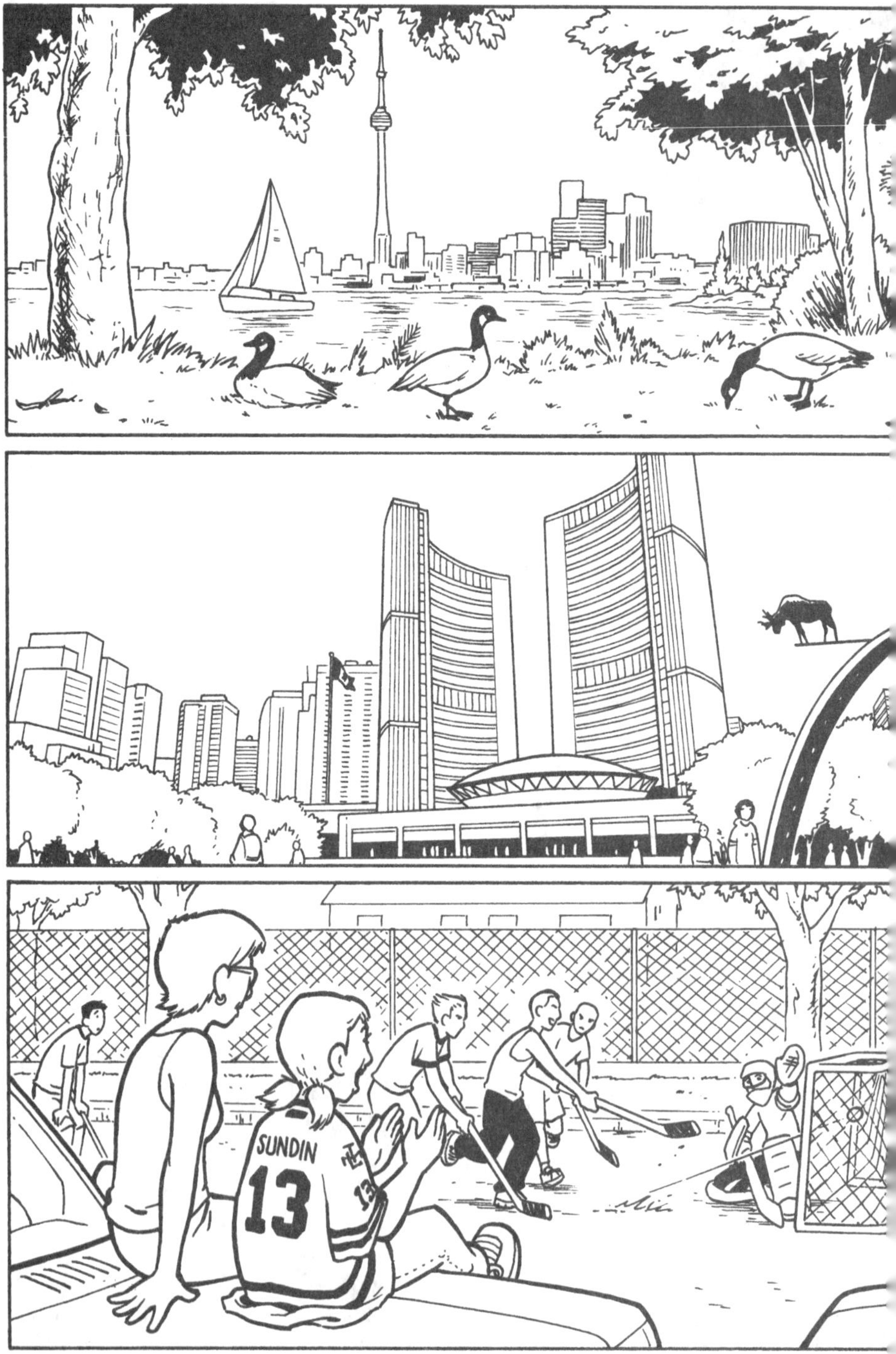
SUNDIN
13

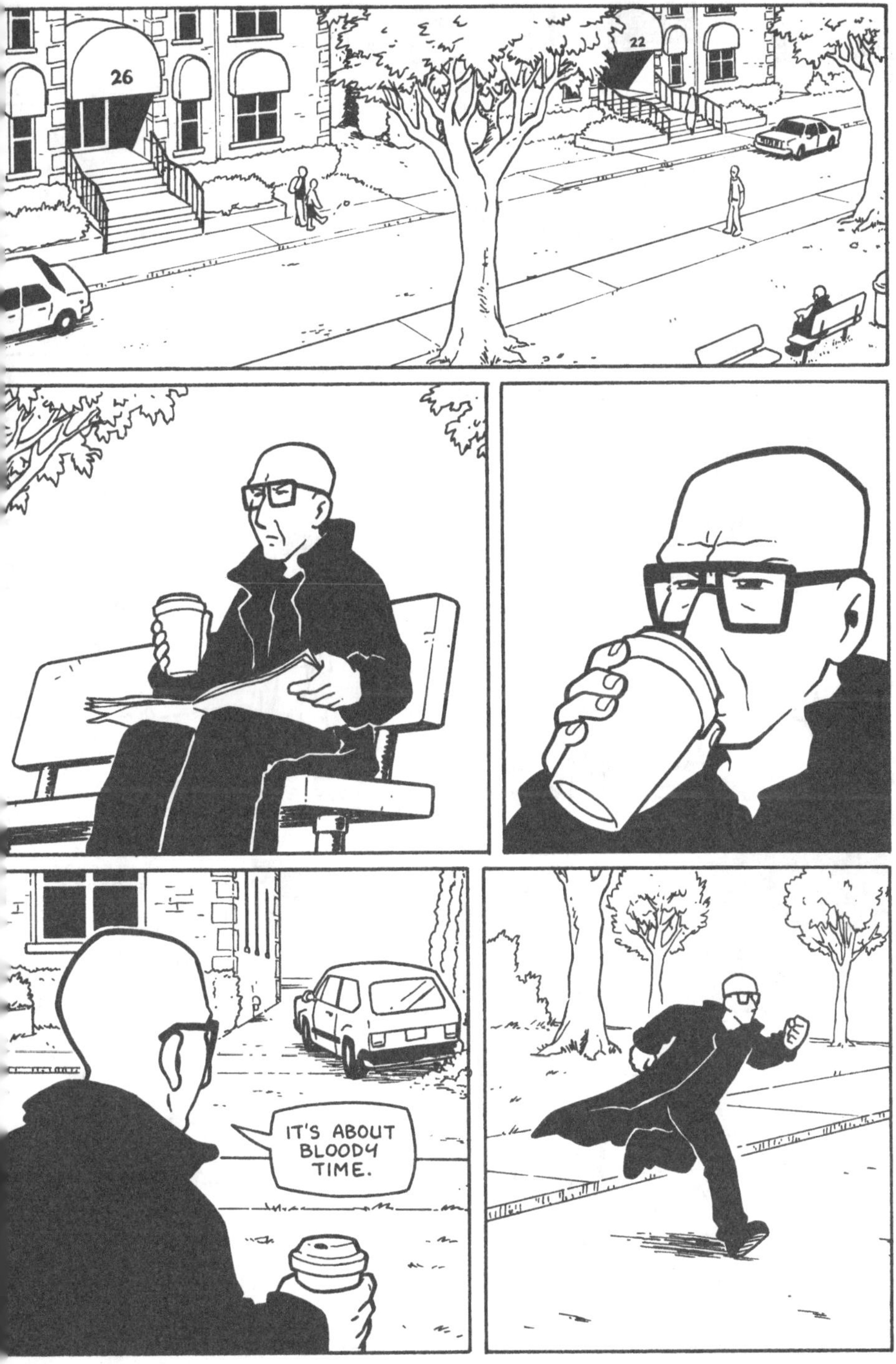
26
22
IT'S ABOUT BLOODY TIME.

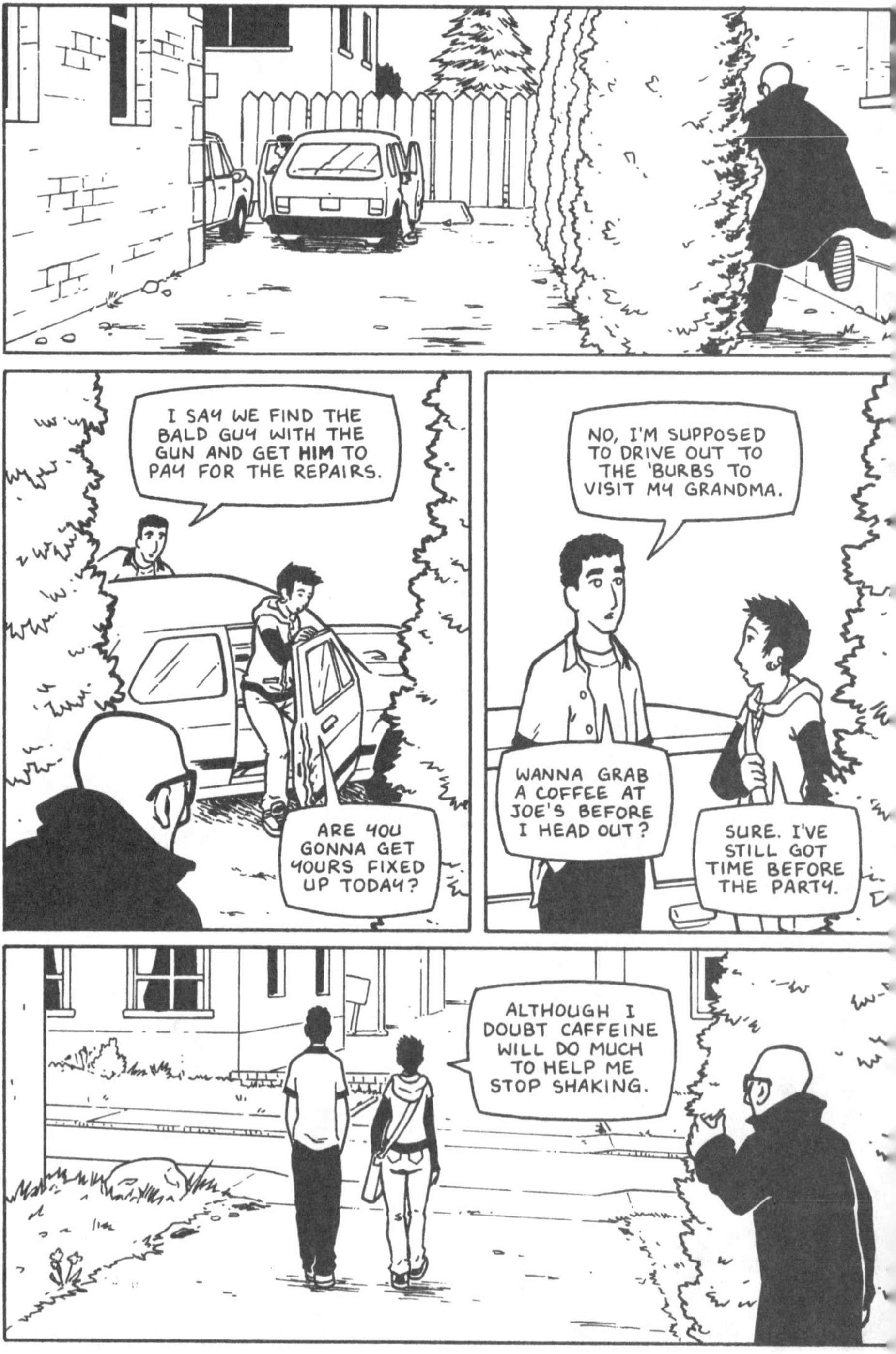
I SAY WE FIND THE BALD GUY WITH THE GUN AND GET **HIM** TO PAY FOR THE REPAIRS.
ARE YOU GONNA GET YOURS FIXED UP TODAY?
NO, I'M SUPPOSED TO DRIVE OUT TO THE 'BURBS TO VISIT MY GRANDMA.
WANNA GRAB A COFFEE AT JOE'S BEFORE I HEAD OUT?
SURE. I'VE STILL GOT TIME BEFORE THE PARTY.
ALTHOUGH I DOUBT CAFFEINE WILL DO MUCH TO HELP ME STOP SHAKING.

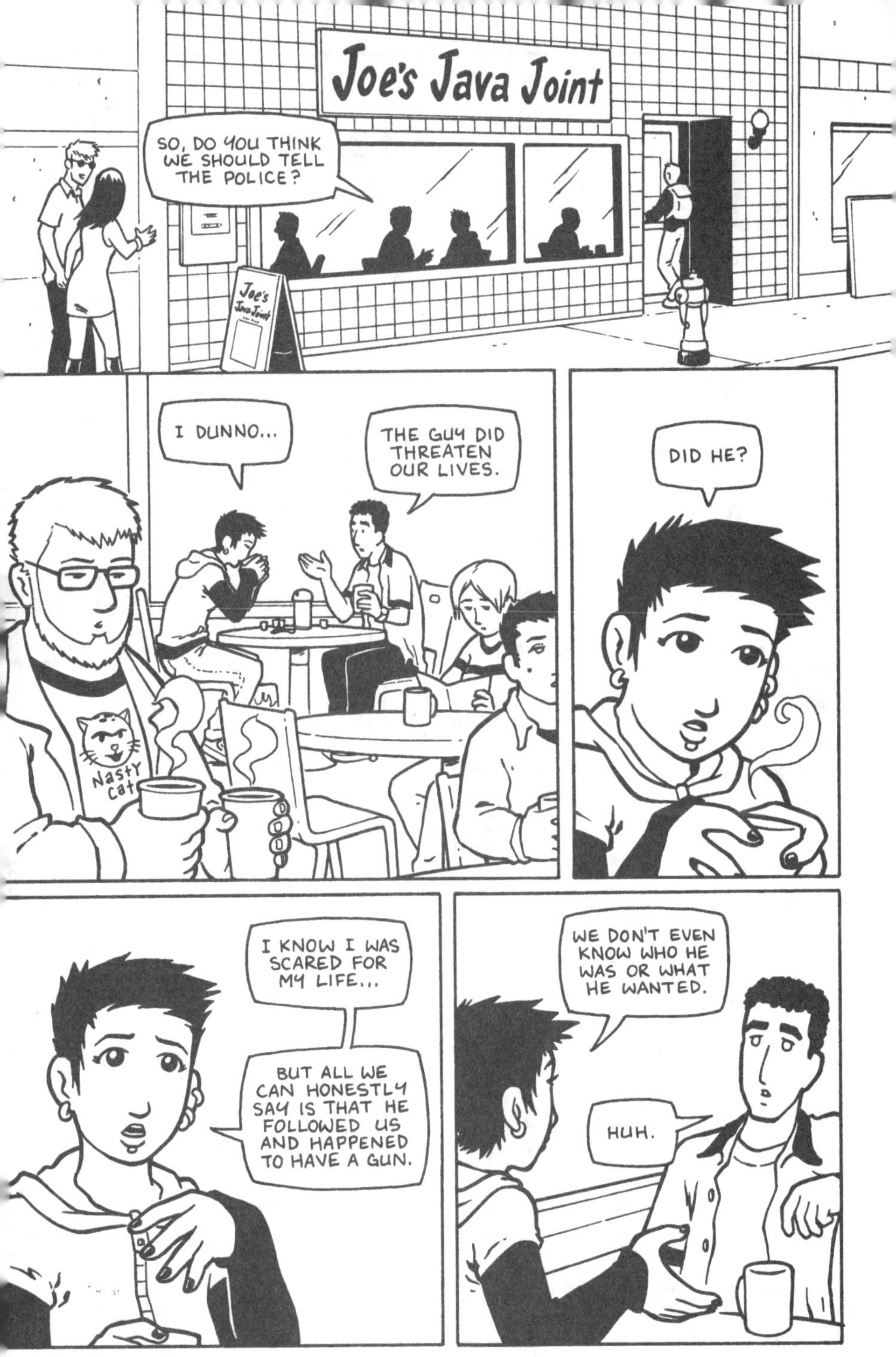
Joe's Java Joint
SO, DO YOU THINK WE SHOULD TELL THE POLICE?
Joe's Java Joint
I DUNNO...
THE GUY DID THREATEN OUR LIVES.
Nasty Cat
DID HE?
I KNOW I WAS SCARED FOR MY LIFE...
BUT ALL WE CAN HONESTLY SAY IS THAT HE FOLLOWED US AND HAPPENED TO HAVE A GUN.
WE DON'T EVEN KNOW WHO HE WAS OR WHAT HE WANTED.
HUH.

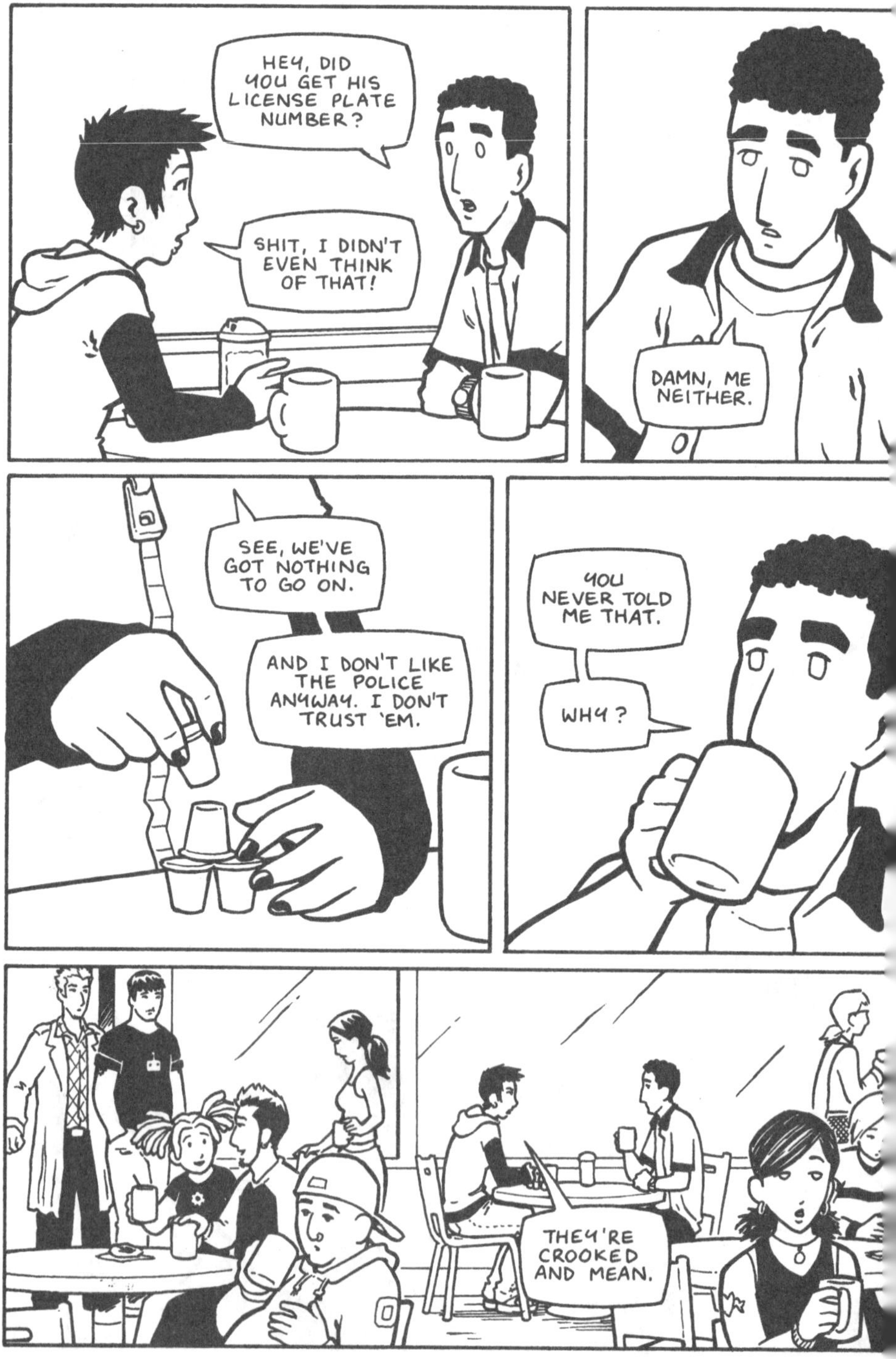
HEY, DID YOU GET HIS LICENSE PLATE NUMBER?
SHIT, I DIDN'T EVEN THINK OF THAT!
DAMN, ME NEITHER.
SEE, WE'VE GOT NOTHING TO GO ON.
AND I DON'T LIKE THE POLICE ANYWAY. I DON'T TRUST 'EM.
YOU NEVER TOLD ME THAT.
WHY?
THEY'RE CROOKED AND MEAN.

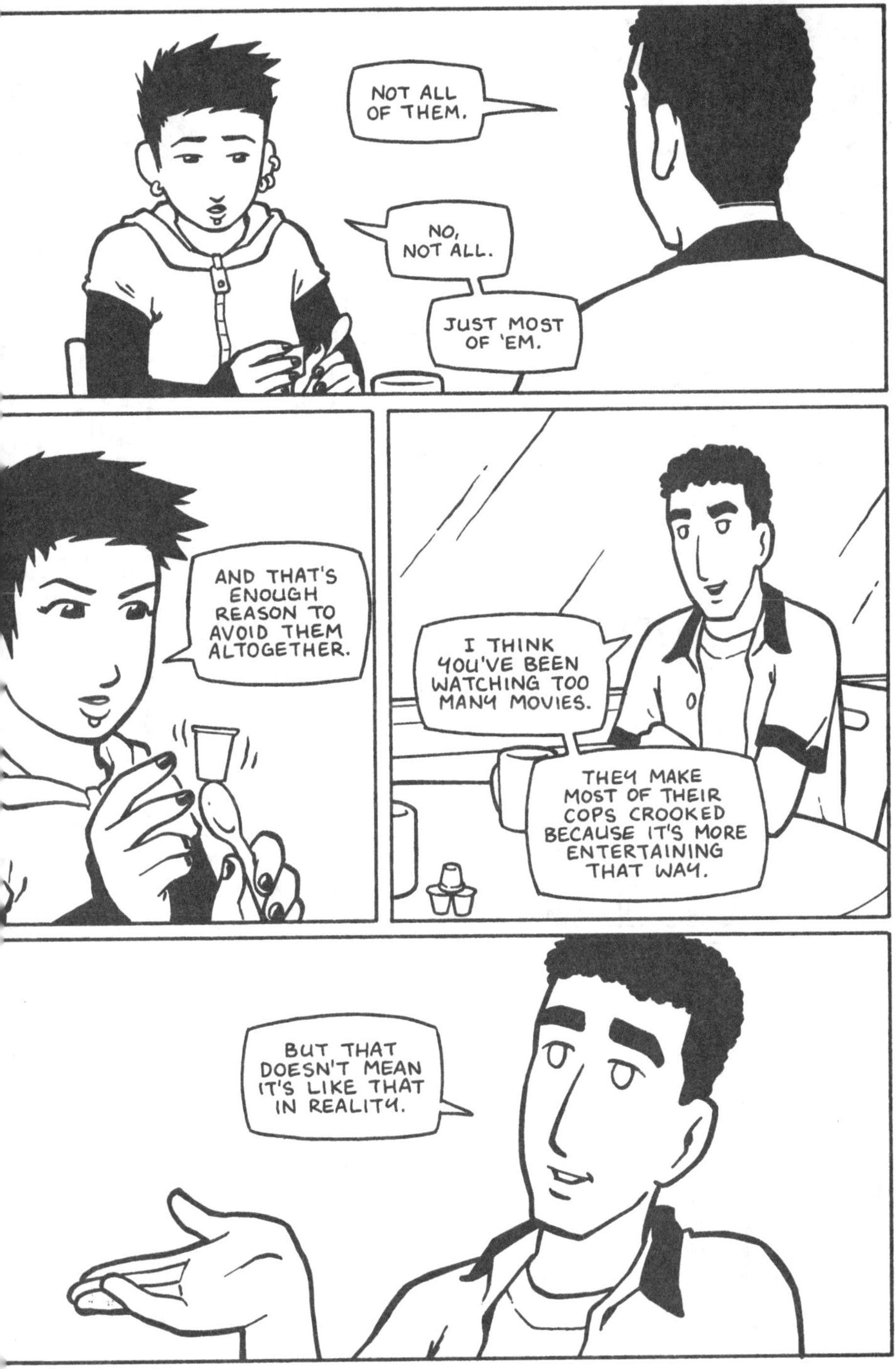
NOT ALL OF THEM.
NO, NOT ALL.
JUST MOST OF 'EM.
AND THAT'S ENOUGH REASON TO AVOID THEM ALTOGETHER.
I THINK YOU'VE BEEN WATCHING TOO MANY MOVIES.
THEY MAKE MOST OF THEIR COPS CROOKED BECAUSE IT'S MORE ENTERTAINING THAT WAY.
BUT THAT DOESN'T MEAN IT'S LIKE THAT IN REALITY.

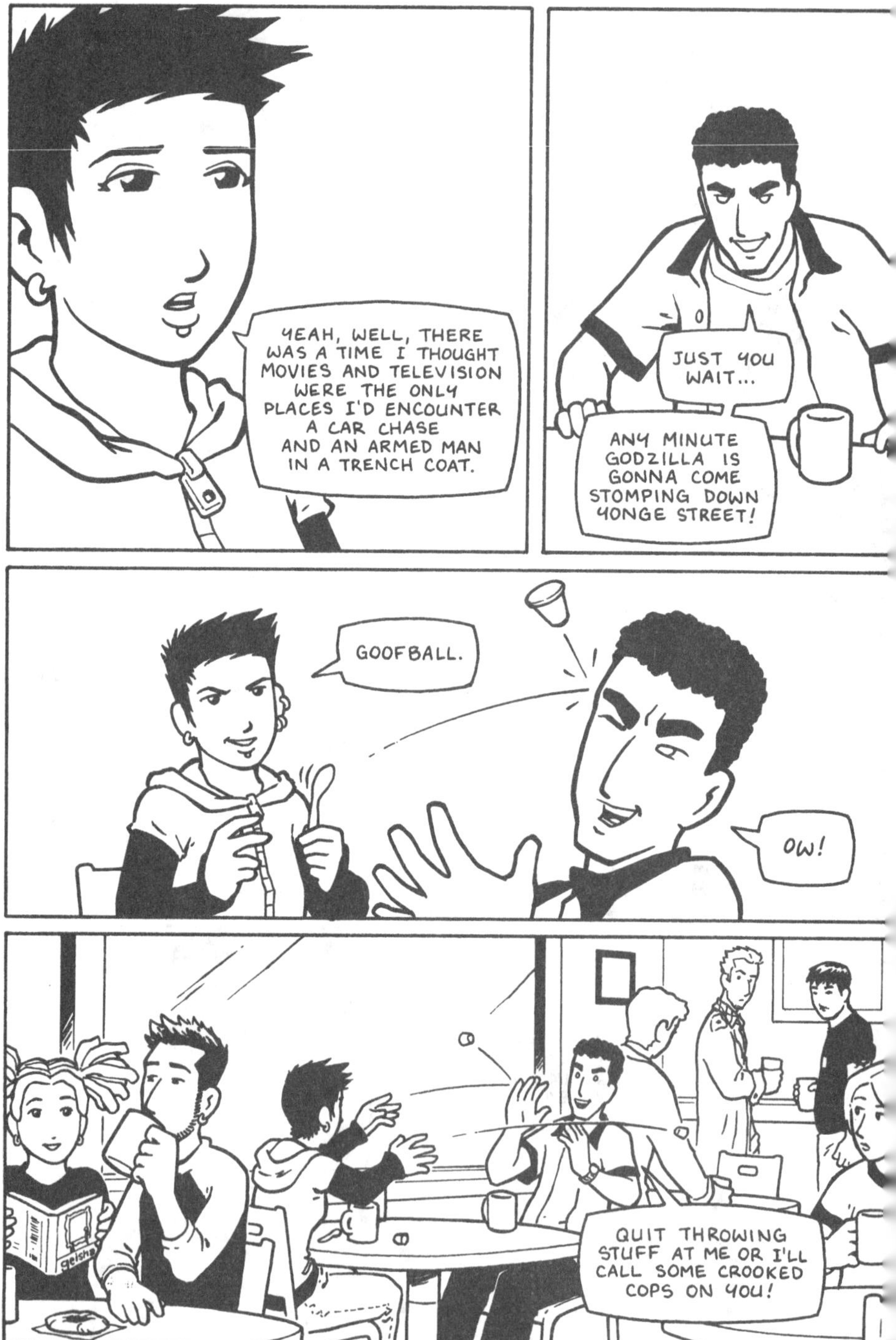
YEAH, WELL, THERE WAS A TIME I THOUGHT MOVIES AND TELEVISION WERE THE ONLY PLACES I'D ENCOUNTER A CAR CHASE AND AN ARMED MAN IN A TRENCH COAT.
JUST YOU WAIT...
ANY MINUTE GODZILLA IS GONNA COME STOMPING DOWN YONGE STREET!
GOOFBALL.
OW!
geisha
QUIT THROWING STUFF AT ME OR I'LL CALL SOME CROOKED COPS ON YOU!

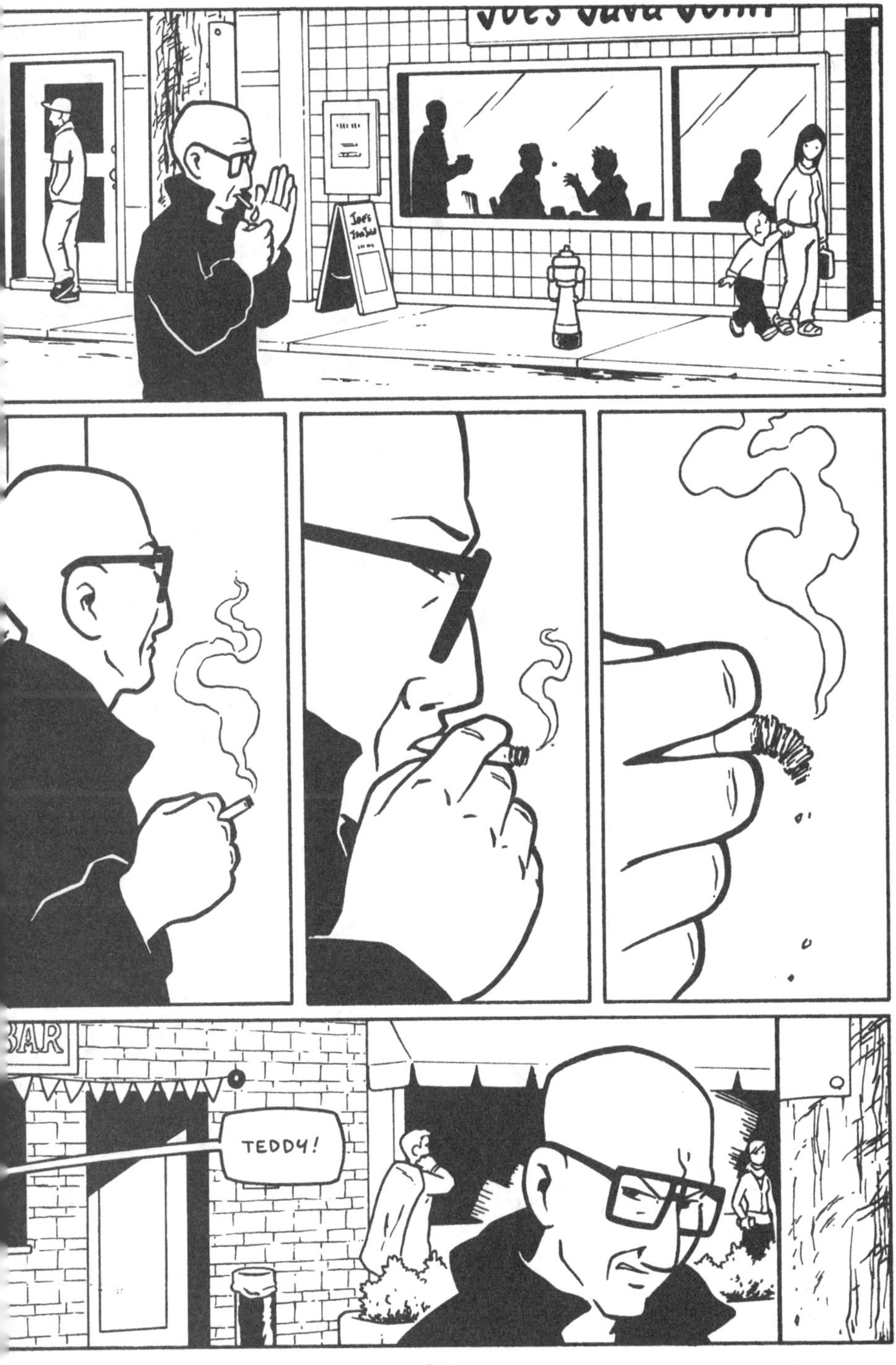
BAR
TEDDY!

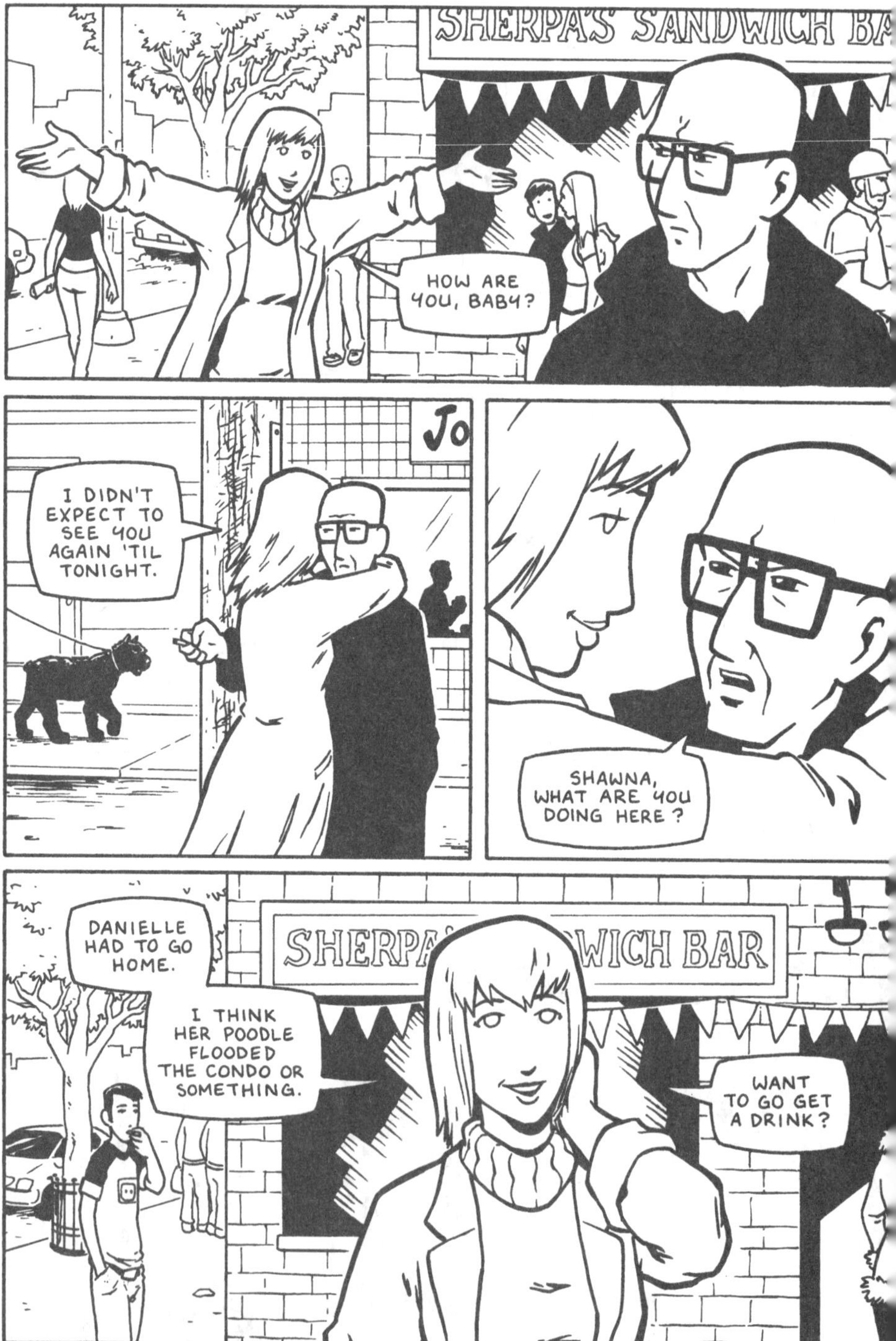
SHERPA'S SANDWICH BA
HOW ARE YOU, BABY?
I DIDN'T EXPECT TO SEE YOU AGAIN 'TIL TONIGHT.
SHAWNA, WHAT ARE YOU DOING HERE?
DANIELLE HAD TO GO HOME.
I THINK HER POODLE FLOODED THE CONDO OR SOMETHING.
WANT TO GO GET A DRINK?

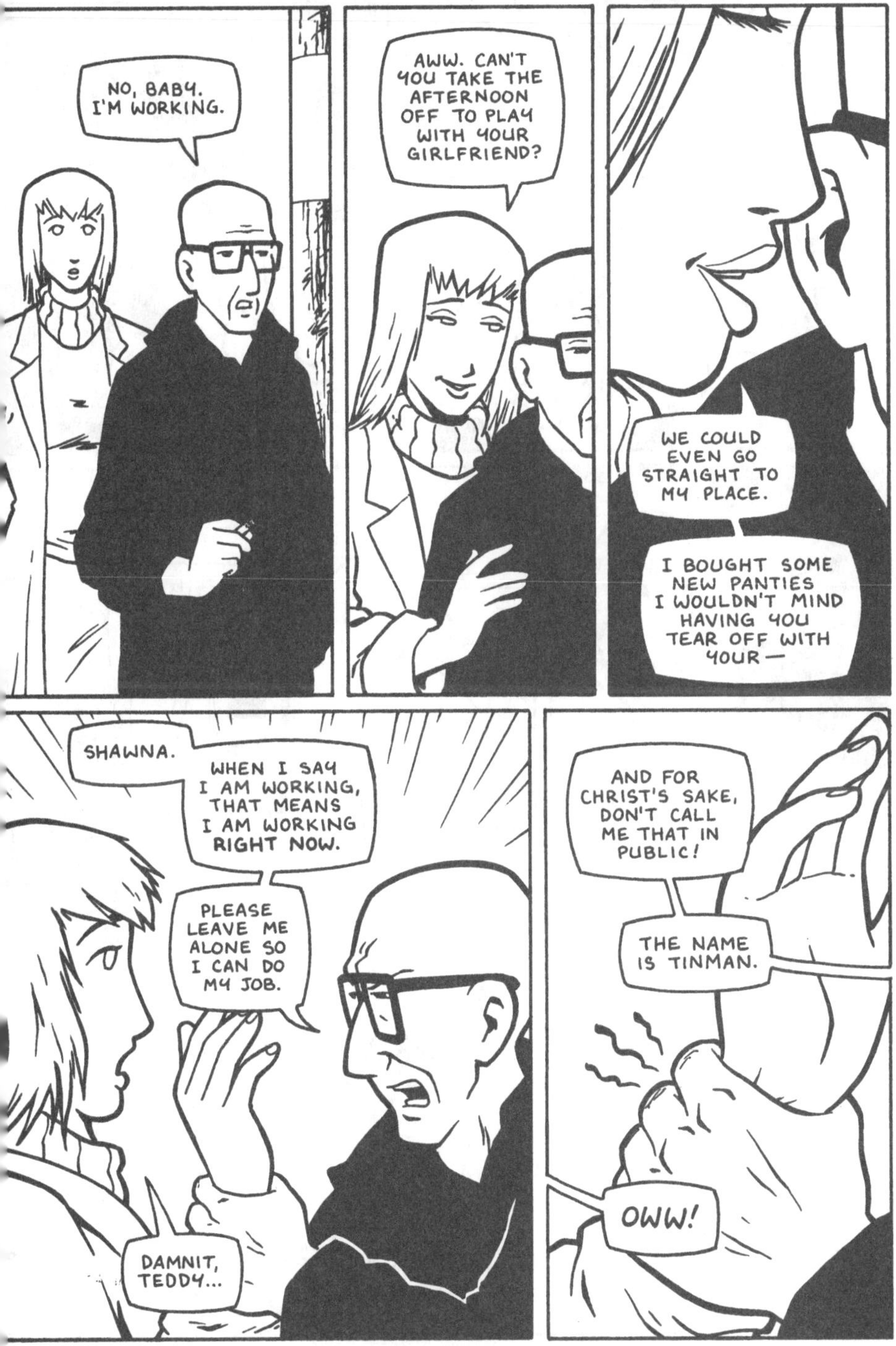

NO, BABY. I'M WORKING.
AWW. CAN'T YOU TAKE THE AFTERNOON OFF TO PLAY WITH YOUR GIRLFRIEND?
WE COULD EVEN GO STRAIGHT TO MY PLACE.
I BOUGHT SOME NEW PANTIES I WOULDN'T MIND HAVING YOU TEAR OFF WITH YOUR—
SHAWNA.
WHEN I SAY I AM WORKING, THAT MEANS I AM WORKING RIGHT NOW.
PLEASE LEAVE ME ALONE SO I CAN DO MY JOB.
DAMNIT, TEDDY...
AND FOR CHRIST'S SAKE, DON'T CALL ME THAT IN PUBLIC!
THE NAME IS TINMAN.
OWW!

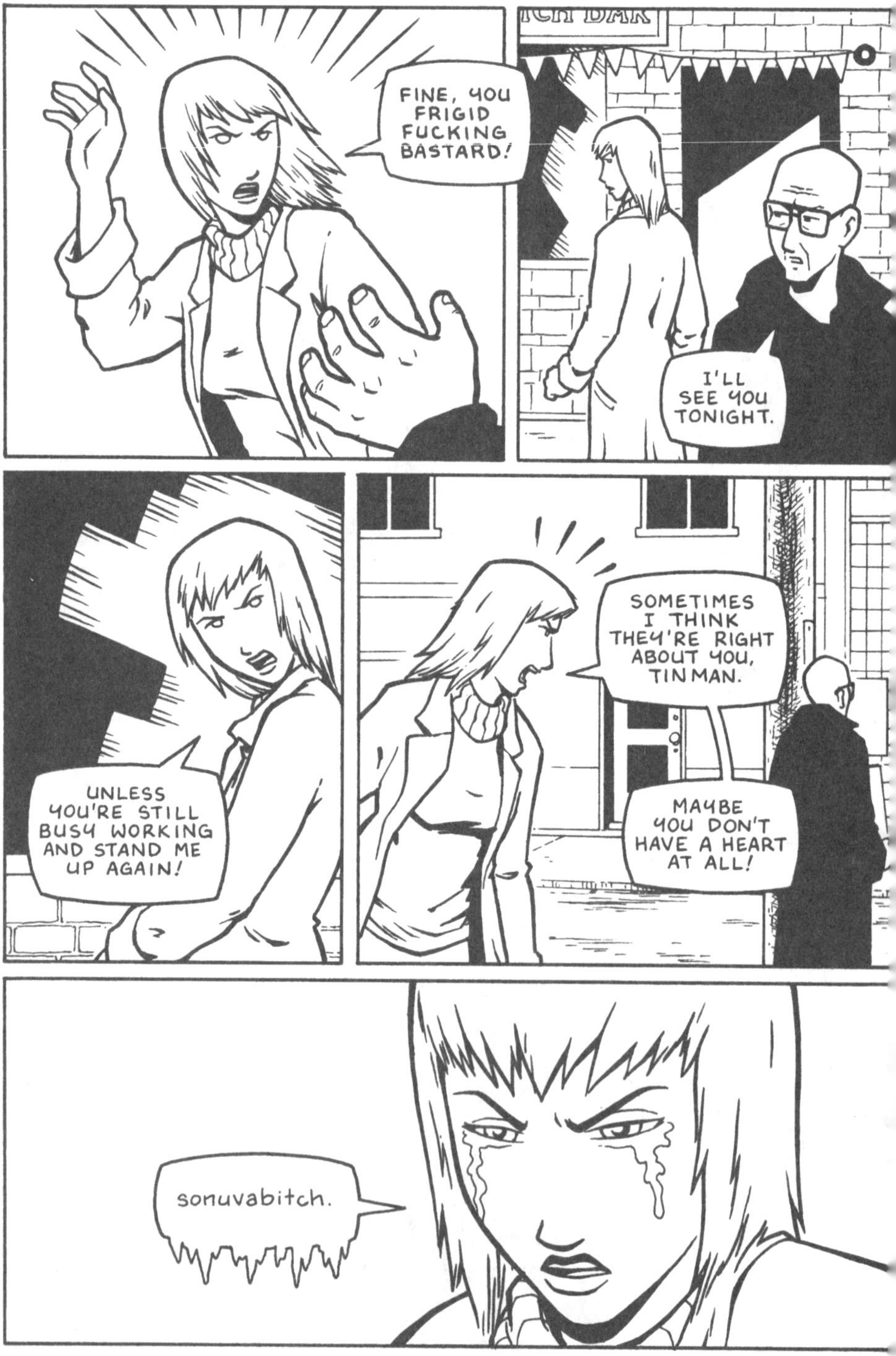
FINE, YOU FRIGID FUCKING BASTARD!
I'LL SEE YOU TONIGHT.
UNLESS YOU'RE STILL BUSY WORKING AND STAND ME UP AGAIN!
SOMETIMES I THINK THEY'RE RIGHT ABOUT YOU, TINMAN.
MAYBE YOU DON'T HAVE A HEART AT ALL!
sonuvabitch.

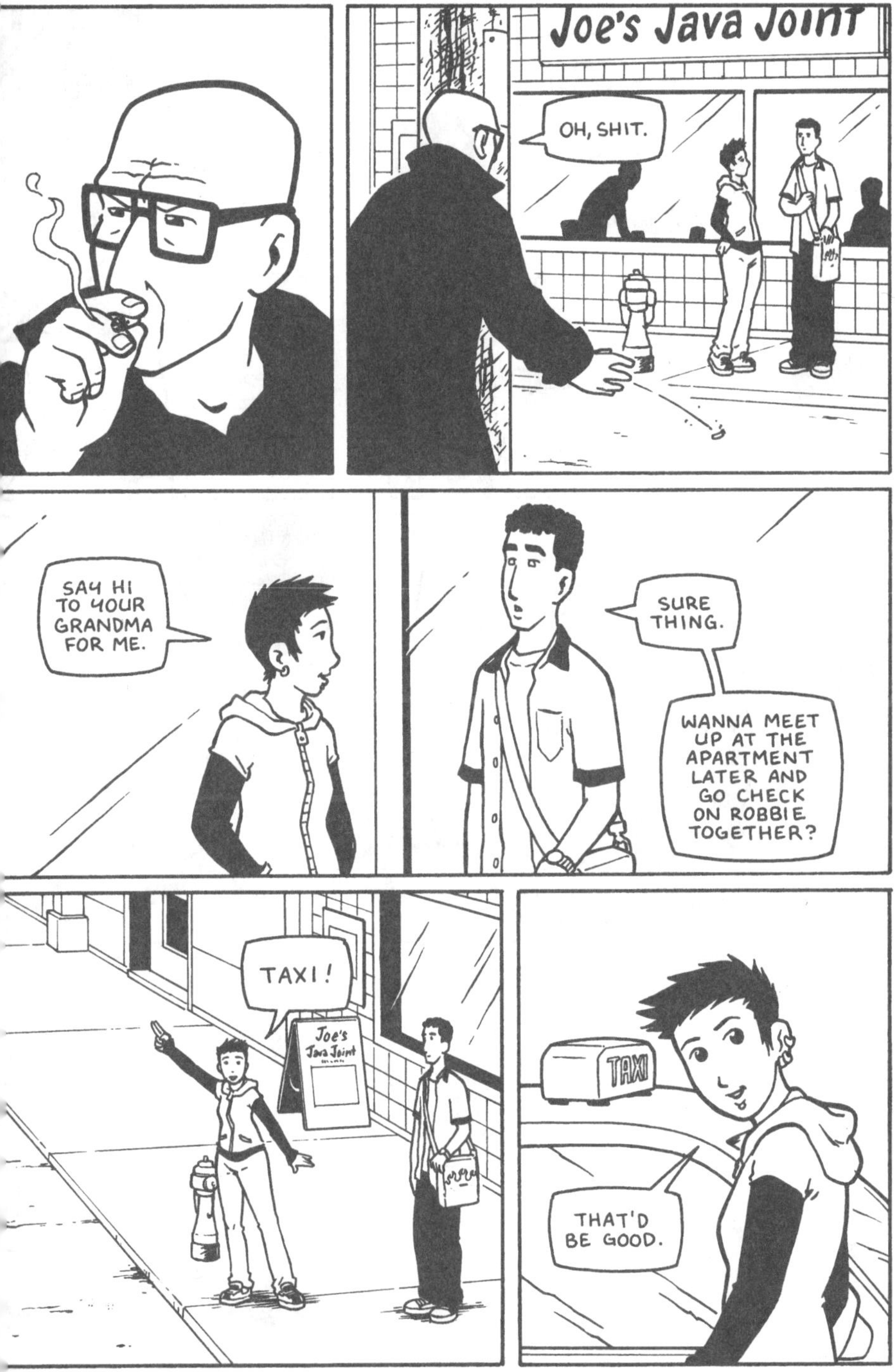
Joe's Java Joint
OH, SHIT.
SAY HI TO YOUR GRANDMA FOR ME.
SURE THING.
WANNA MEET UP AT THE APARTMENT LATER AND GO CHECK ON ROBBIE TOGETHER?
TAXI!
Joe's Java Joint
TAXI
THAT'D BE GOOD.

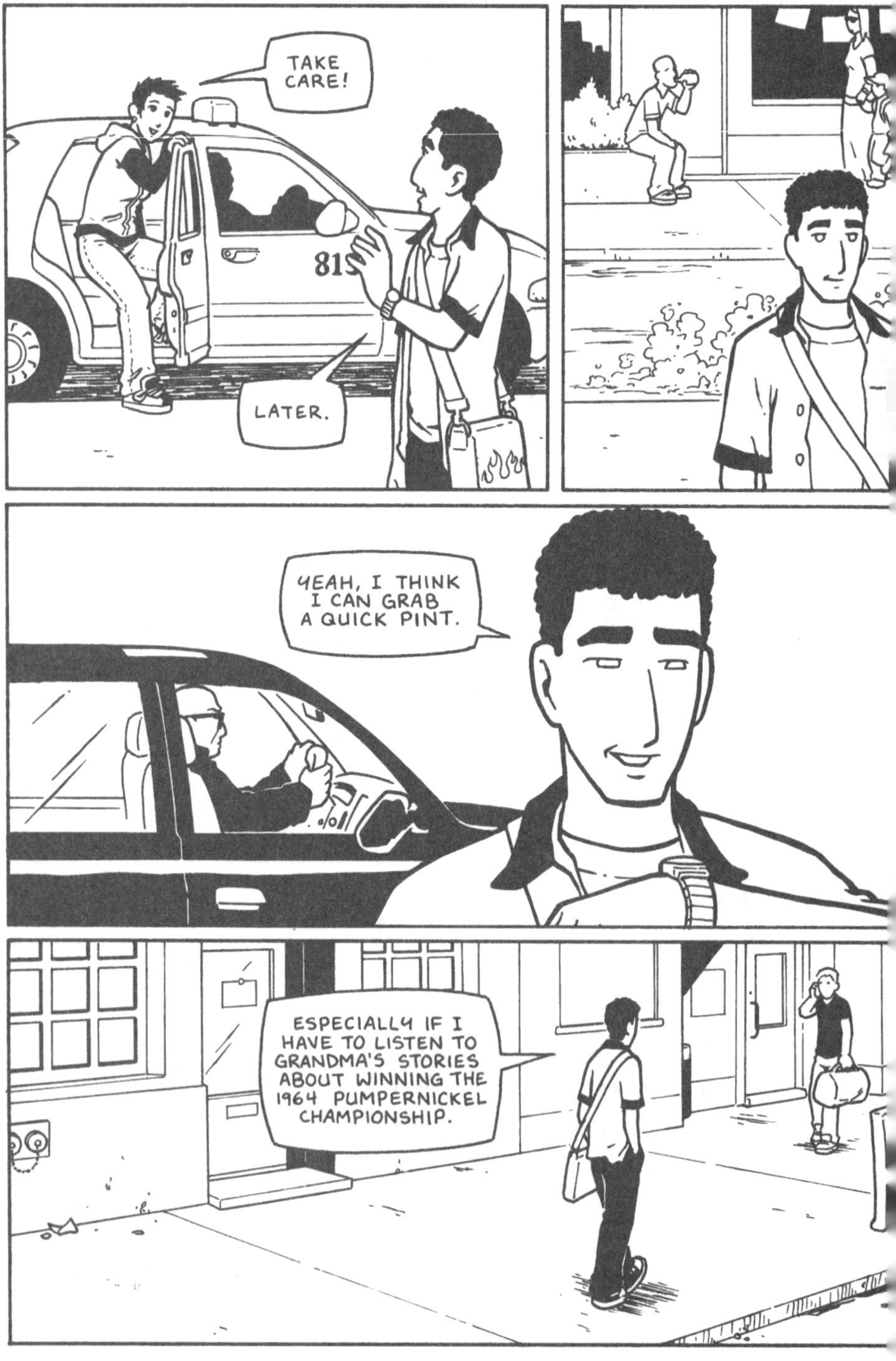
TAKE CARE!
LATER.
YEAH, I THINK I CAN GRAB A QUICK PINT.
ESPECIALLY IF I HAVE TO LISTEN TO GRANDMA'S STORIES ABOUT WINNING THE 1964 PUMPERNICKEL CHAMPIONSHIP.

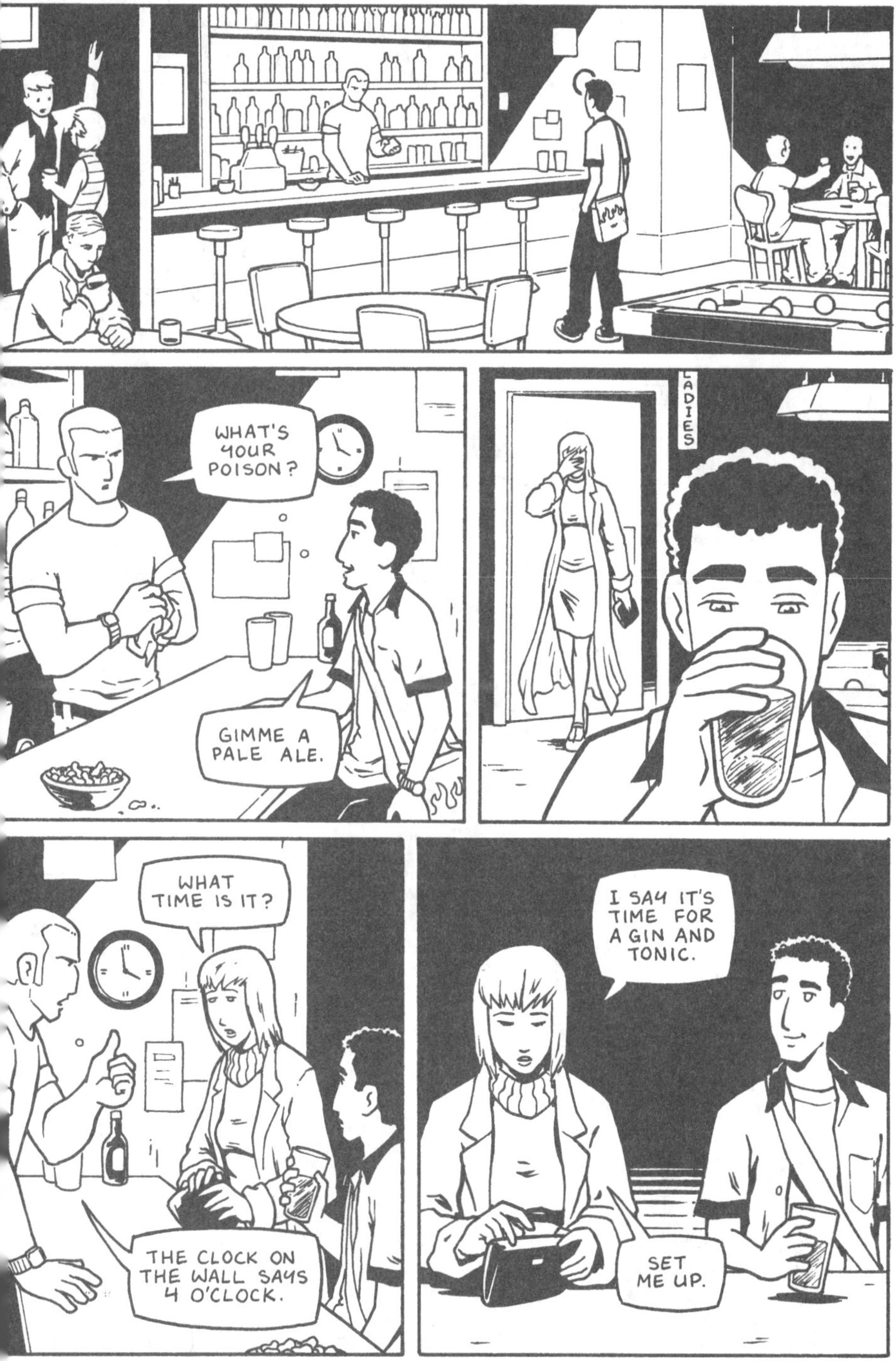
LADIES
WHAT'S YOUR POISON?
GIMME A PALE ALE.
WHAT TIME IS IT?
THE CLOCK ON THE WALL SAYS 4 O'CLOCK.
I SAY IT'S TIME FOR A GIN AND TONIC.
SET ME UP.

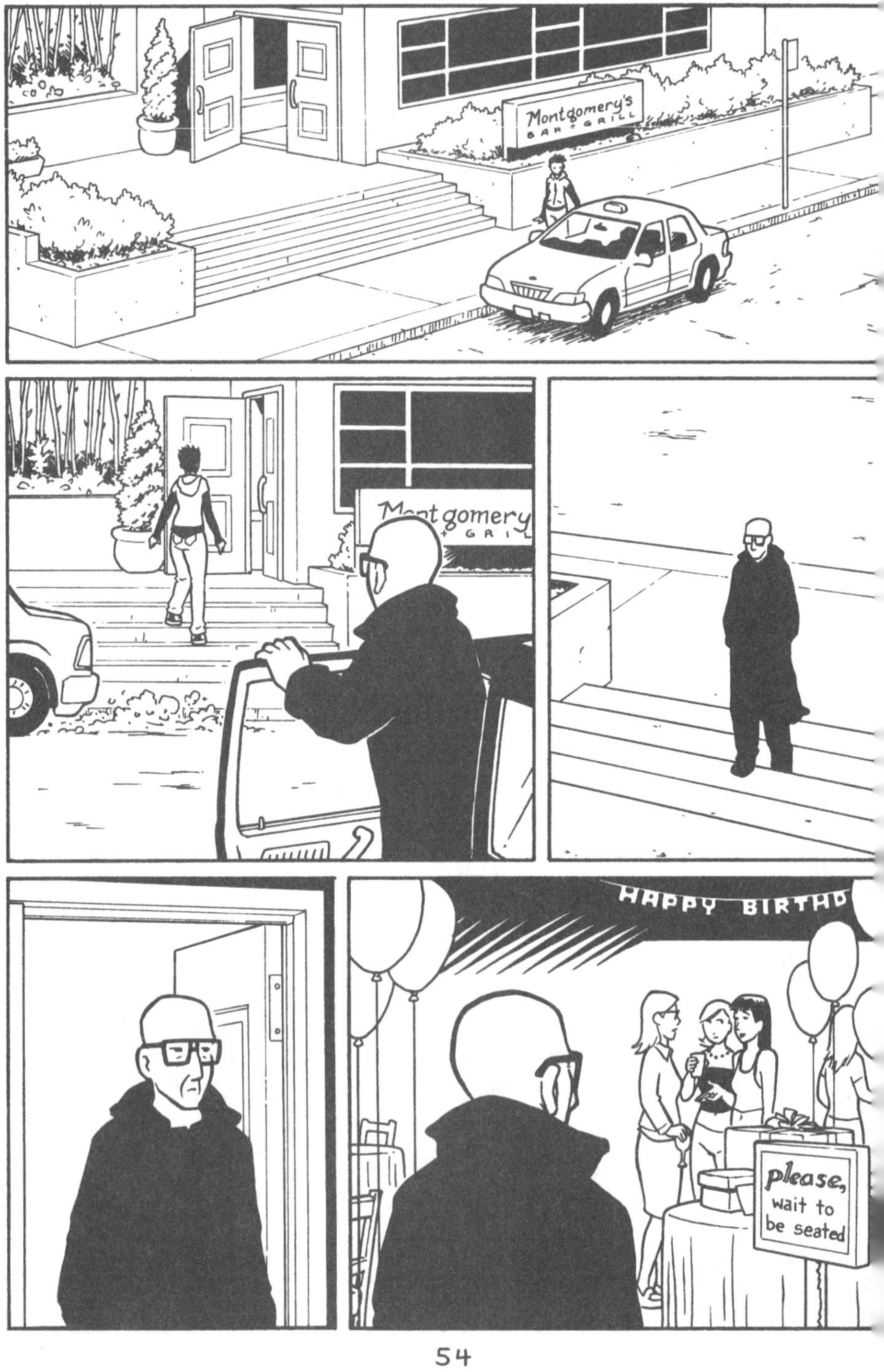
Montgomery's
BAR + GRILL
Montgomery
HAPPY BIRTHD
please,
wait to
be seated

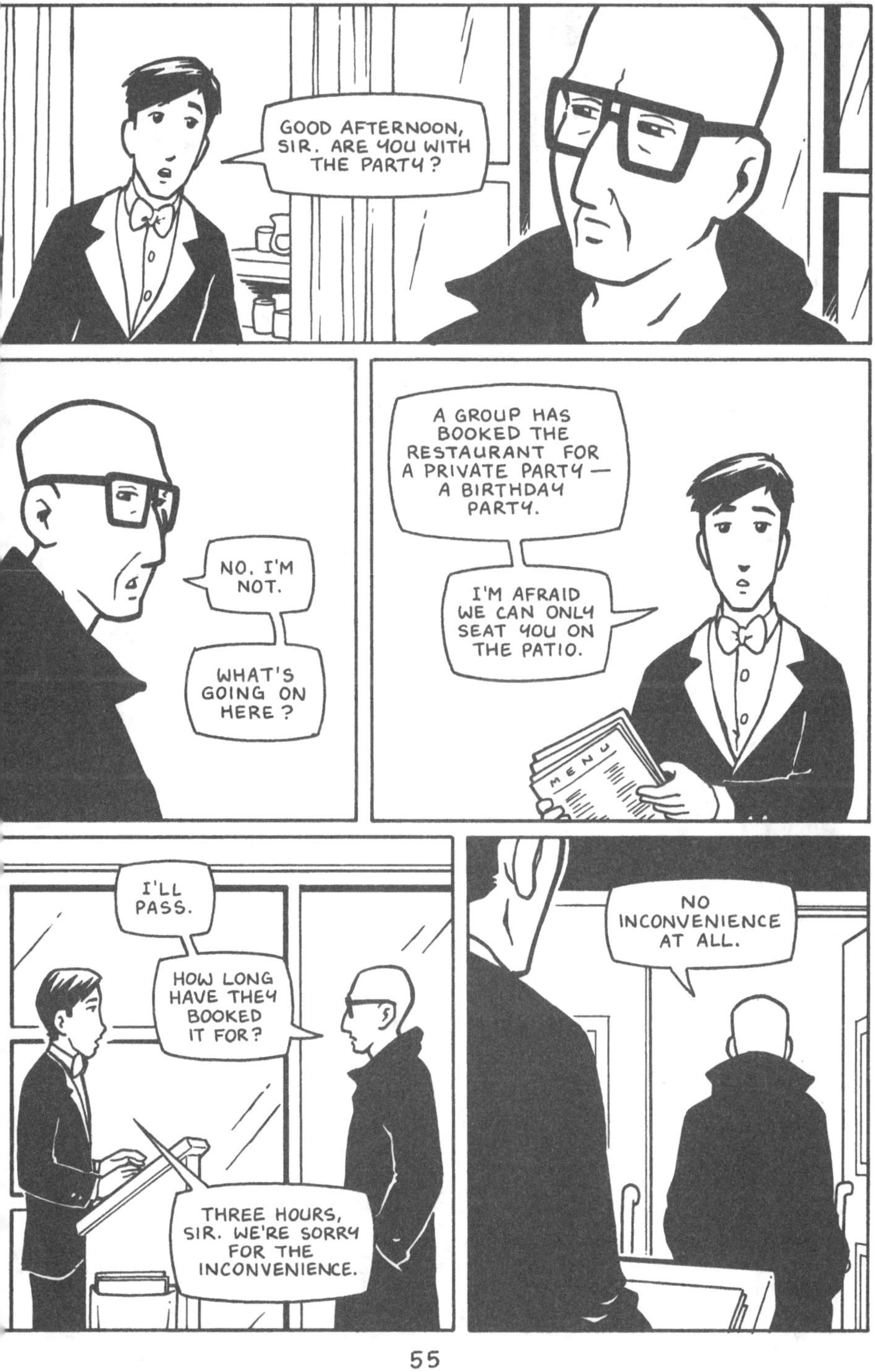
GOOD AFTERNOON, SIR. ARE YOU WITH THE PARTY?
NO. I'M NOT.
WHAT'S GOING ON HERE?
A GROUP HAS BOOKED THE RESTAURANT FOR A PRIVATE PARTY — A BIRTHDAY PARTY.
I'M AFRAID WE CAN ONLY SEAT YOU ON THE PATIO.
MENU
I'LL PASS.
HOW LONG HAVE THEY BOOKED IT FOR?
THREE HOURS, SIR. WE'RE SORRY FOR THE INCONVENIENCE.
NO INCONVENIENCE AT ALL.

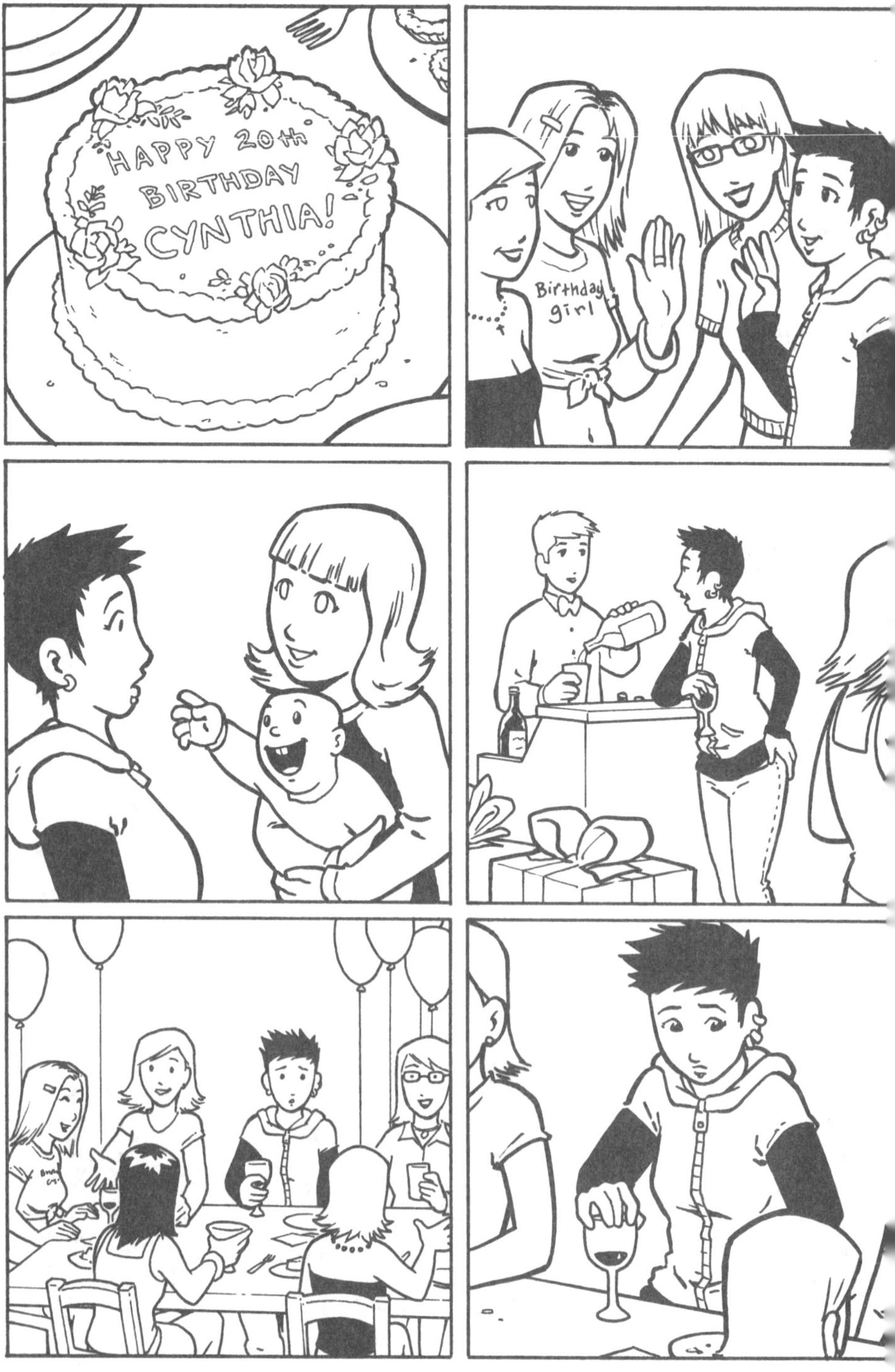
HAPPY 20th BIRTHDAY CYNTHIA!
Birthday girl

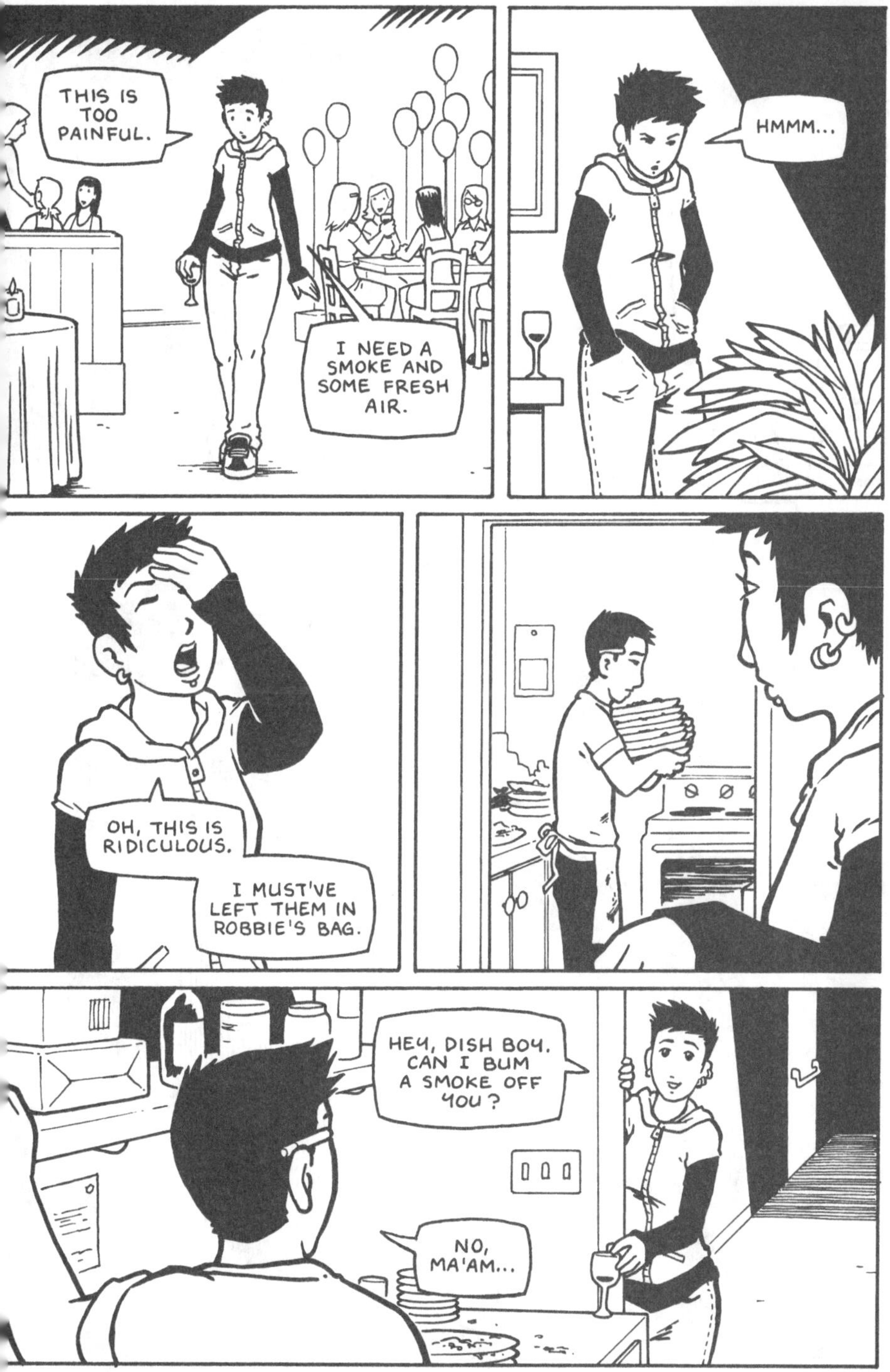
THIS IS TOO PAINFUL.
I NEED A SMOKE AND SOME FRESH AIR.
HMMM...
OH, THIS IS RIDICULOUS.
I MUST'VE LEFT THEM IN ROBBIE'S BAG.
HEY, DISH BOY. CAN I BUM A SMOKE OFF YOU?
NO, MA'AM...

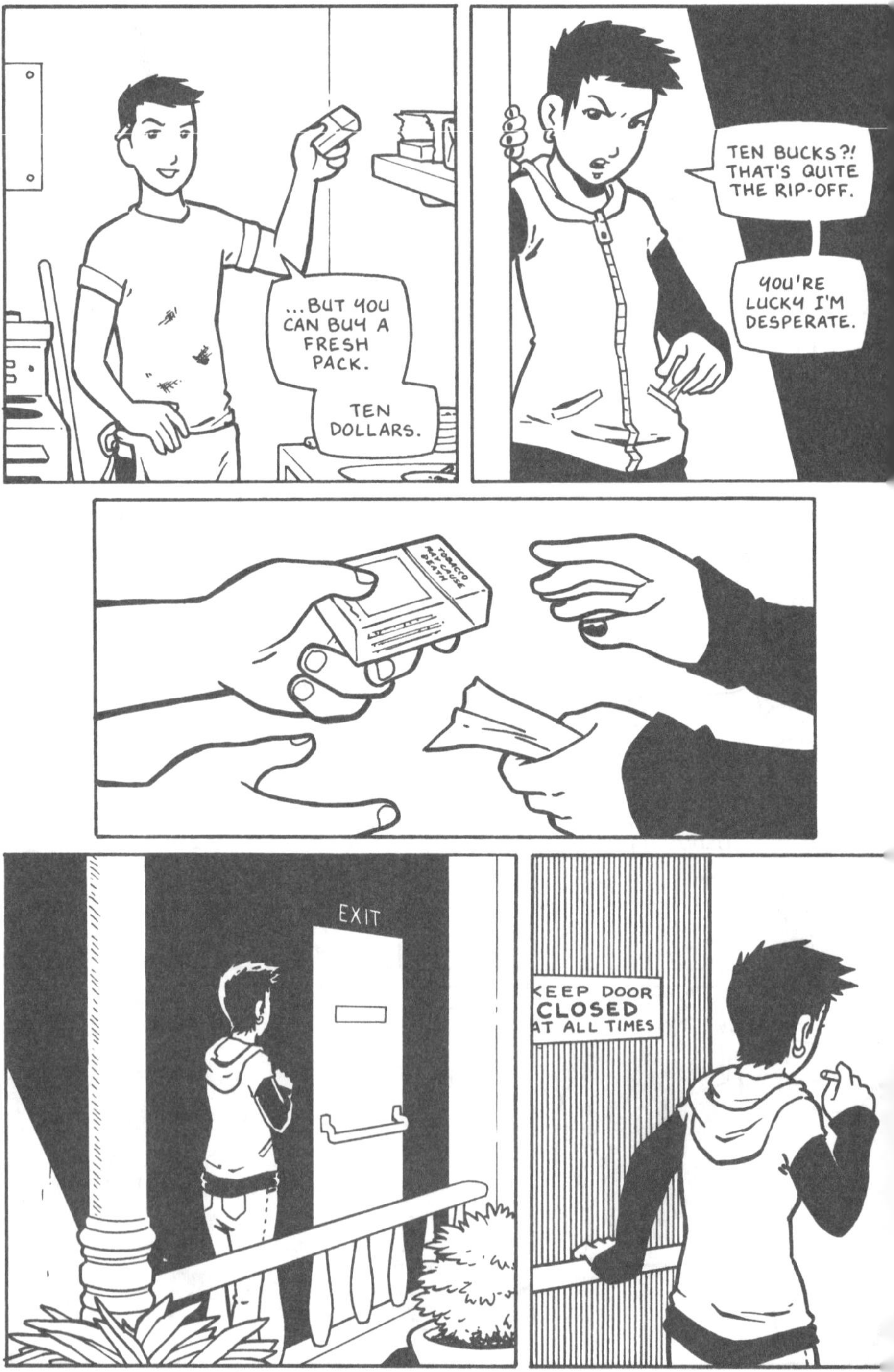
...BUT YOU CAN BUY A FRESH PACK.
TEN DOLLARS.
TEN BUCKS?! THAT'S QUITE THE RIP-OFF.
YOU'RE LUCKY I'M DESPERATE.
TOBACCO MAY CAUSE DEATH
EXIT
KEEP DOOR CLOSED AT ALL TIMES

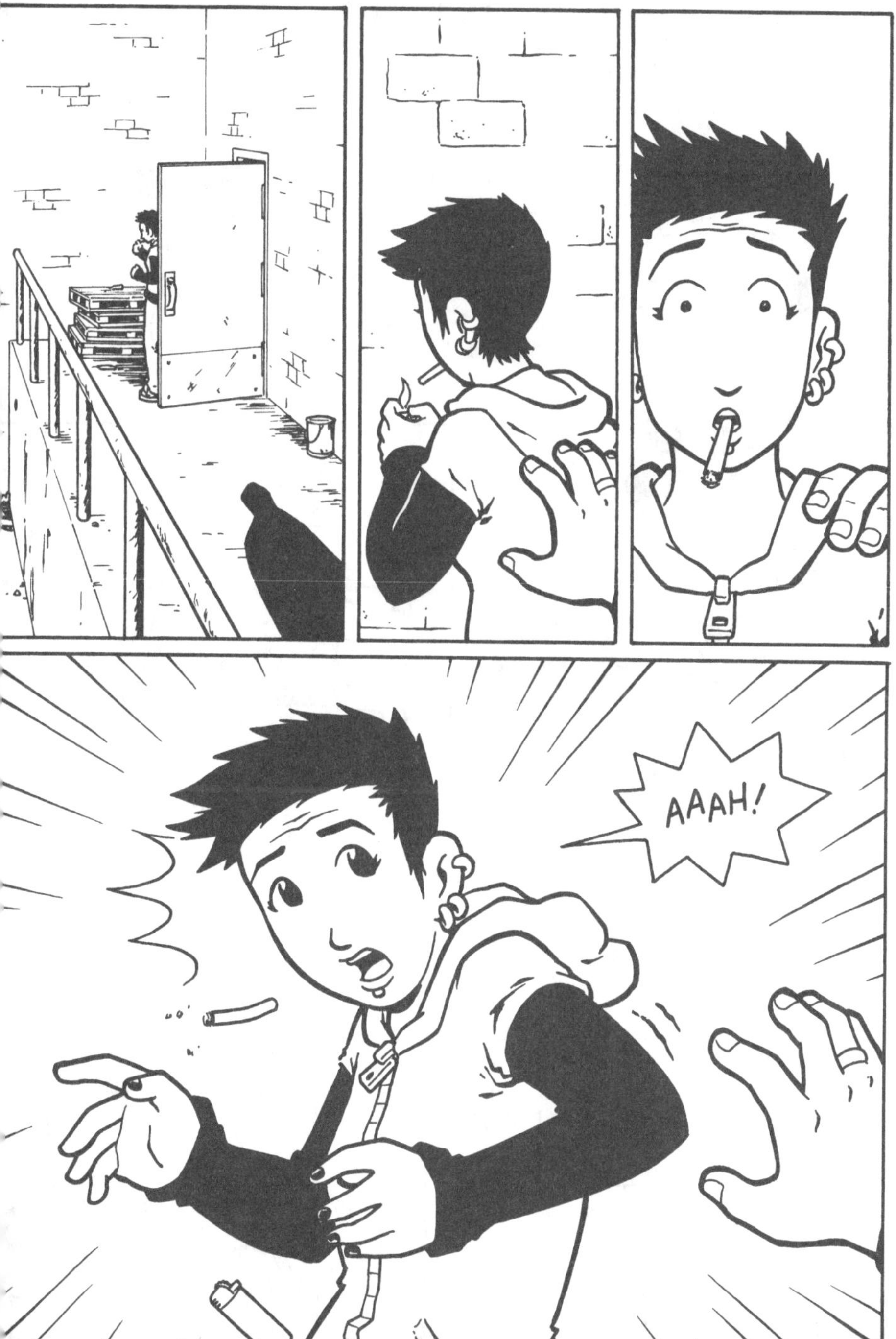
AAAH!

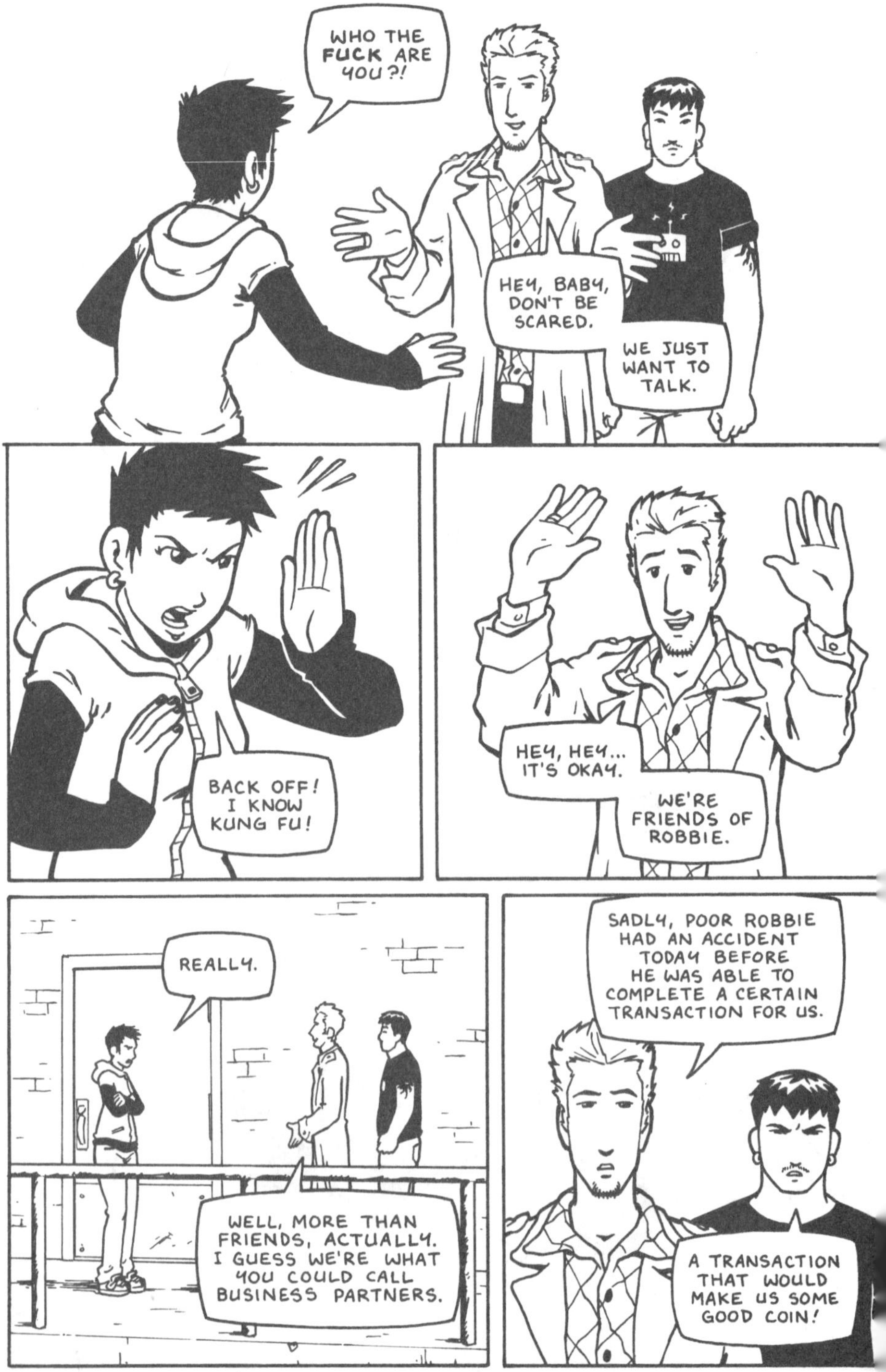
WHO THE FUCK ARE YOU?!
HEY, BABY, DON'T BE SCARED.
WE JUST WANT TO TALK.
BACK OFF! I KNOW KUNG FU!
HEY, HEY... IT'S OKAY.
WE'RE FRIENDS OF ROBBIE.
REALLY.
WELL, MORE THAN FRIENDS, ACTUALLY. I GUESS WE'RE WHAT YOU COULD CALL BUSINESS PARTNERS.
SADLY, POOR ROBBIE HAD AN ACCIDENT TODAY BEFORE HE WAS ABLE TO COMPLETE A CERTAIN TRANSACTION FOR US.
A TRANSACTION THAT WOULD MAKE US SOME GOOD COIN!

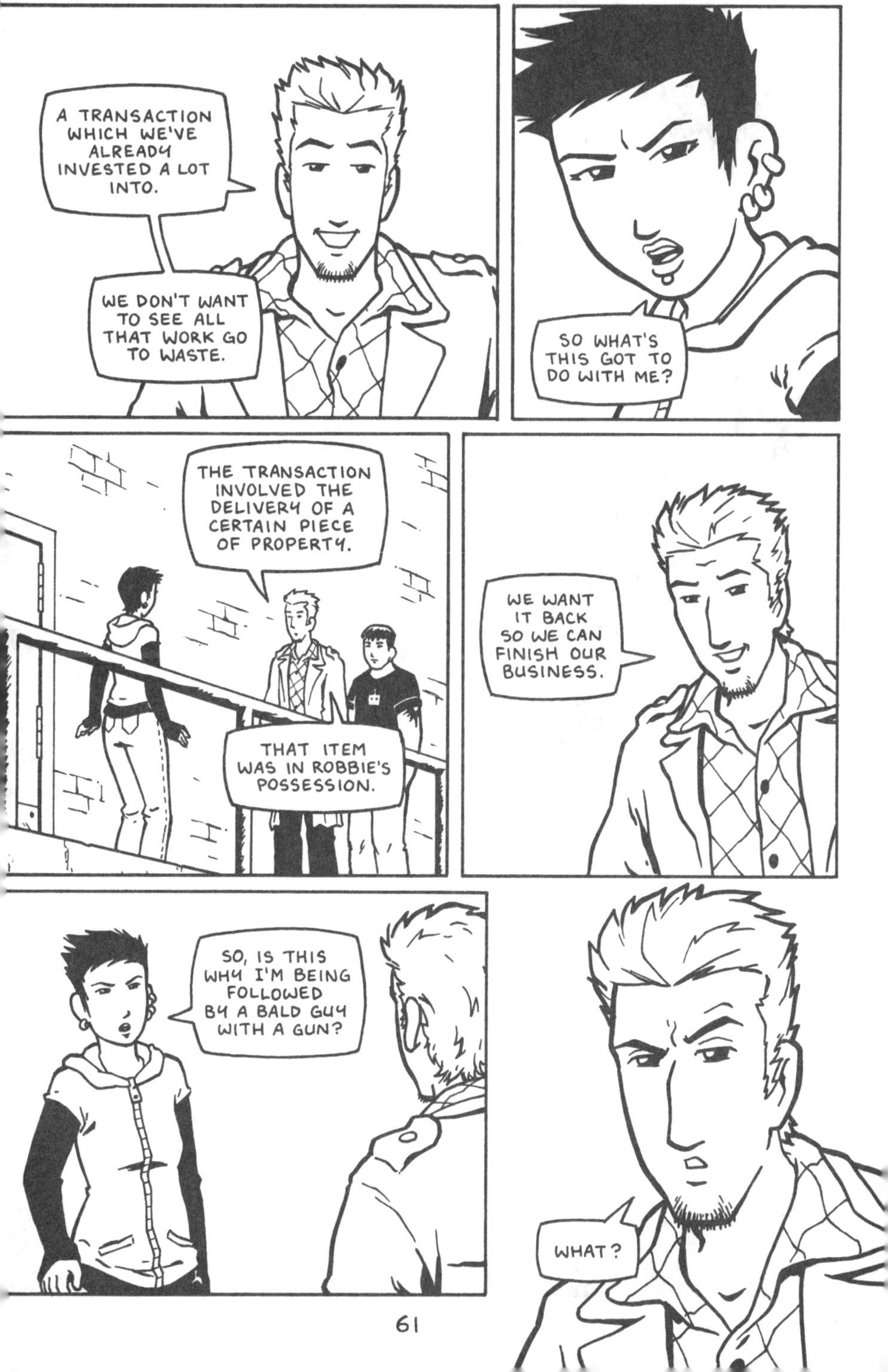
A TRANSACTION WHICH WE'VE ALREADY INVESTED A LOT INTO.
WE DON'T WANT TO SEE ALL THAT WORK GO TO WASTE.
SO WHAT'S THIS GOT TO DO WITH ME?
THE TRANSACTION INVOLVED THE DELIVERY OF A CERTAIN PIECE OF PROPERTY.
THAT ITEM WAS IN ROBBIE'S POSSESSION.
WE WANT IT BACK SO WE CAN FINISH OUR BUSINESS.
SO, IS THIS WHY I'M BEING FOLLOWED BY A BALD GUY WITH A GUN?
WHAT?

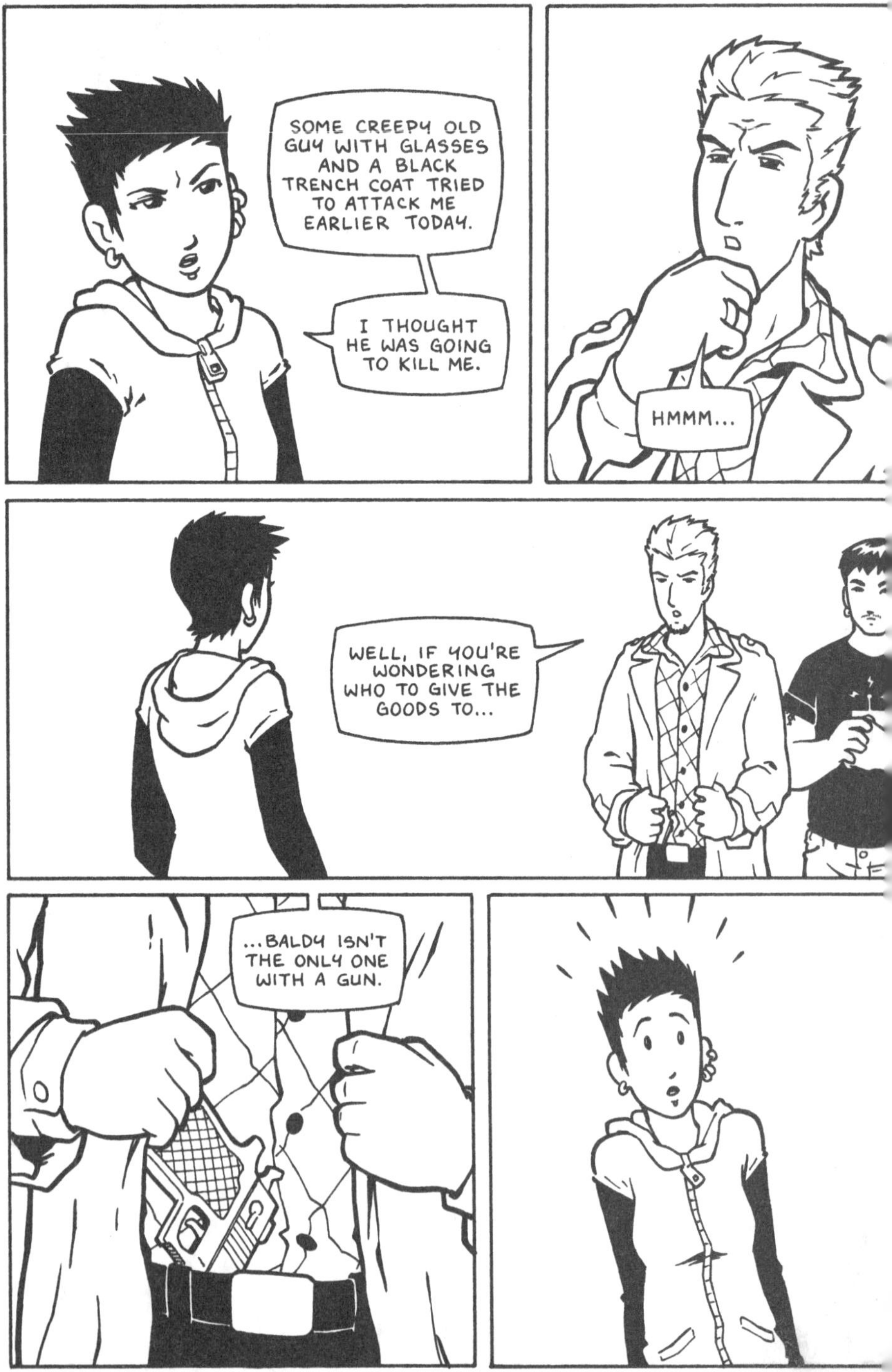
SOME CREEPY OLD GUY WITH GLASSES AND A BLACK TRENCH COAT TRIED TO ATTACK ME EARLIER TODAY.
I THOUGHT HE WAS GOING TO KILL ME.
HMMM...
WELL, IF YOU'RE WONDERING WHO TO GIVE THE GOODS TO...
...BALDY ISN'T THE ONLY ONE WITH A GUN.

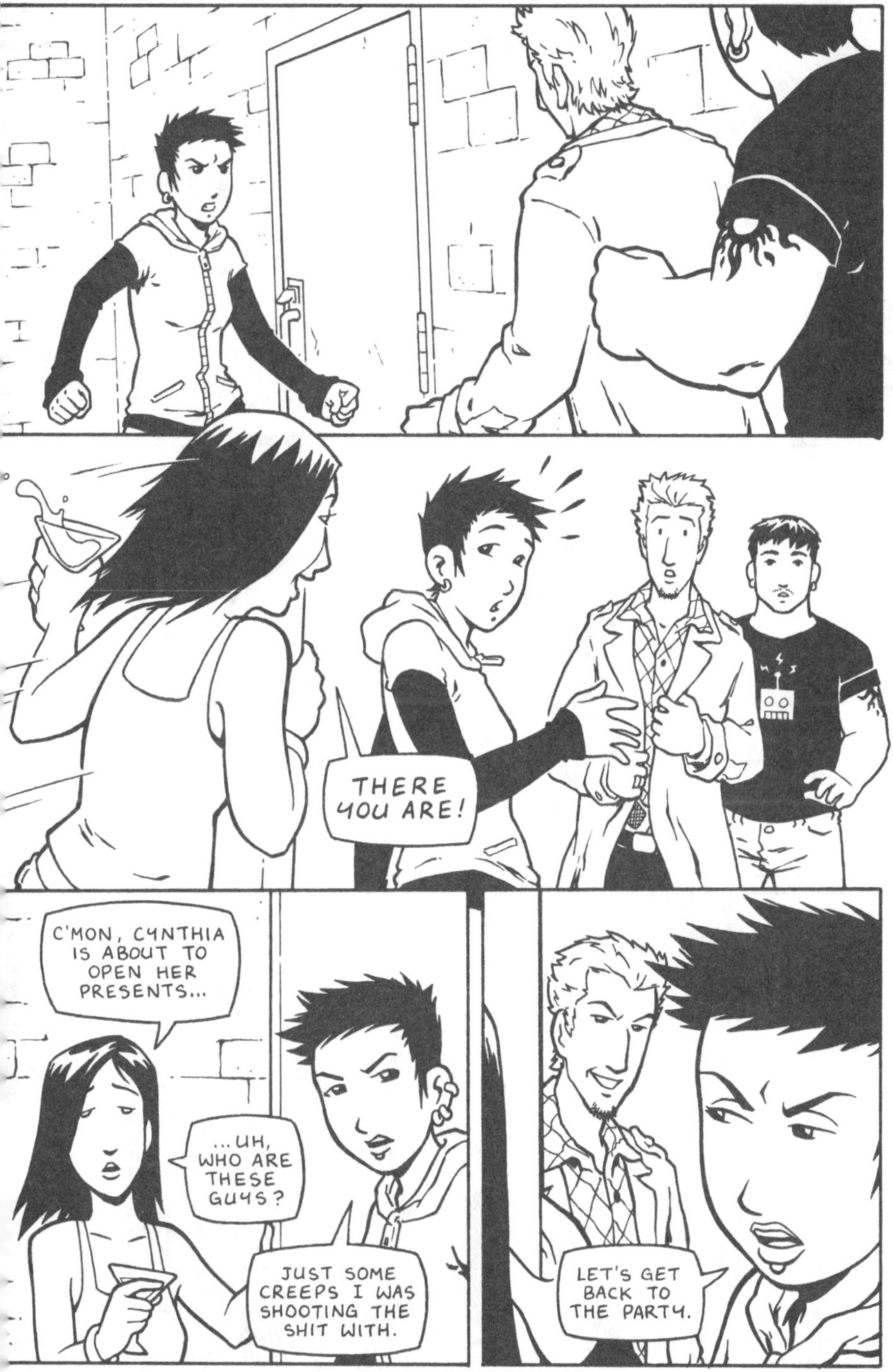
THERE YOU ARE!
C'MON, CYNTHIA IS ABOUT TO OPEN HER PRESENTS...
...UH, WHO ARE THESE GUYS?
JUST SOME CREEPS I WAS SHOOTING THE SHIT WITH.
LET'S GET BACK TO THE PARTY.

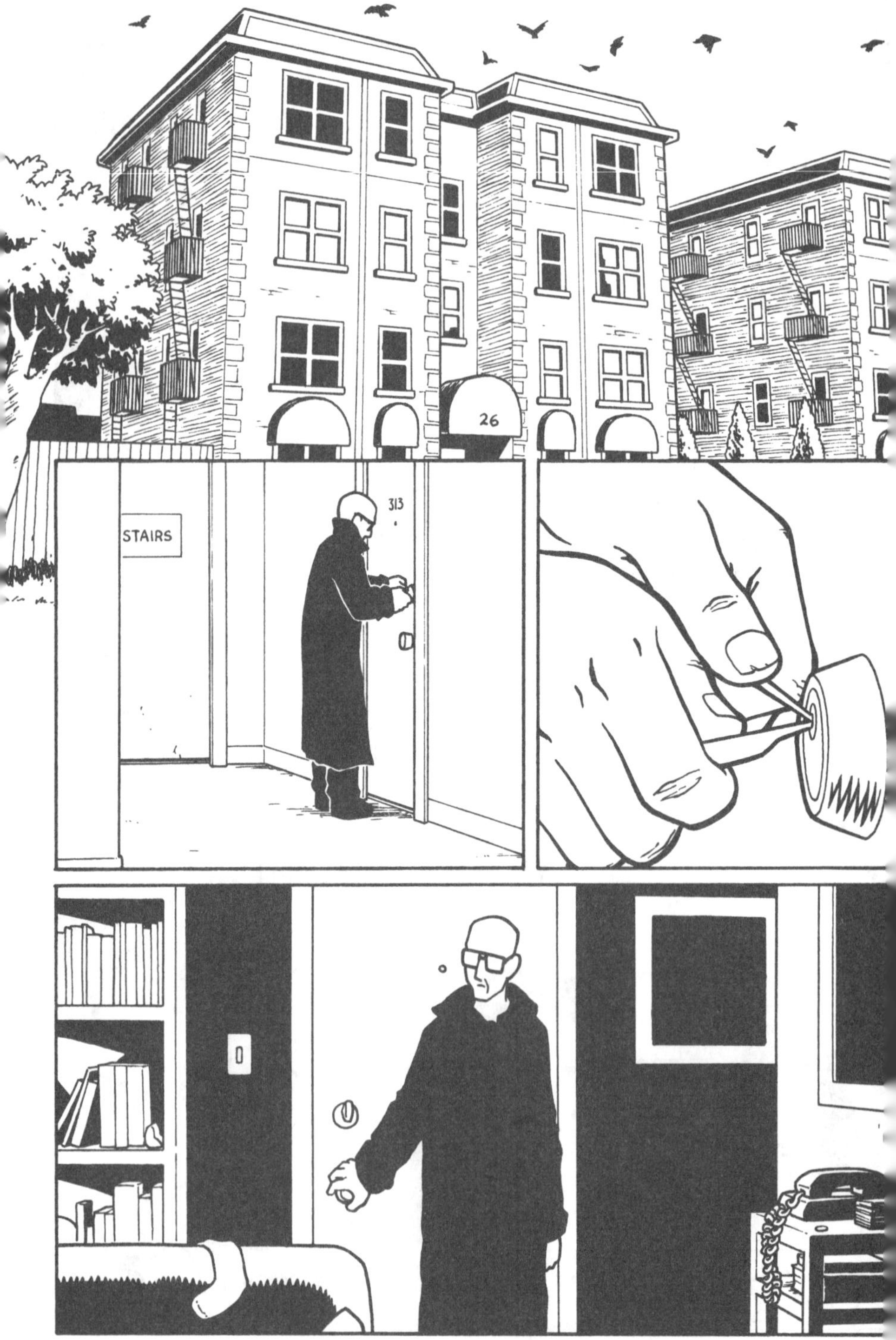
26
313
STAIRS

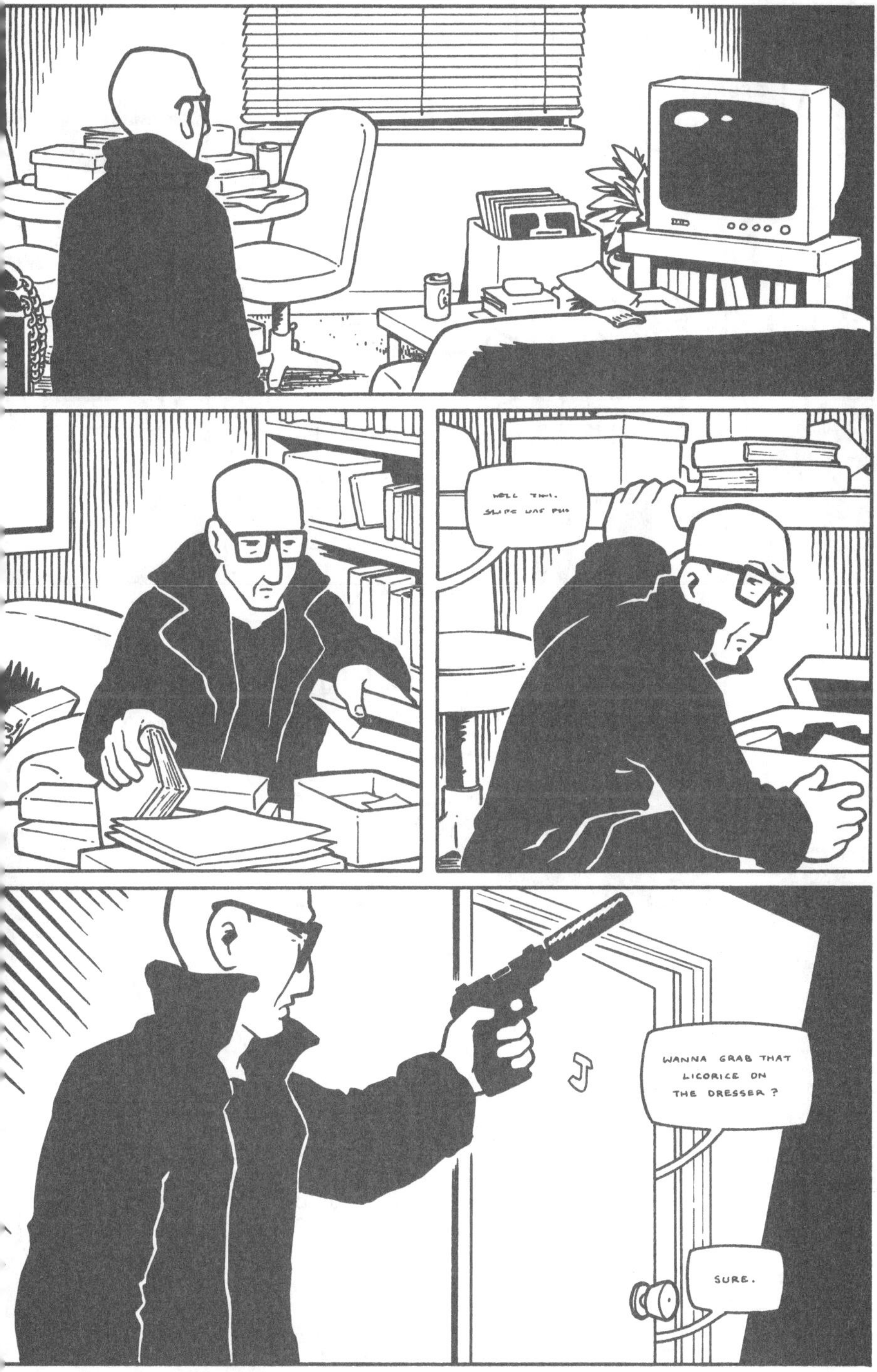
WANNA GRAB THAT LICORICE ON THE DRESSER?
SURE.

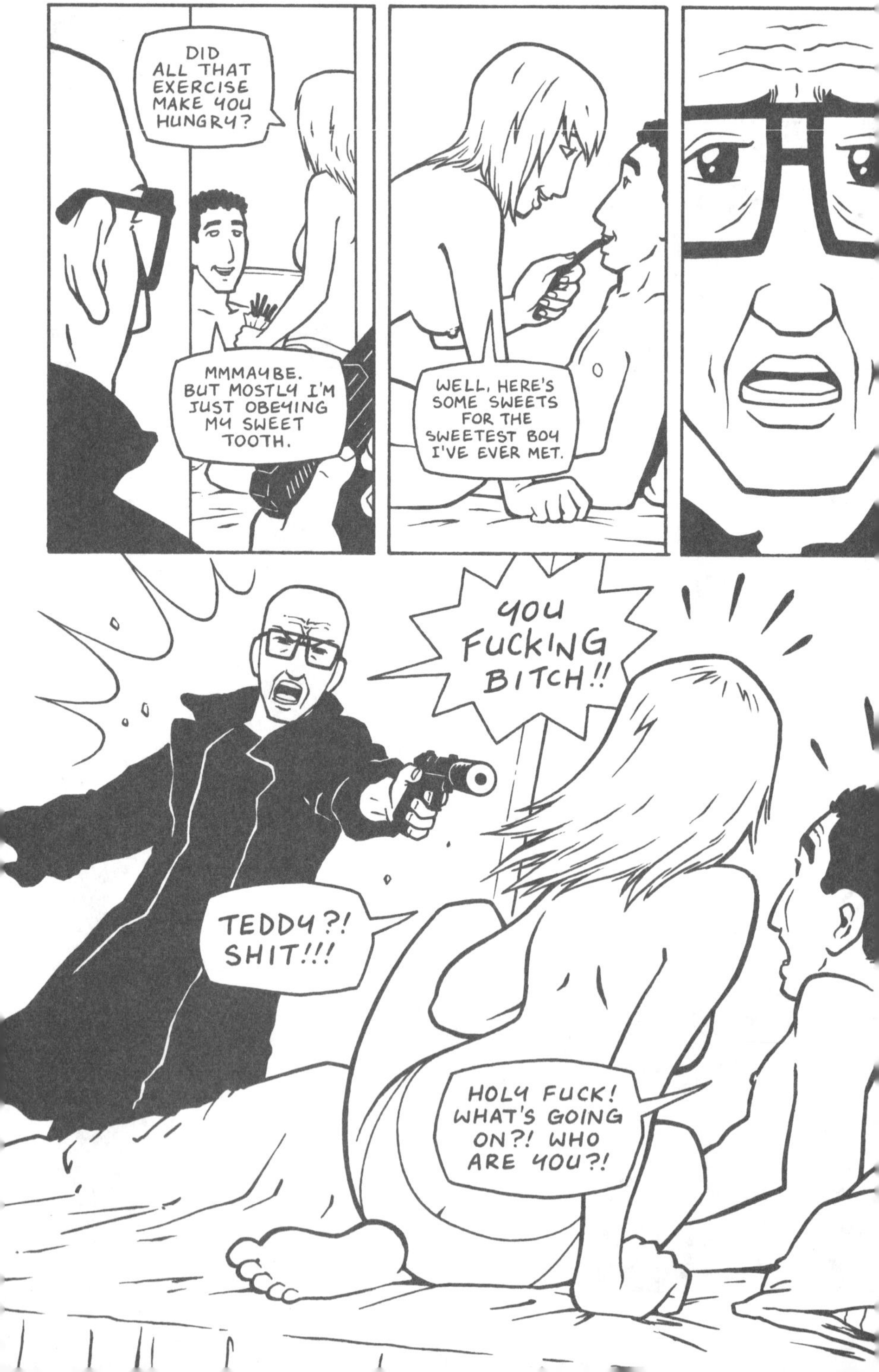
DID ALL THAT EXERCISE MAKE YOU HUNGRY?
MMMAYBE. BUT MOSTLY I'M JUST OBEYING MY SWEET TOOTH.
WELL, HERE'S SOME SWEETS FOR THE SWEETEST BOY I'VE EVER MET.
YOU FUCKING BITCH!!
TEDDY?! SHIT!!!
HOLY FUCK! WHAT'S GOING ON?! WHO ARE YOU?!

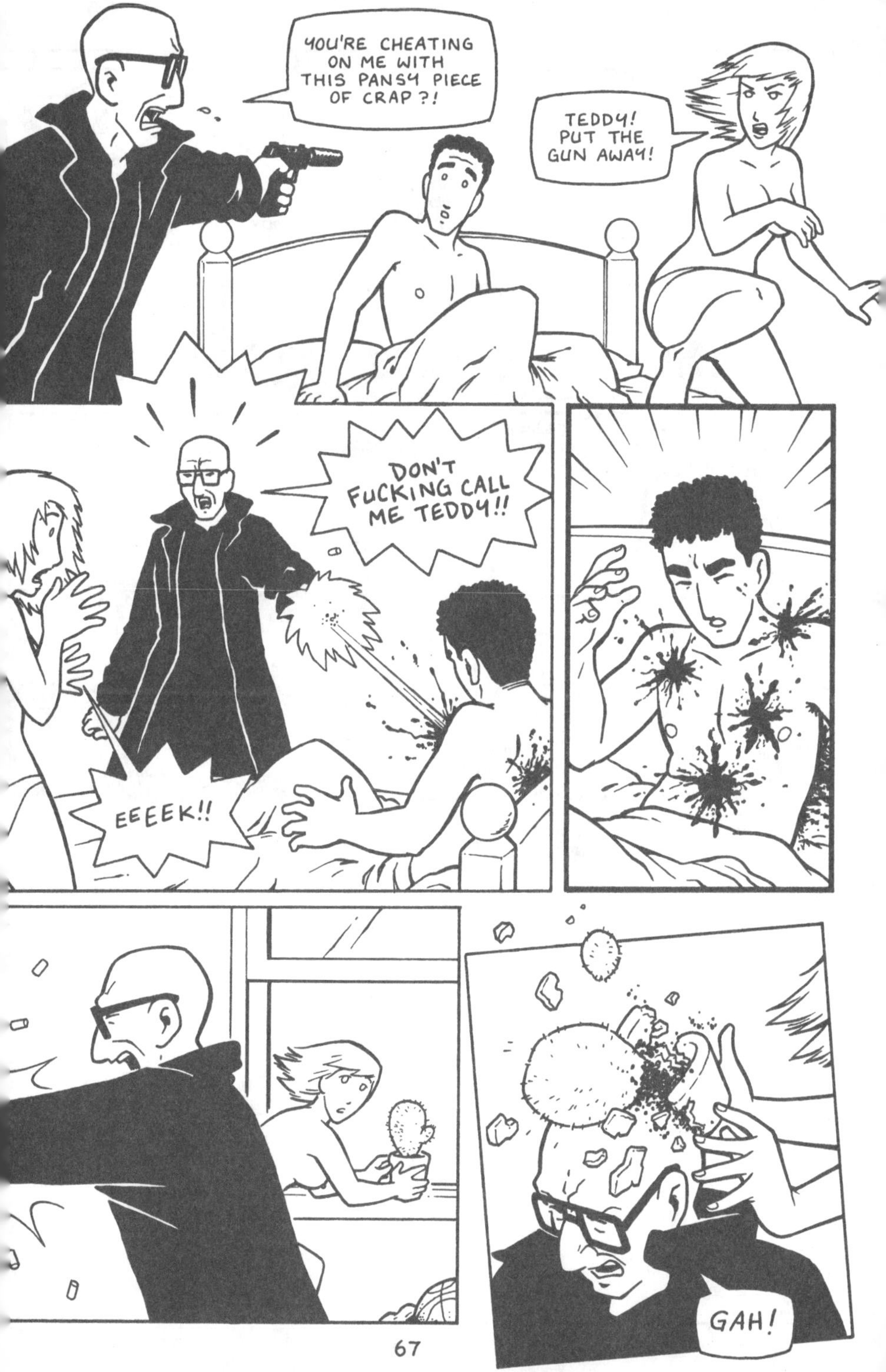
YOU'RE CHEATING ON ME WITH THIS PANSY PIECE OF CRAP?!
TEDDY! PUT THE GUN AWAY!
DON'T FUCKING CALL ME TEDDY!!
EEEEK!!
GAH!

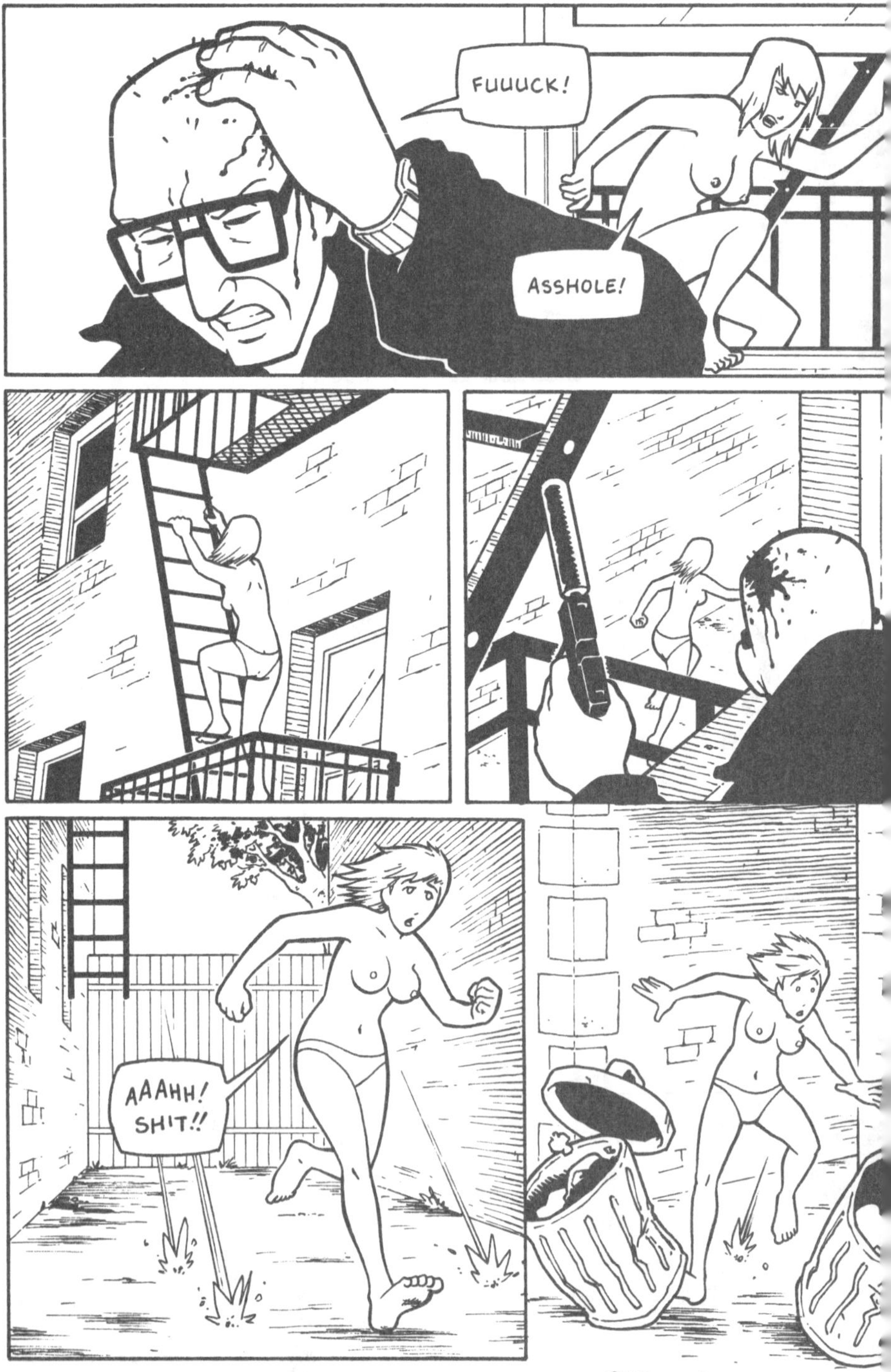
FUUUCK!
ASSHOLE!
AAAHH! SHIT!!

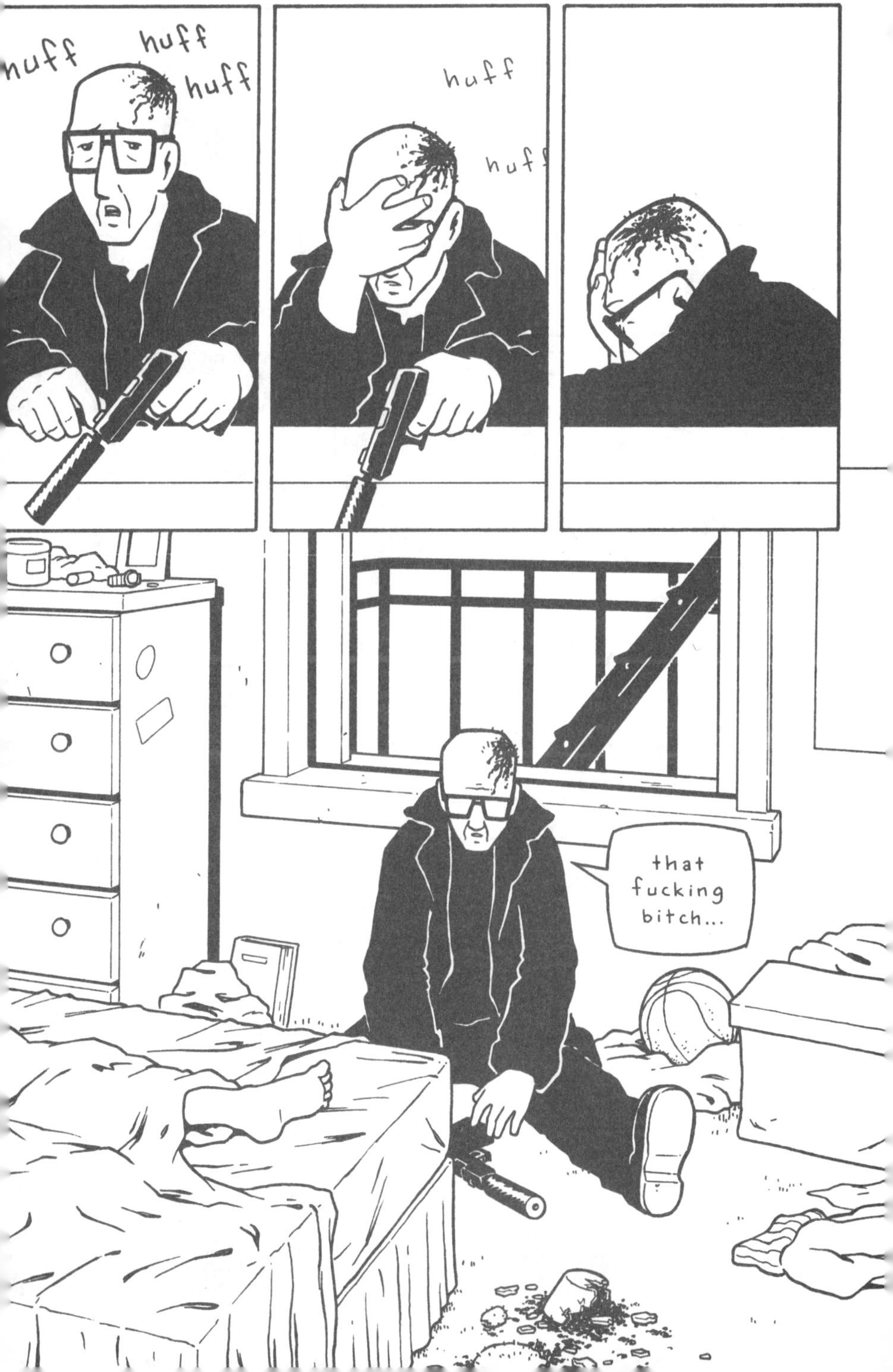
huff
huff
huff
huff
huf
that fucking bitch...

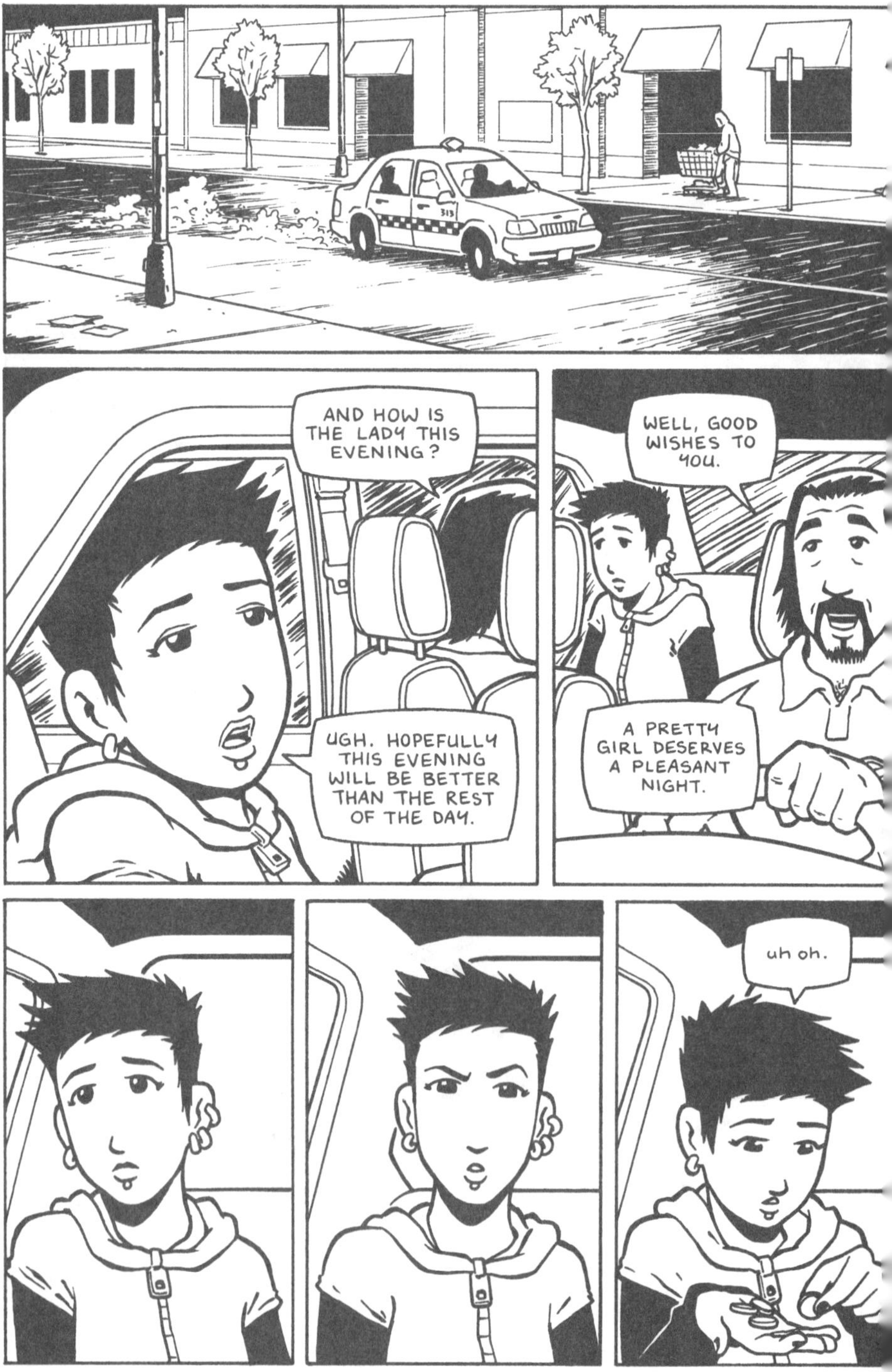
AND HOW IS THE LADY THIS EVENING?
UGH. HOPEFULLY THIS EVENING WILL BE BETTER THAN THE REST OF THE DAY.
WELL, GOOD WISHES TO YOU.
A PRETTY GIRL DESERVES A PLEASANT NIGHT.
uh oh.

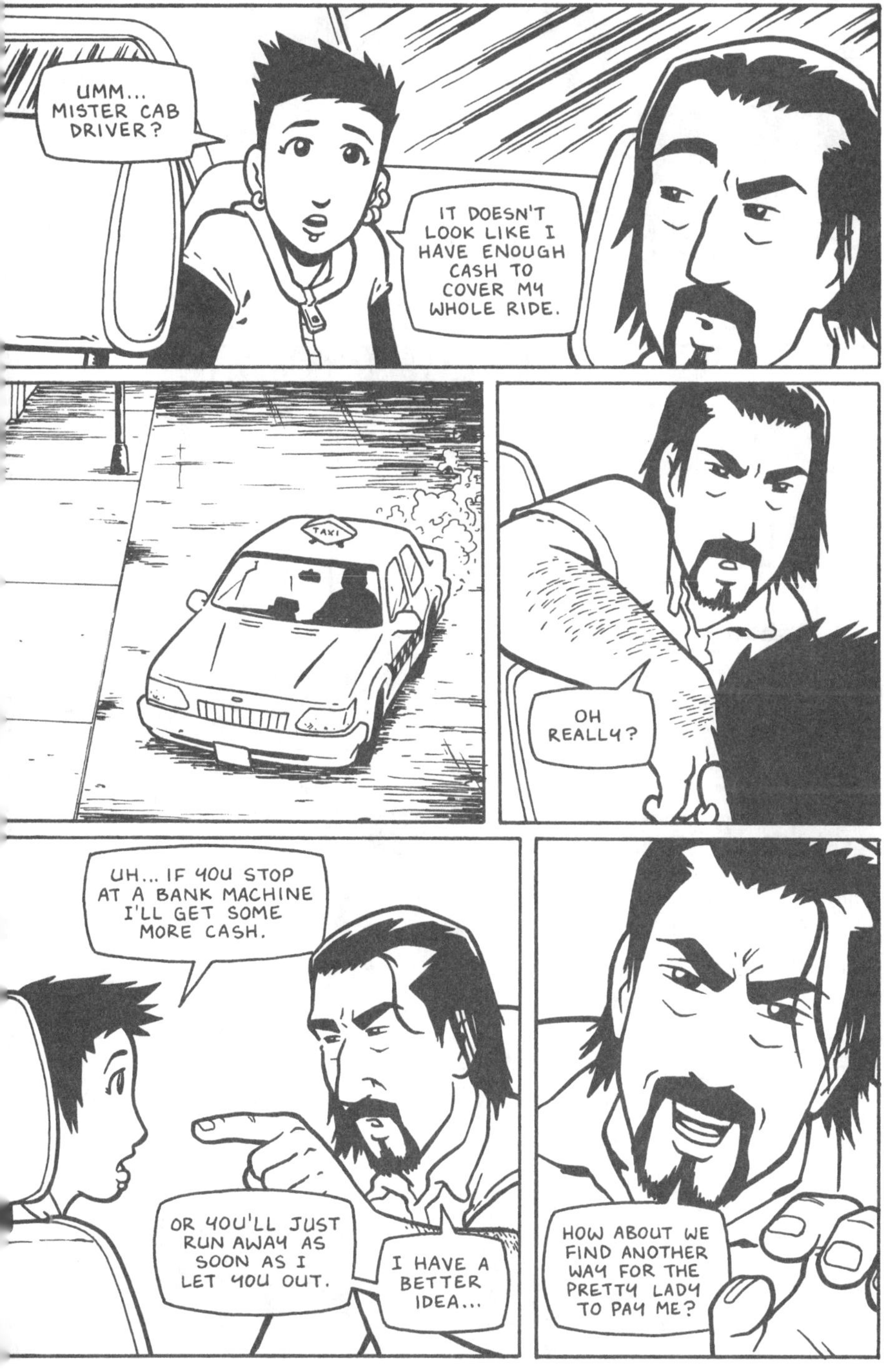
UMM... MISTER CAB DRIVER?
IT DOESN'T LOOK LIKE I HAVE ENOUGH CASH TO COVER MY WHOLE RIDE.
TAXI
OH REALLY?
UH... IF YOU STOP AT A BANK MACHINE I'LL GET SOME MORE CASH.
OR YOU'LL JUST RUN AWAY AS SOON AS I LET YOU OUT.
I HAVE A BETTER IDEA...
HOW ABOUT WE FIND ANOTHER WAY FOR THE PRETTY LADY TO PAY ME?

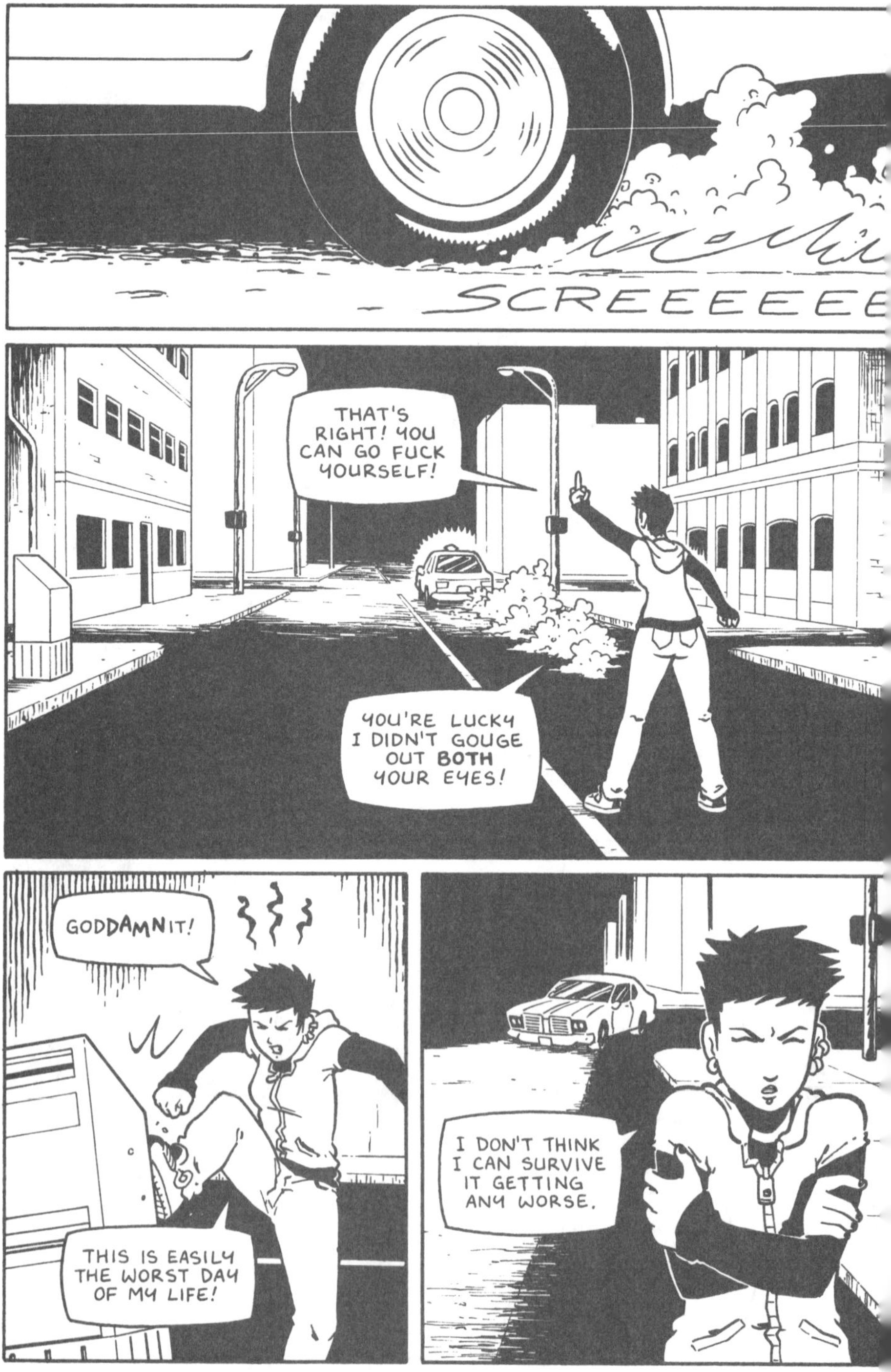
SCREEEEEE
THAT'S RIGHT! YOU CAN GO FUCK YOURSELF!
YOU'RE LUCKY I DIDN'T GOUGE OUT **BOTH** YOUR EYES!
GODDAMNIT!
THIS IS EASILY THE WORST DAY OF MY LIFE!
I DON'T THINK I CAN SURVIVE IT GETTING ANY WORSE.

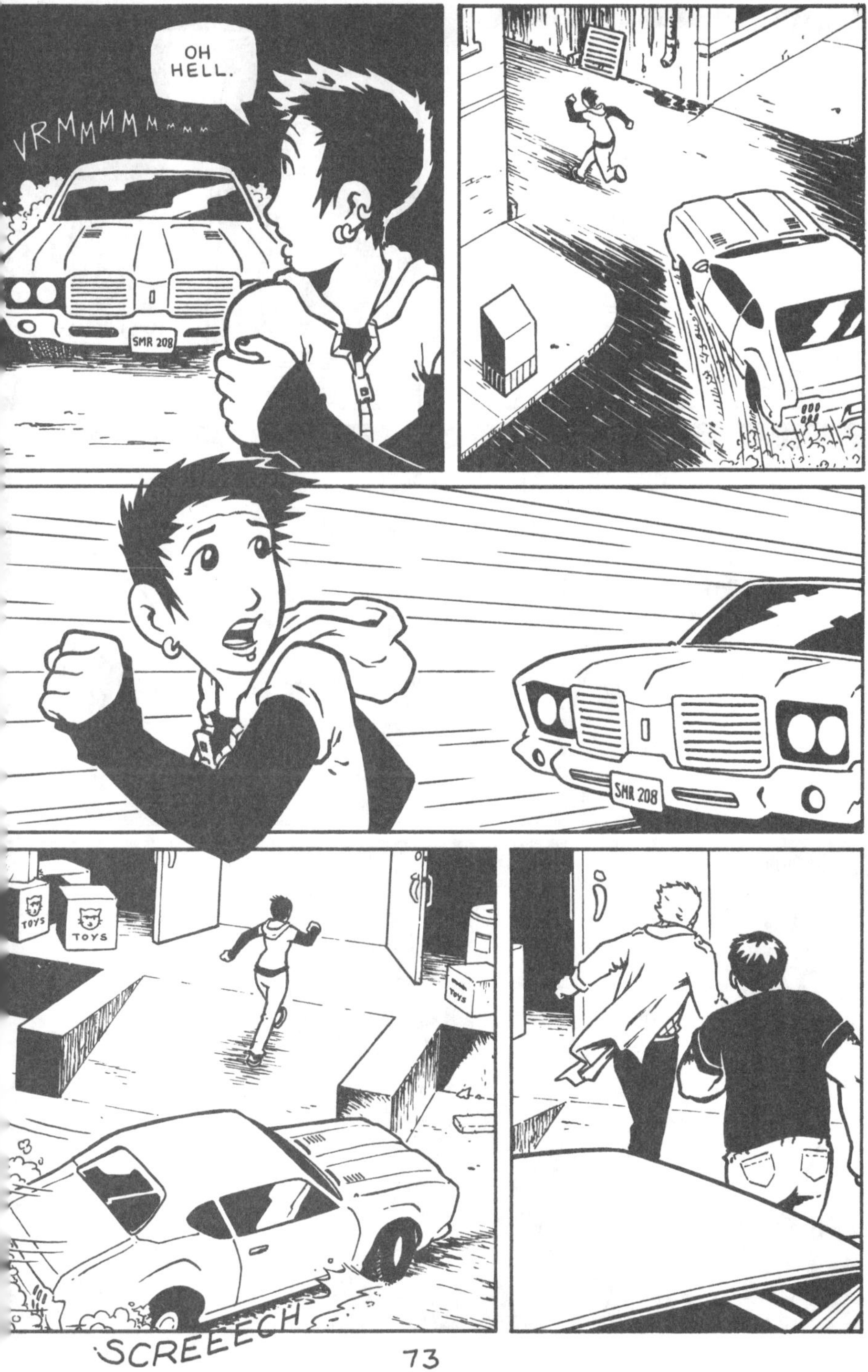
OH HELL.
VRMMMMMmmmm
SMR 208
SMR 208
TOYS
TOYS
TOYS
SCREEECH

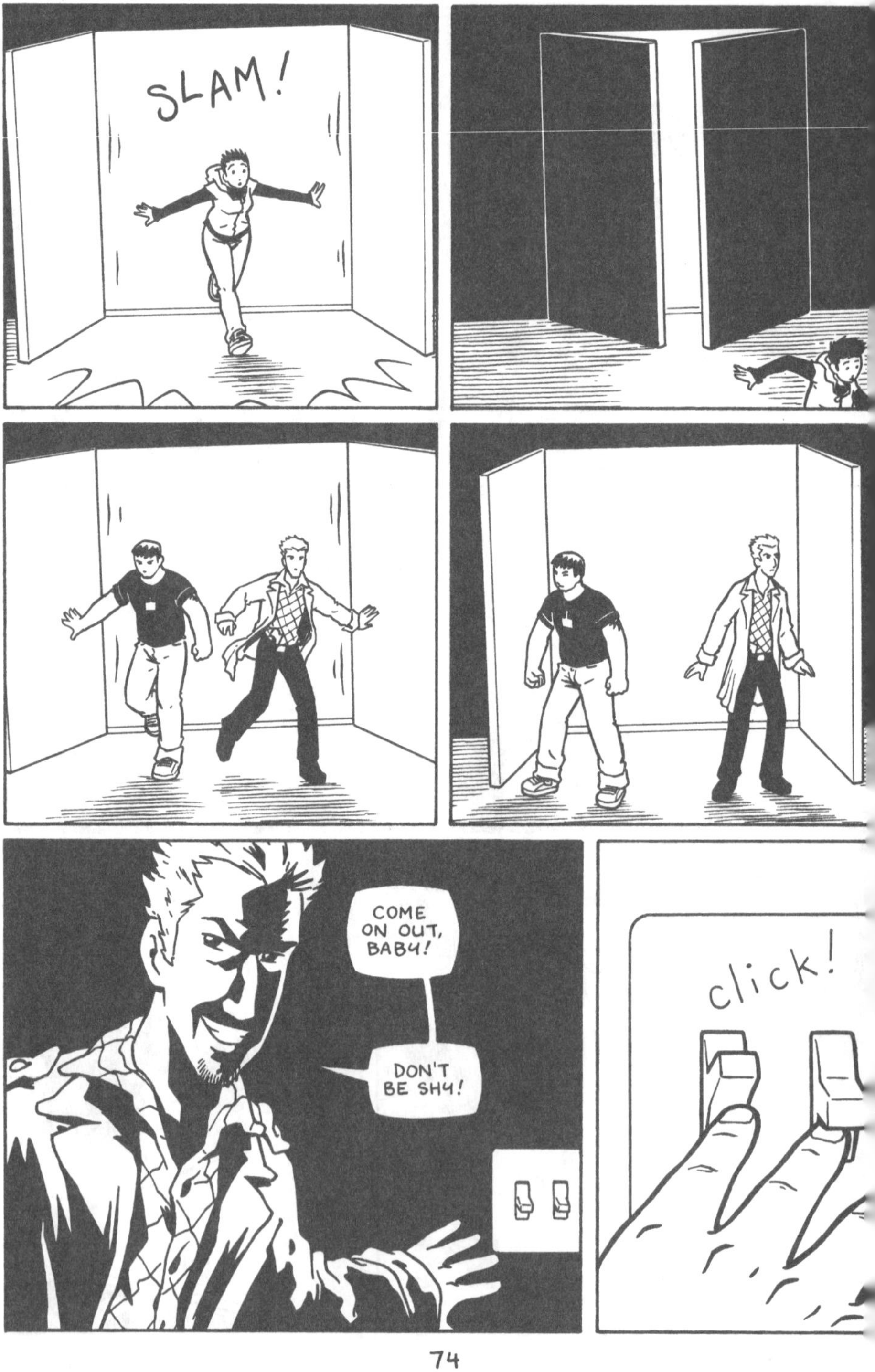
SLAM!
COME ON OUT, BABY!
DON'T BE SHY!
click!

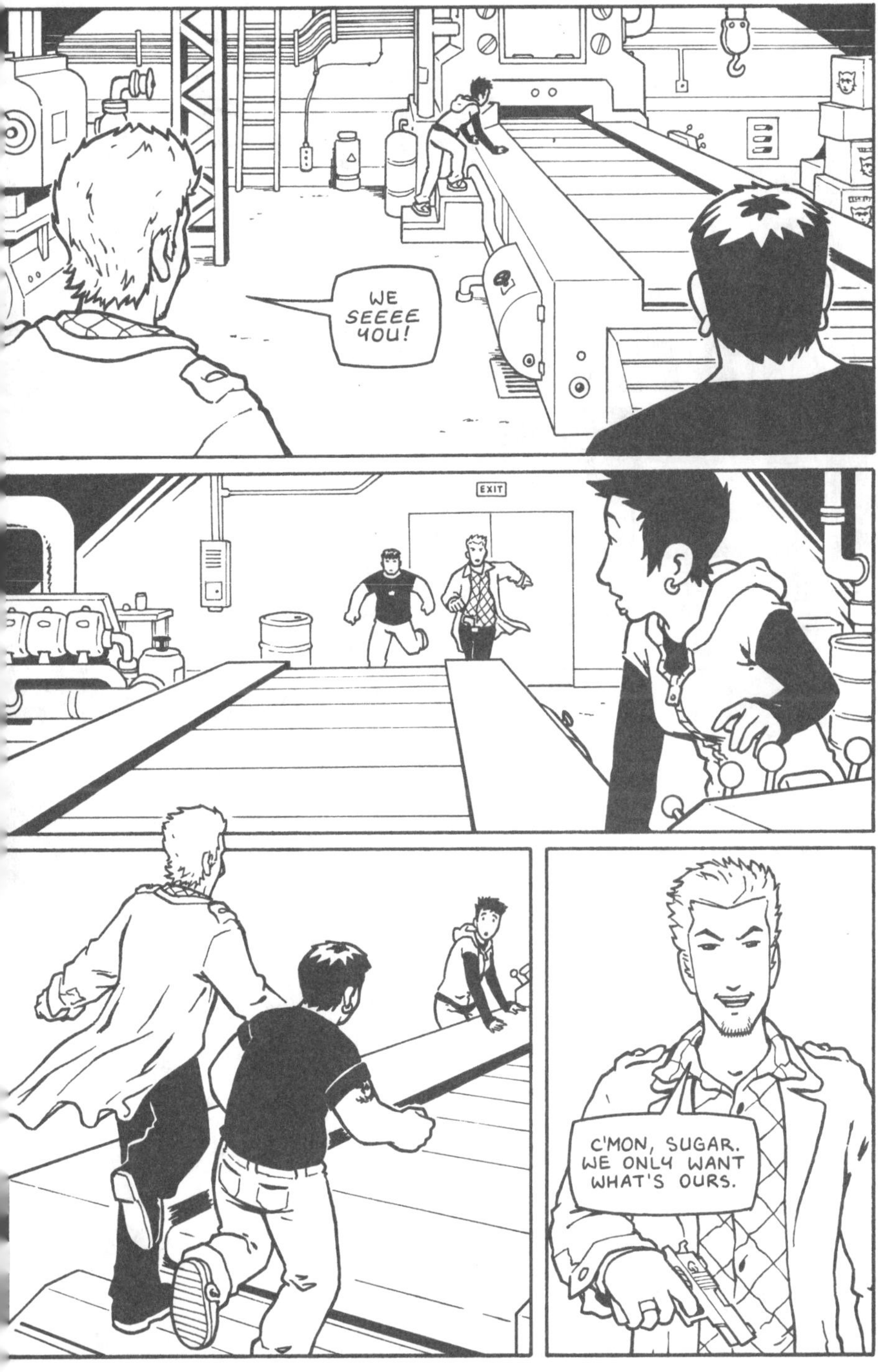
WE SEEEE YOU!
EXIT
C'MON, SUGAR. WE ONLY WANT WHAT'S OURS.

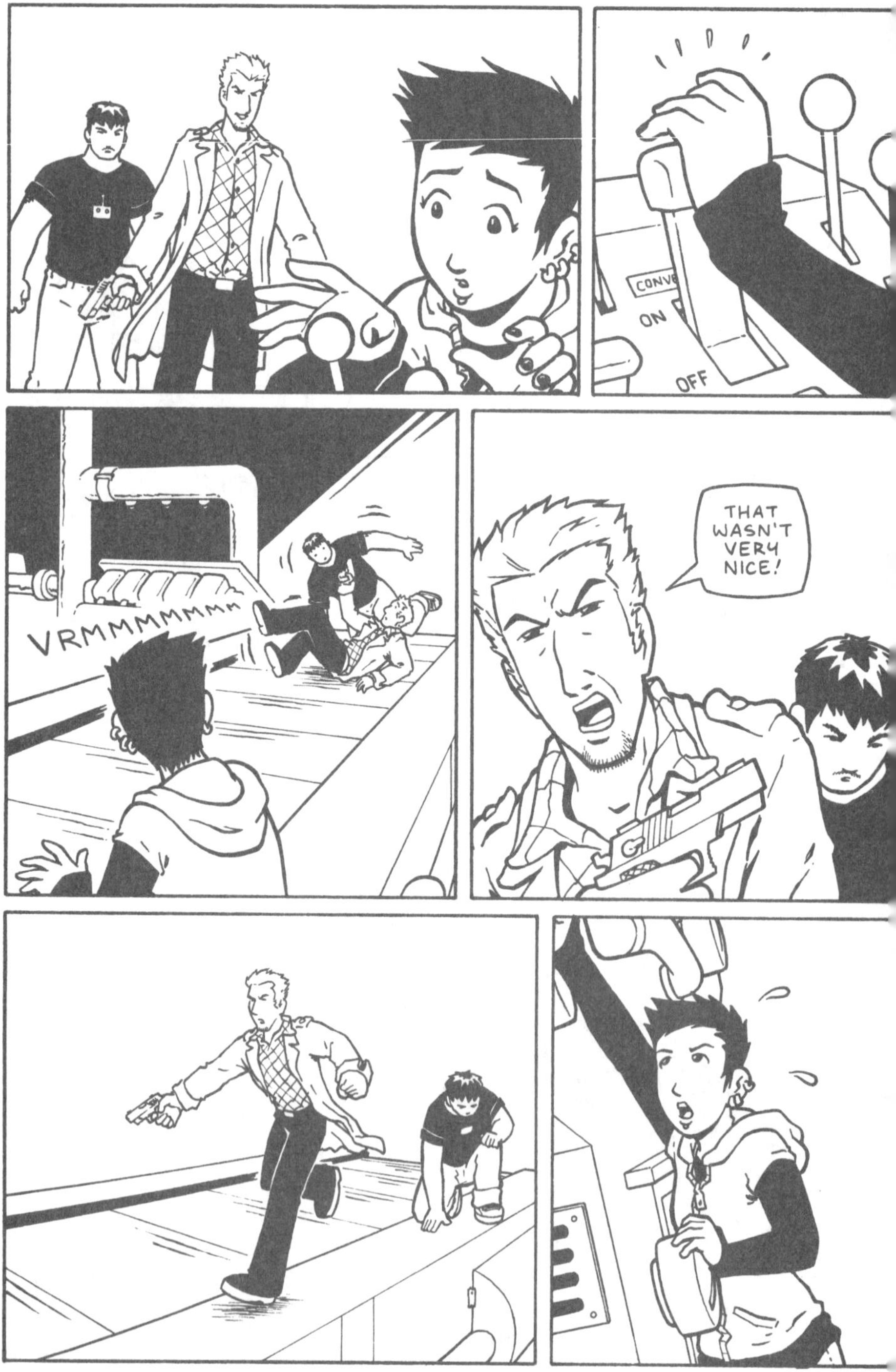
CONVE
ON
OFF
VRMMMMMMM
THAT WASN'T VERY NICE!

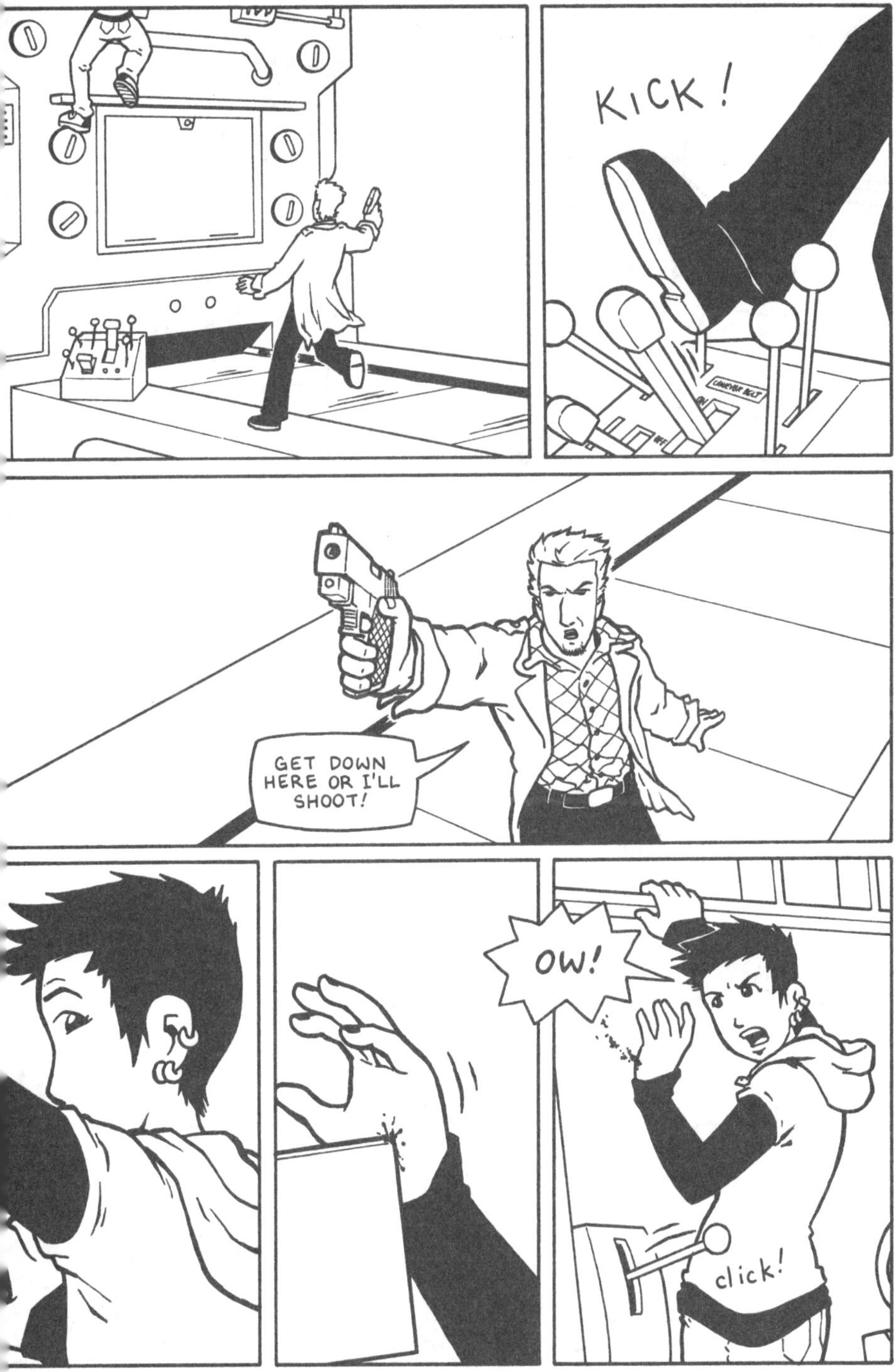
KICK!
CONVEYOR BELT
ON
OFF
GET DOWN HERE OR I'LL SHOOT!
OW!
click!

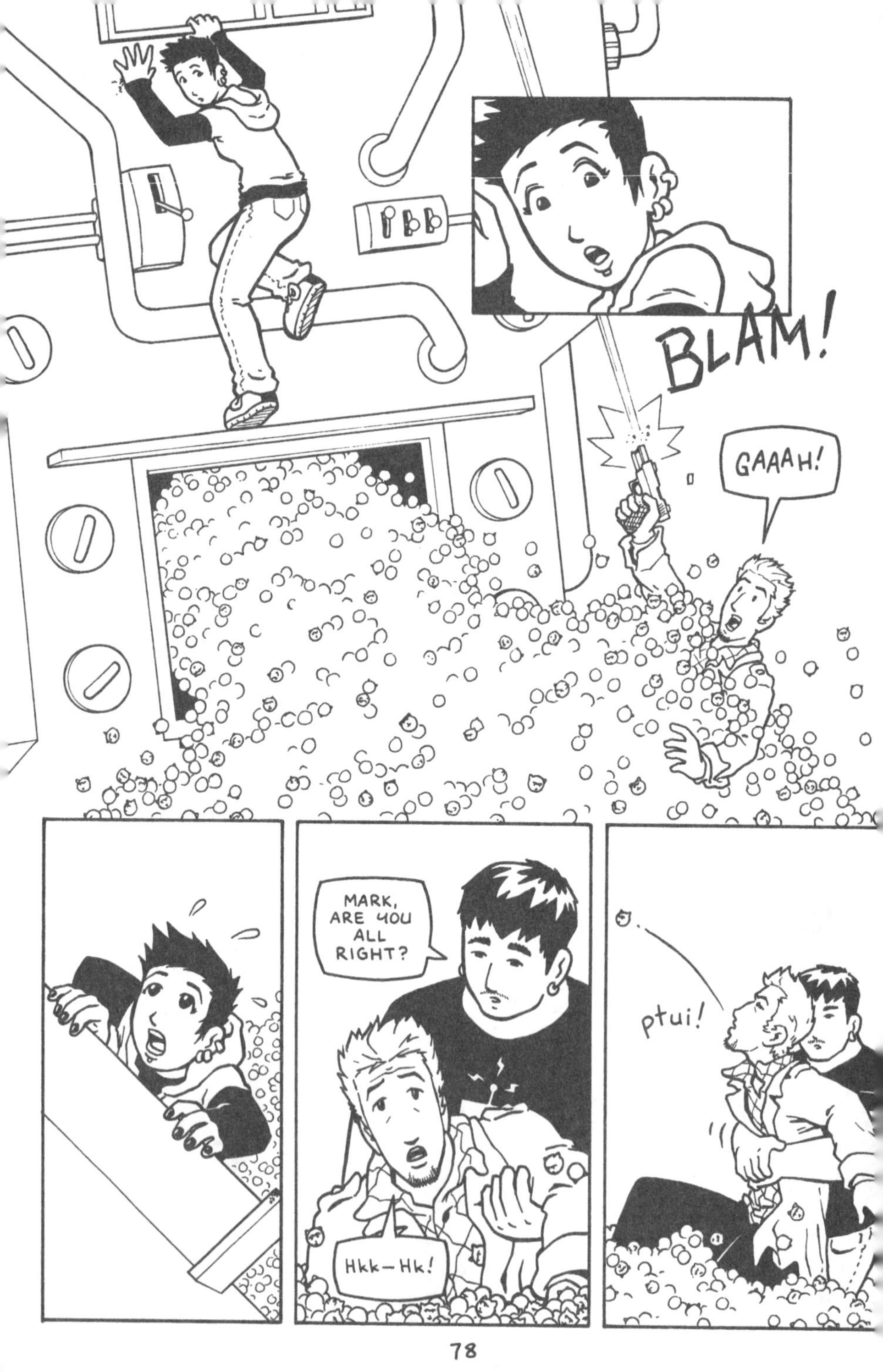
BLAM!
GAAAH!
MARK, ARE YOU ALL RIGHT?
Hkk-Hk!
ptui!

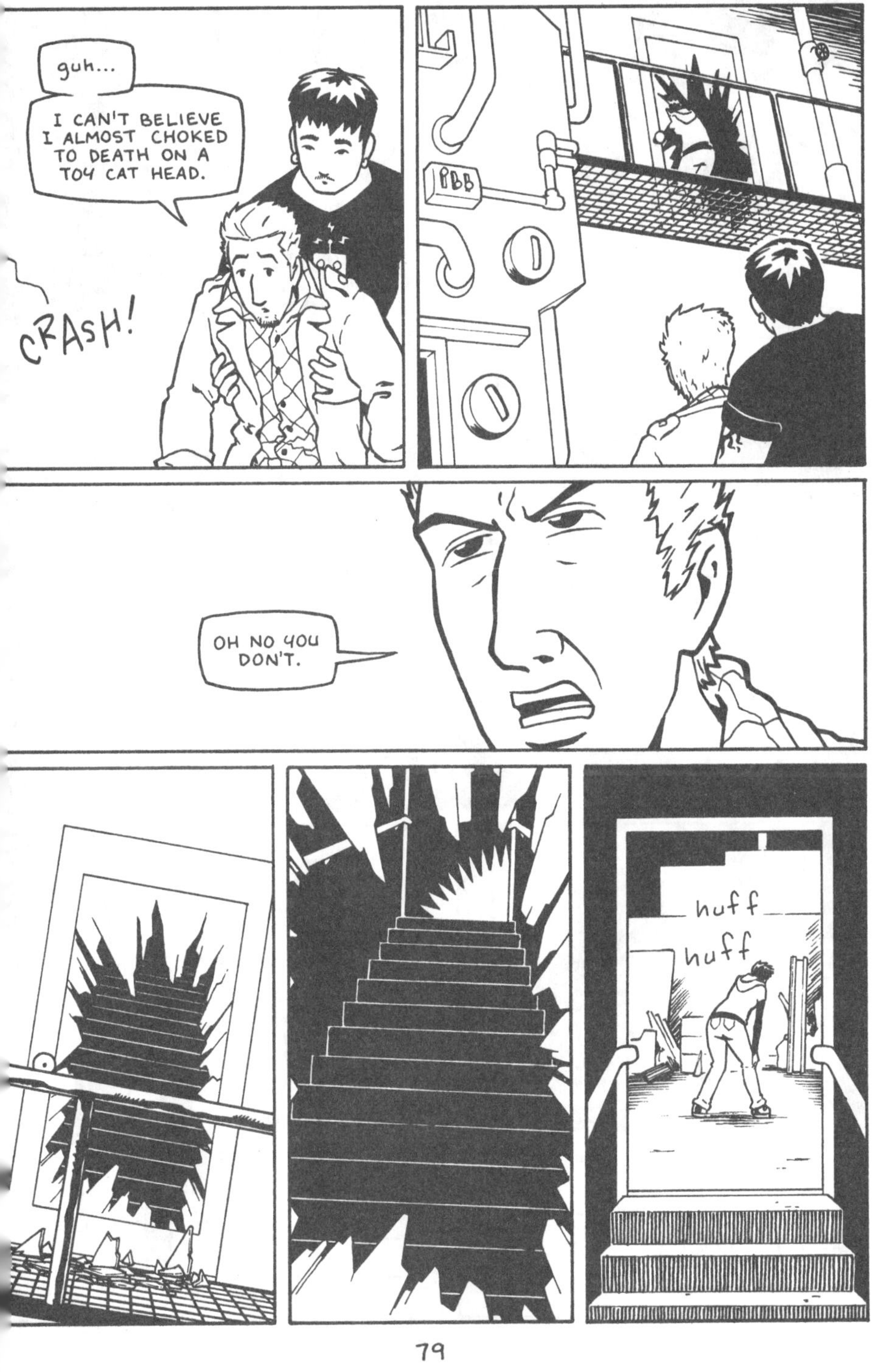
guh...
I CAN'T BELIEVE I ALMOST CHOKED TO DEATH ON A TOY CAT HEAD.
CRASH!
OH NO YOU DON'T.
huff
huff

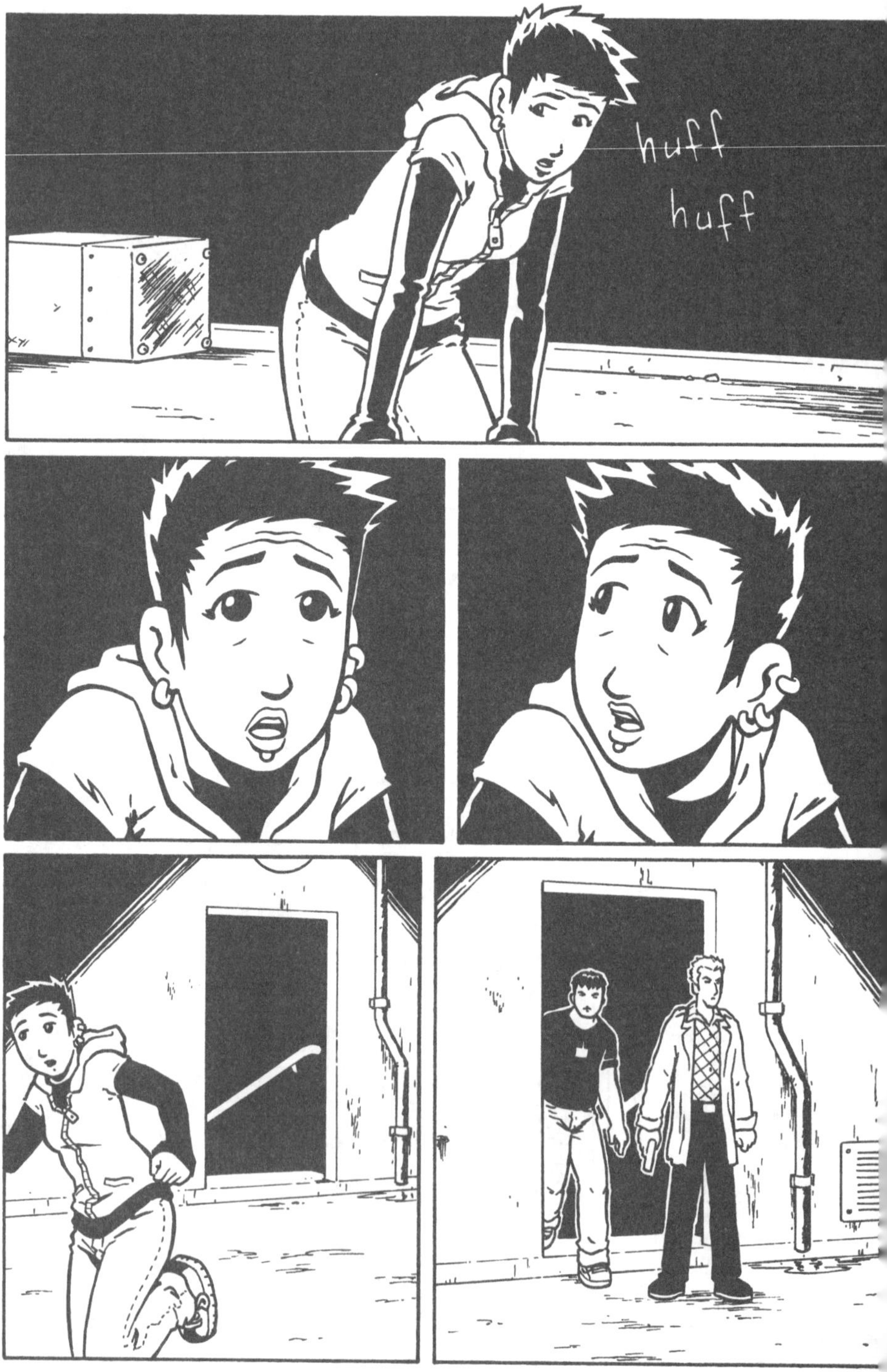
huff
huff

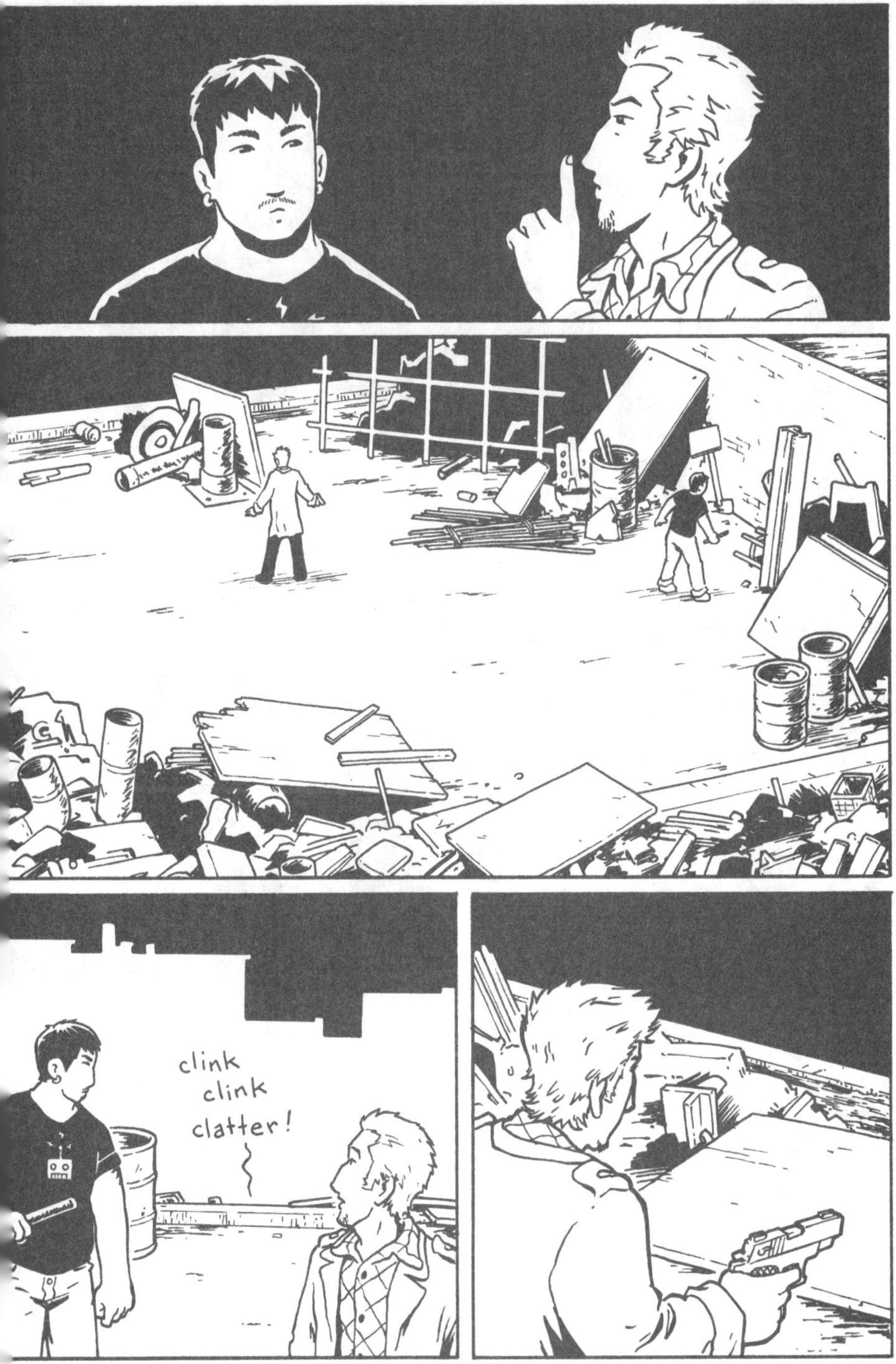
clink
clink
clatter!

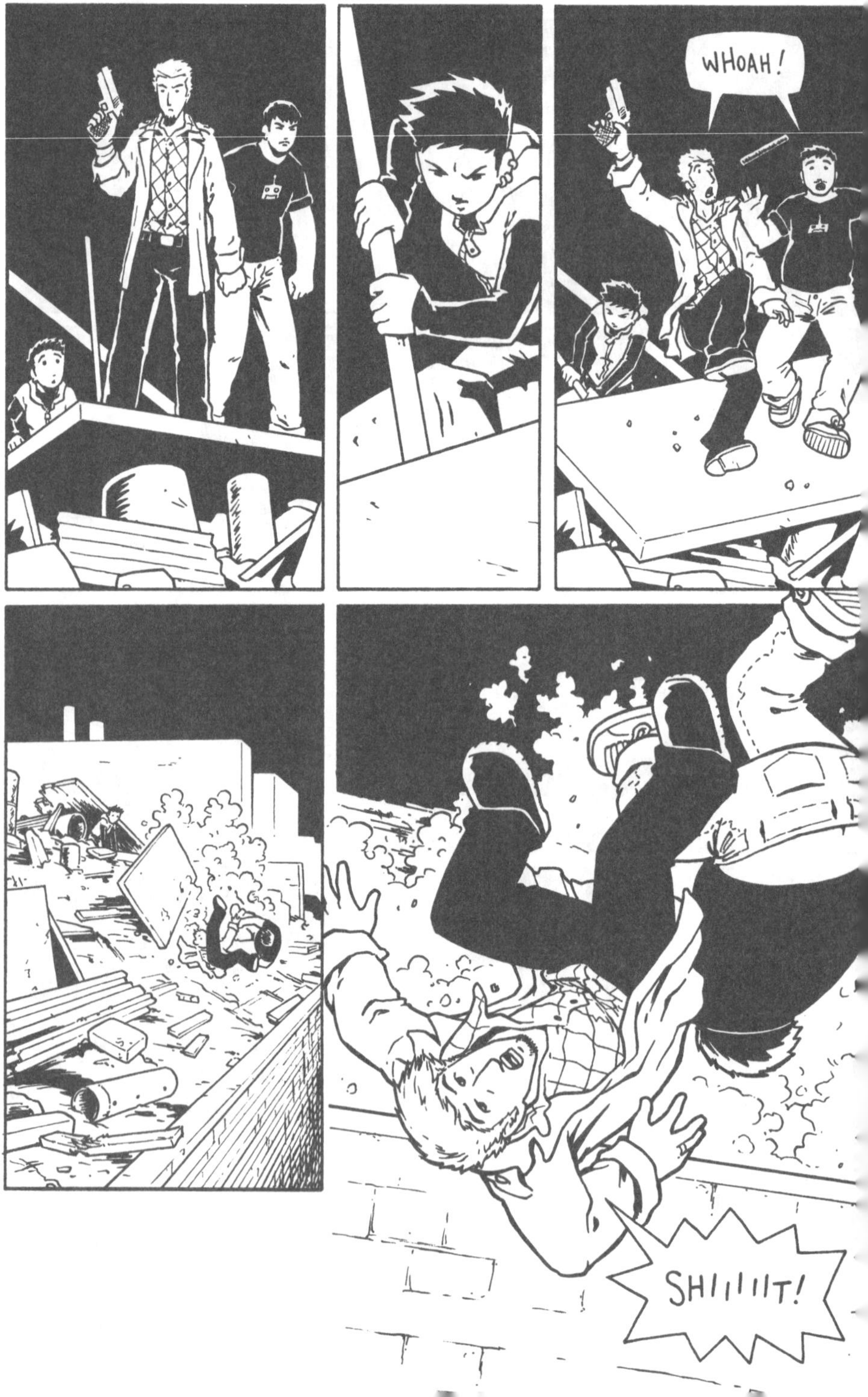
WHOAH!
SHIIIIIT!

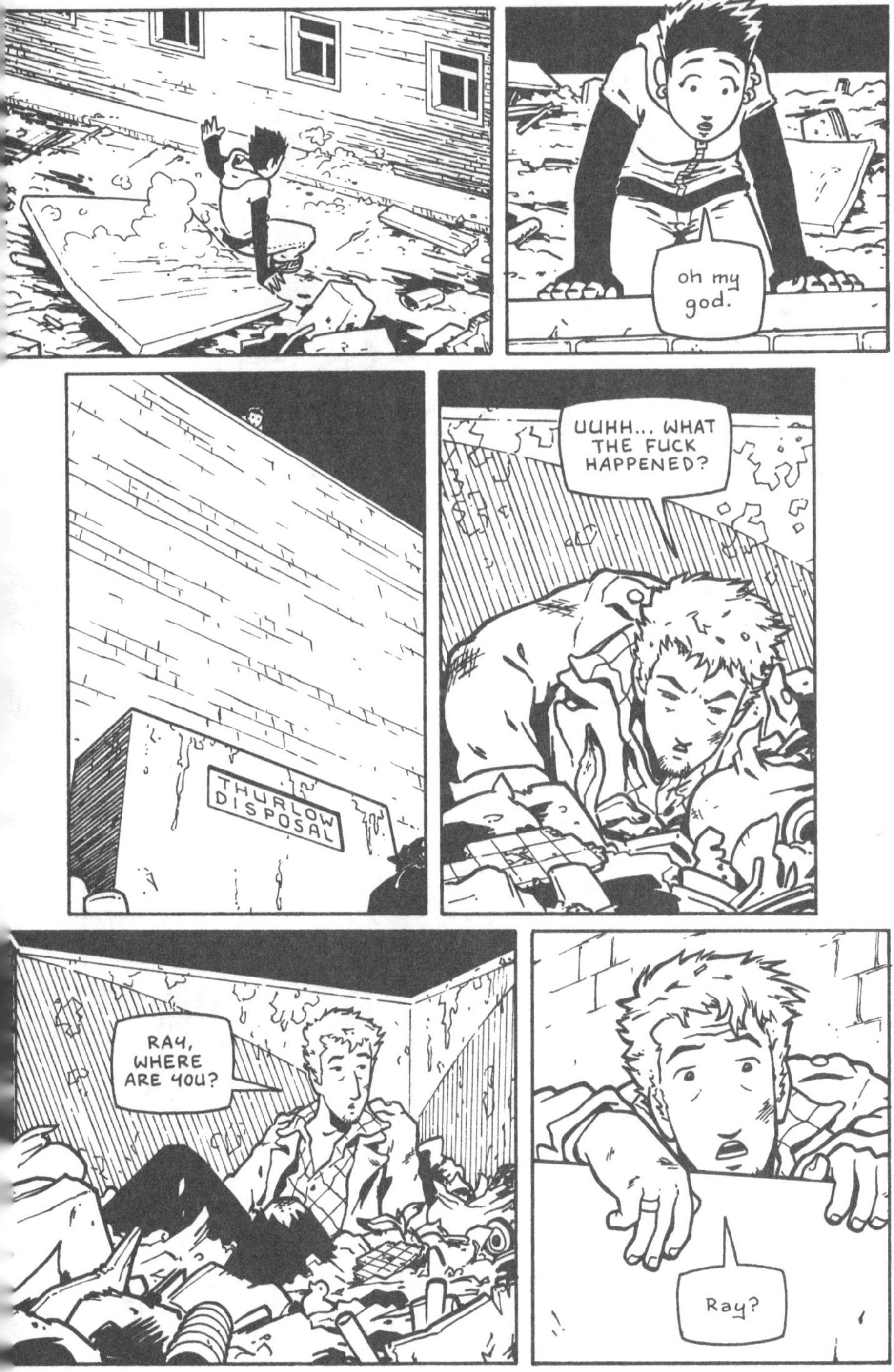
oh my god.
UUHH... WHAT THE FUCK HAPPENED?
THURLOW DISPOSAL
RAY, WHERE ARE YOU?
Ray?

RAY? YOU ALIVE?

DUDE...

...I DON'T FEEL SO GOOD...

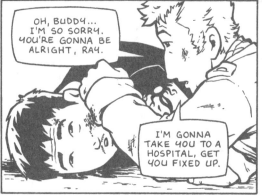

OH, BUDDY... I'M SO SORRY. YOU'RE GONNA BE ALRIGHT, RAY.

I'M GONNA TAKE YOU TO A HOSPITAL, GET YOU FIXED UP.

AND THEN I'LL SLIT THAT BITCH'S THROAT!

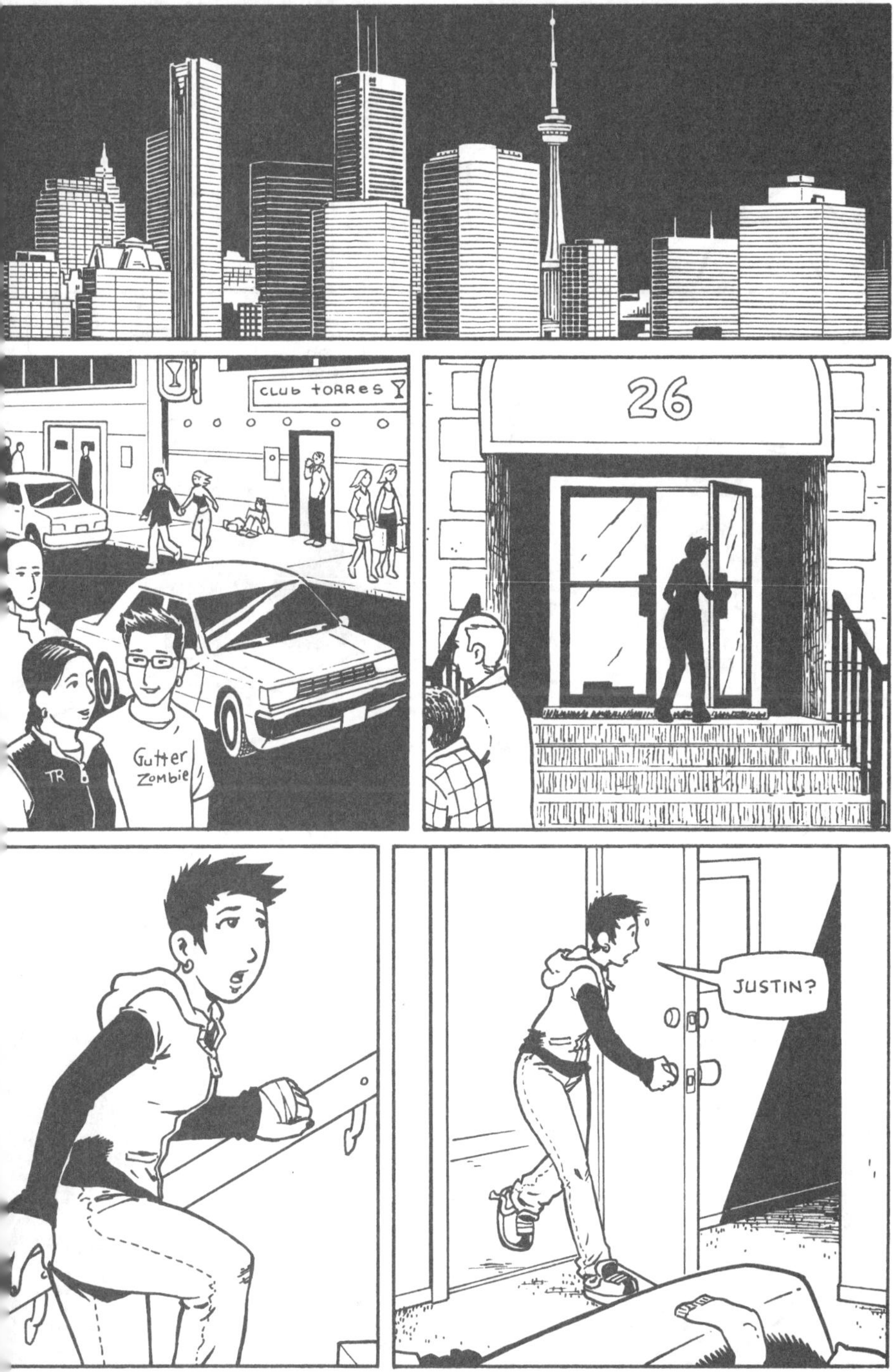
CLUB TORRES
26
Gutter Zombie
TR
JUSTIN?

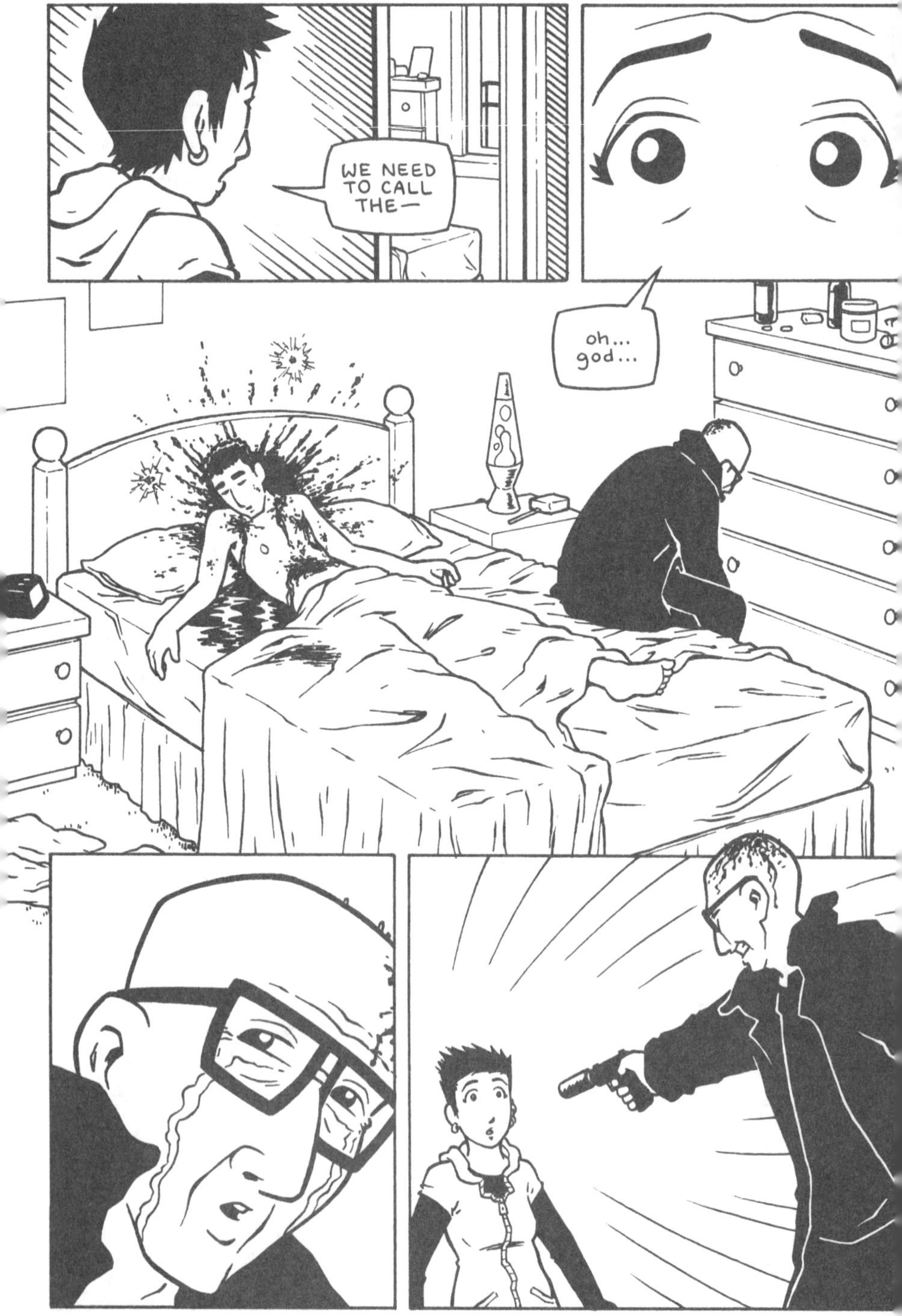
WE NEED TO CALL THE—
oh... god...

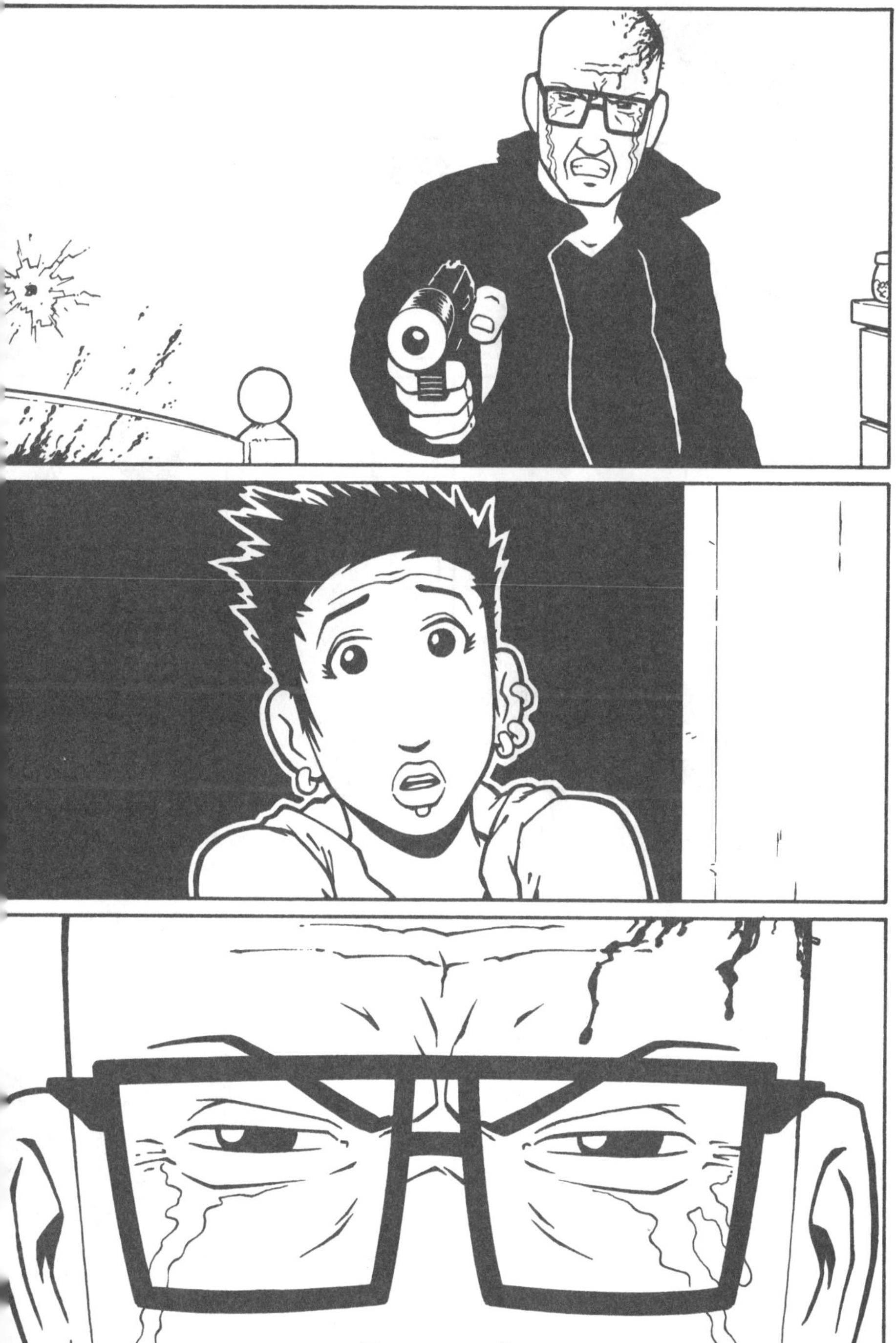

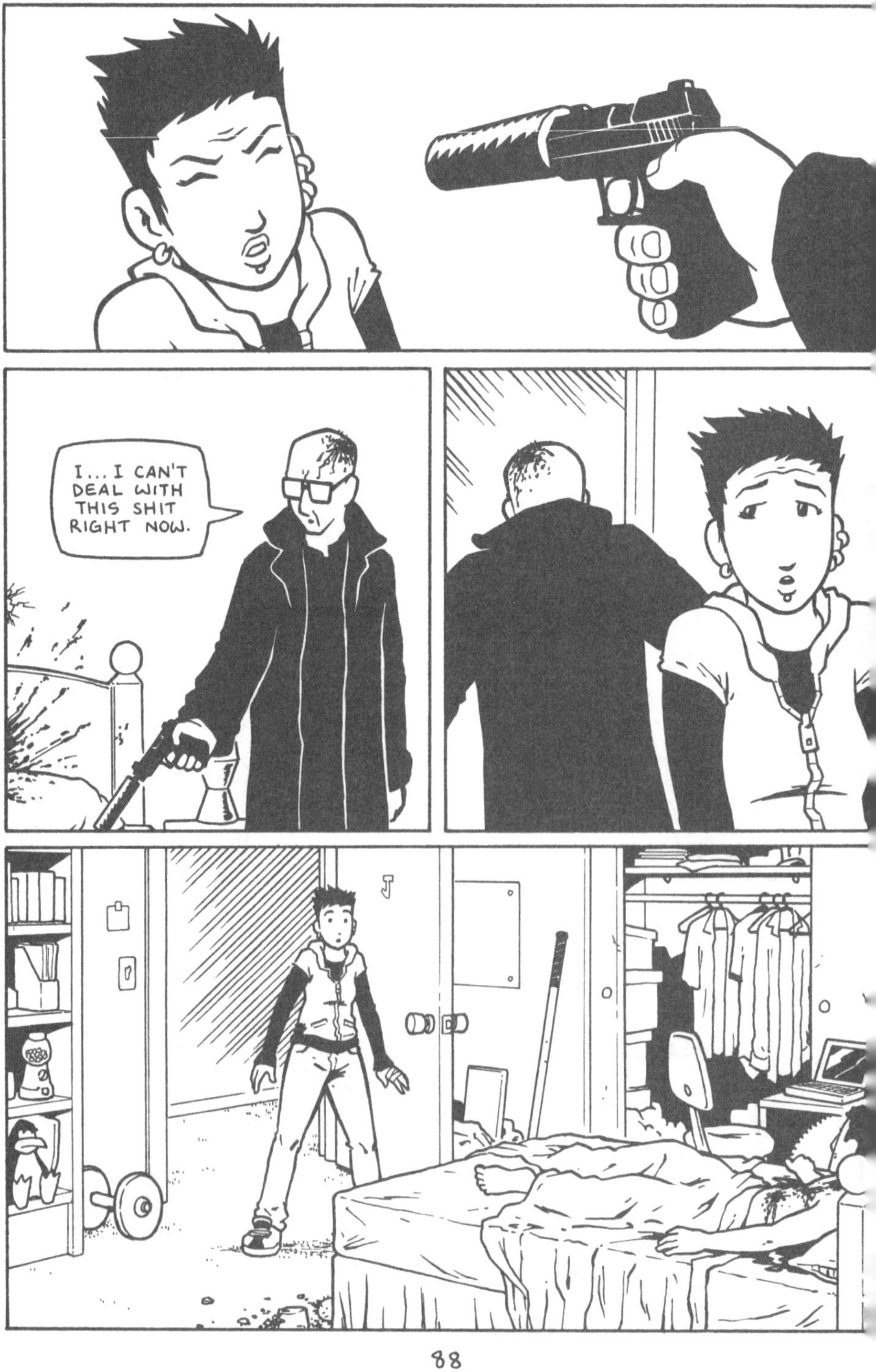
I... I CAN'T DEAL WITH THIS SHIT RIGHT NOW.

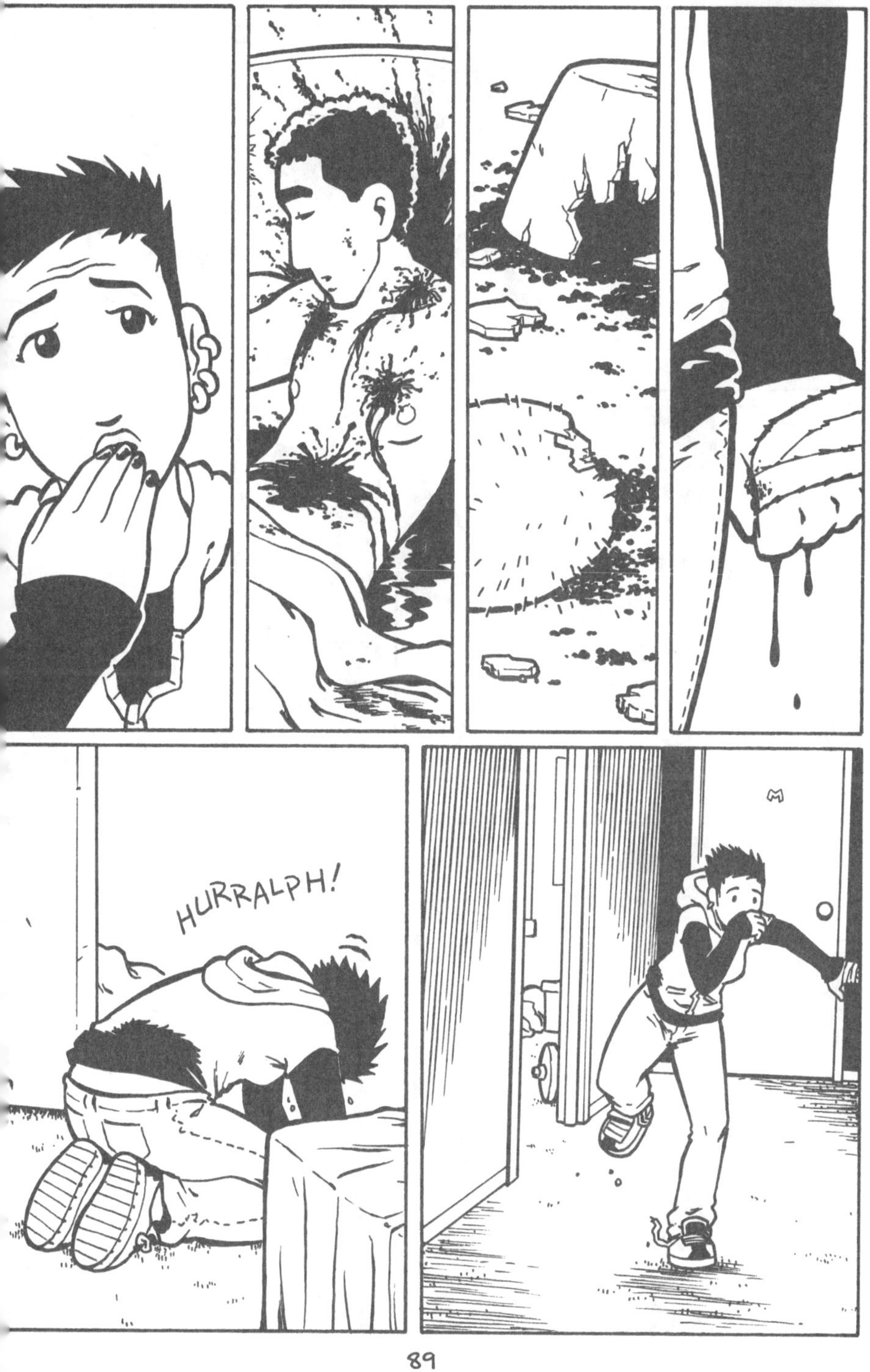
HURRALPH!
M

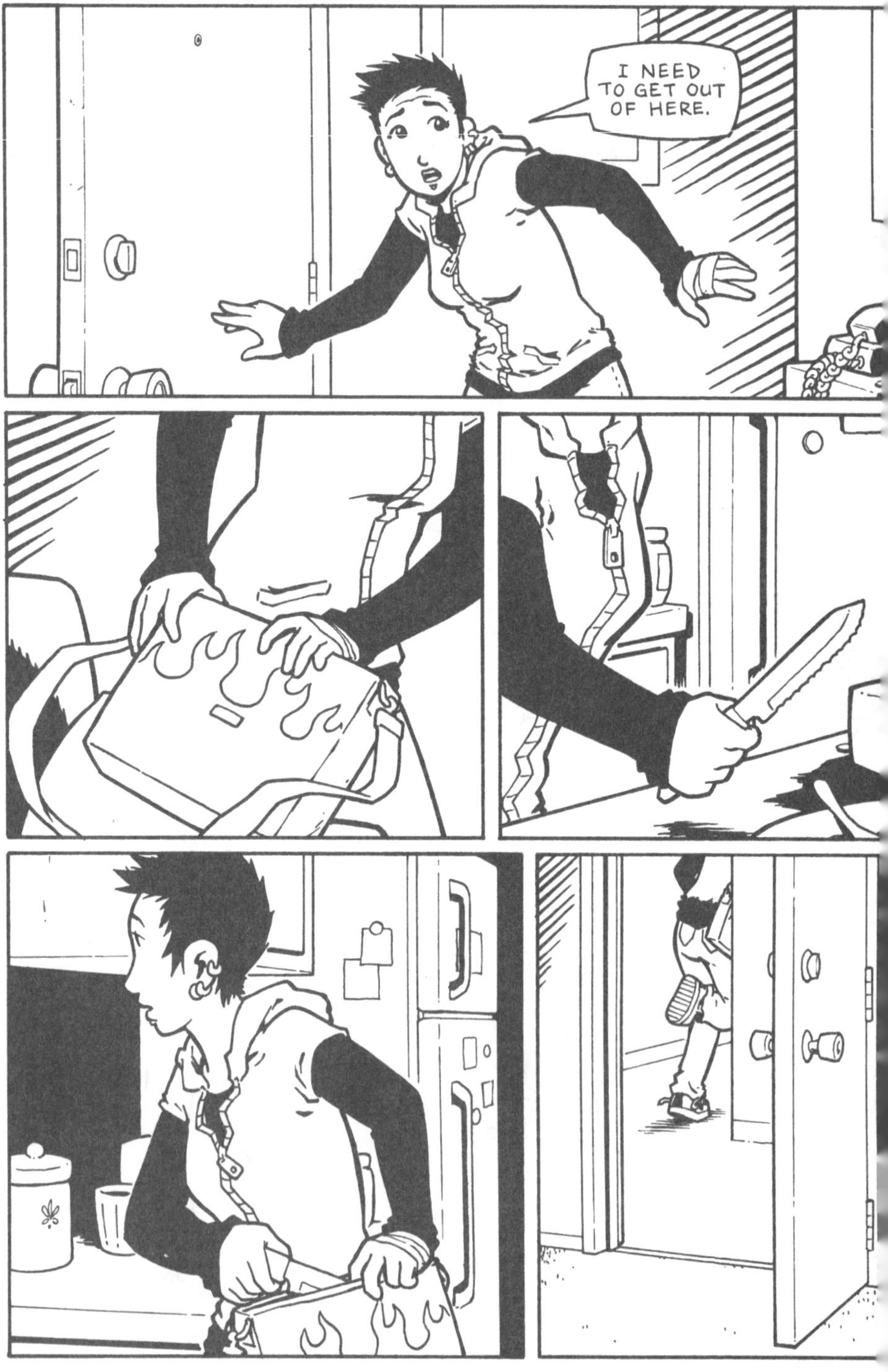
I NEED TO GET OUT OF HERE.

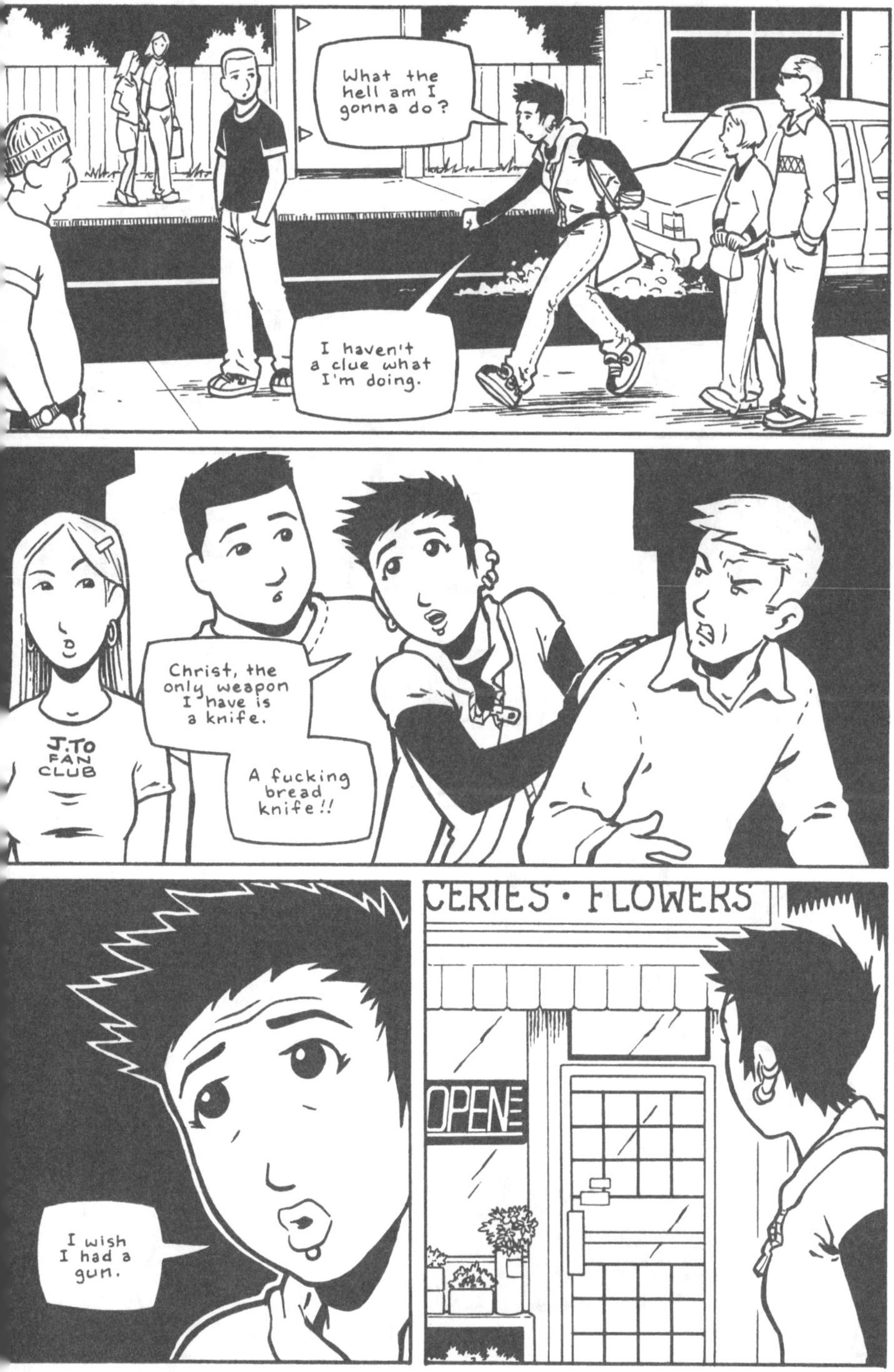
What the hell am I gonna do?
I haven't a clue what I'm doing.
J.TO FAN CLUB
Christ, the only weapon I have is a knife.
A fucking bread knife!!
I wish I had a gun.
CERIES • FLOWERS
OPEN

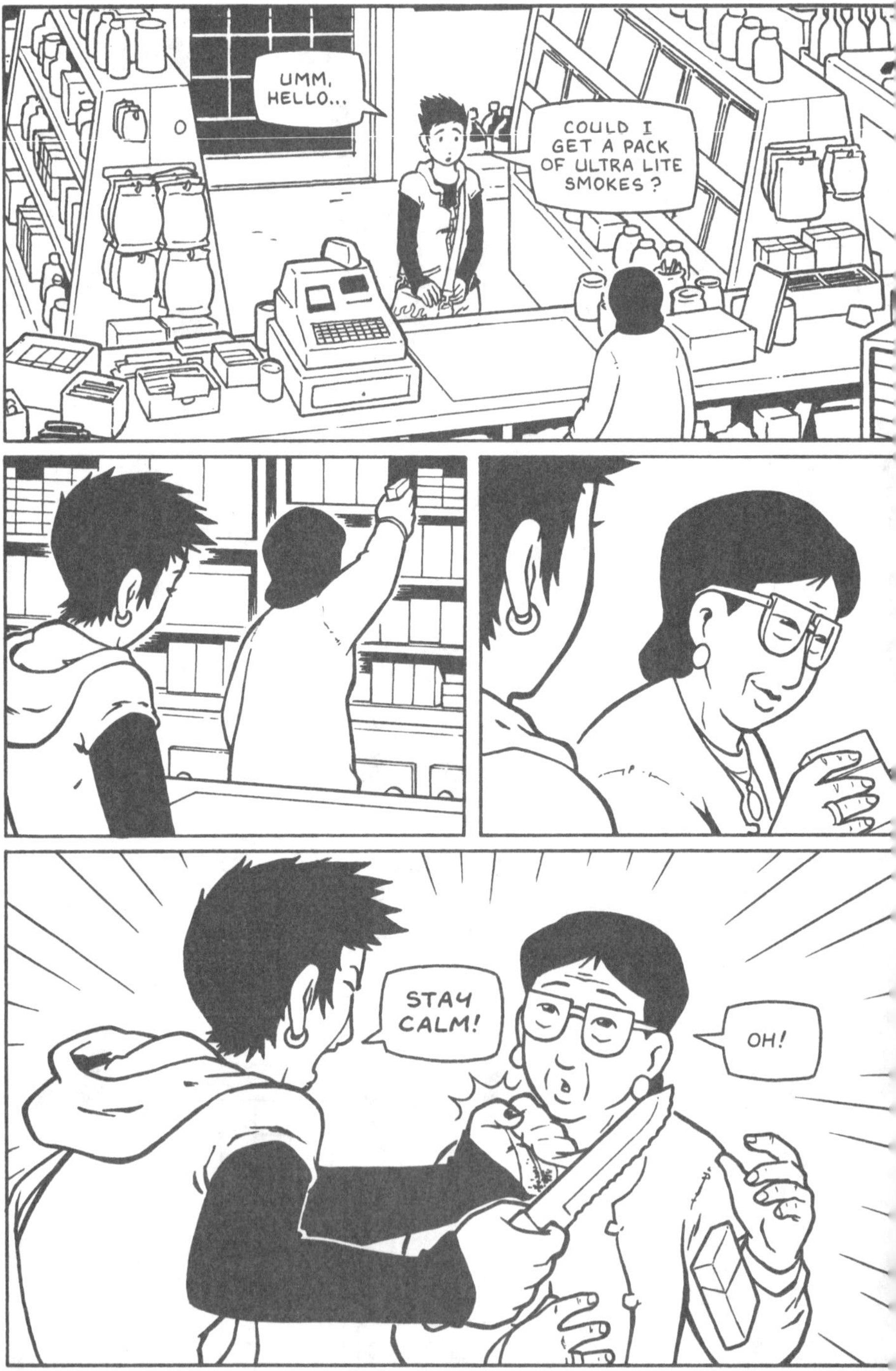

UMM, HELLO...
COULD I GET A PACK OF ULTRA LITE SMOKES?
STAY CALM!
OH!

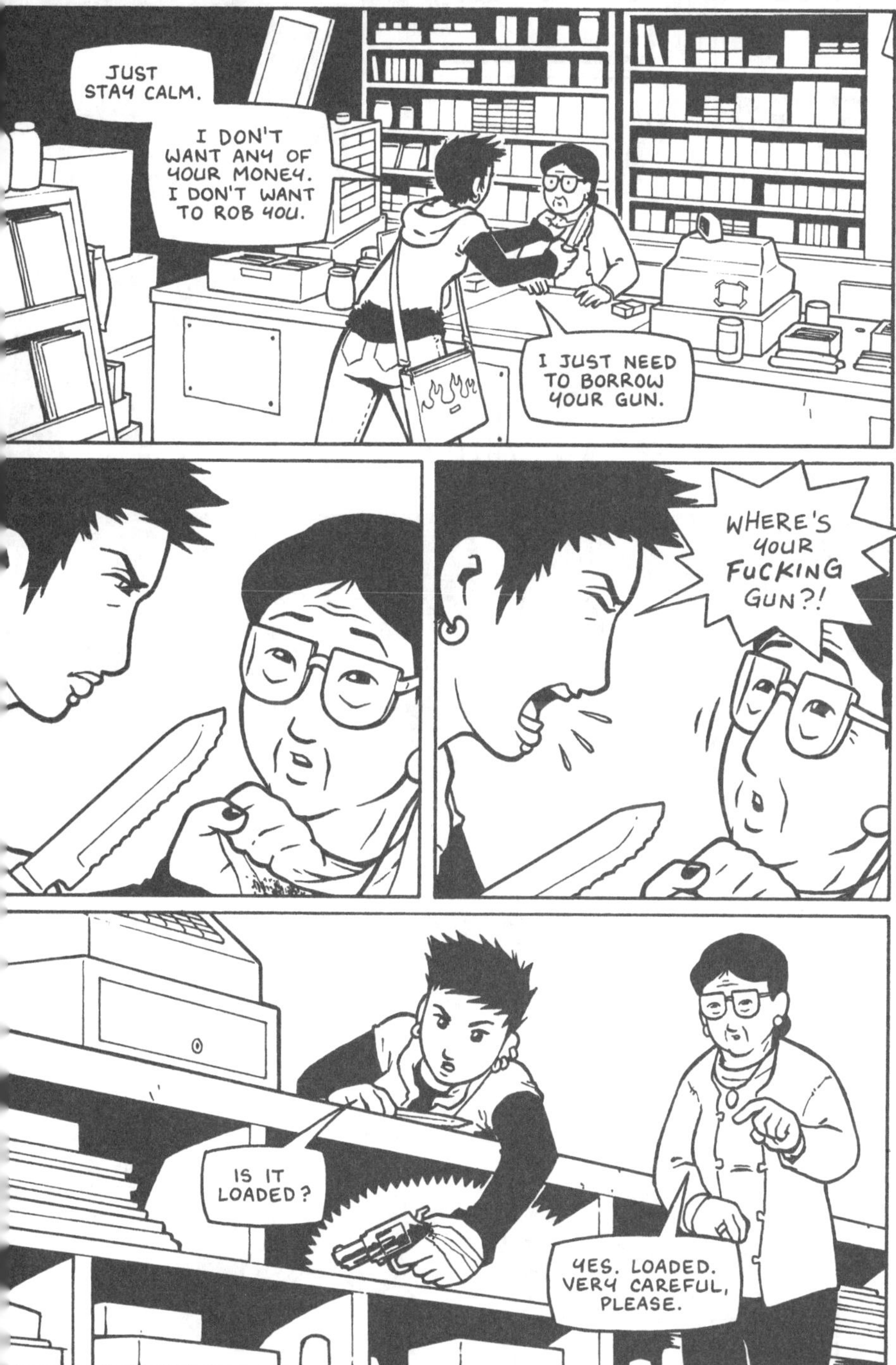
JUST STAY CALM.
I DON'T WANT ANY OF YOUR MONEY. I DON'T WANT TO ROB YOU.
I JUST NEED TO BORROW YOUR GUN.
WHERE'S YOUR FUCKING GUN?!
IS IT LOADED?
YES. LOADED. VERY CAREFUL, PLEASE.

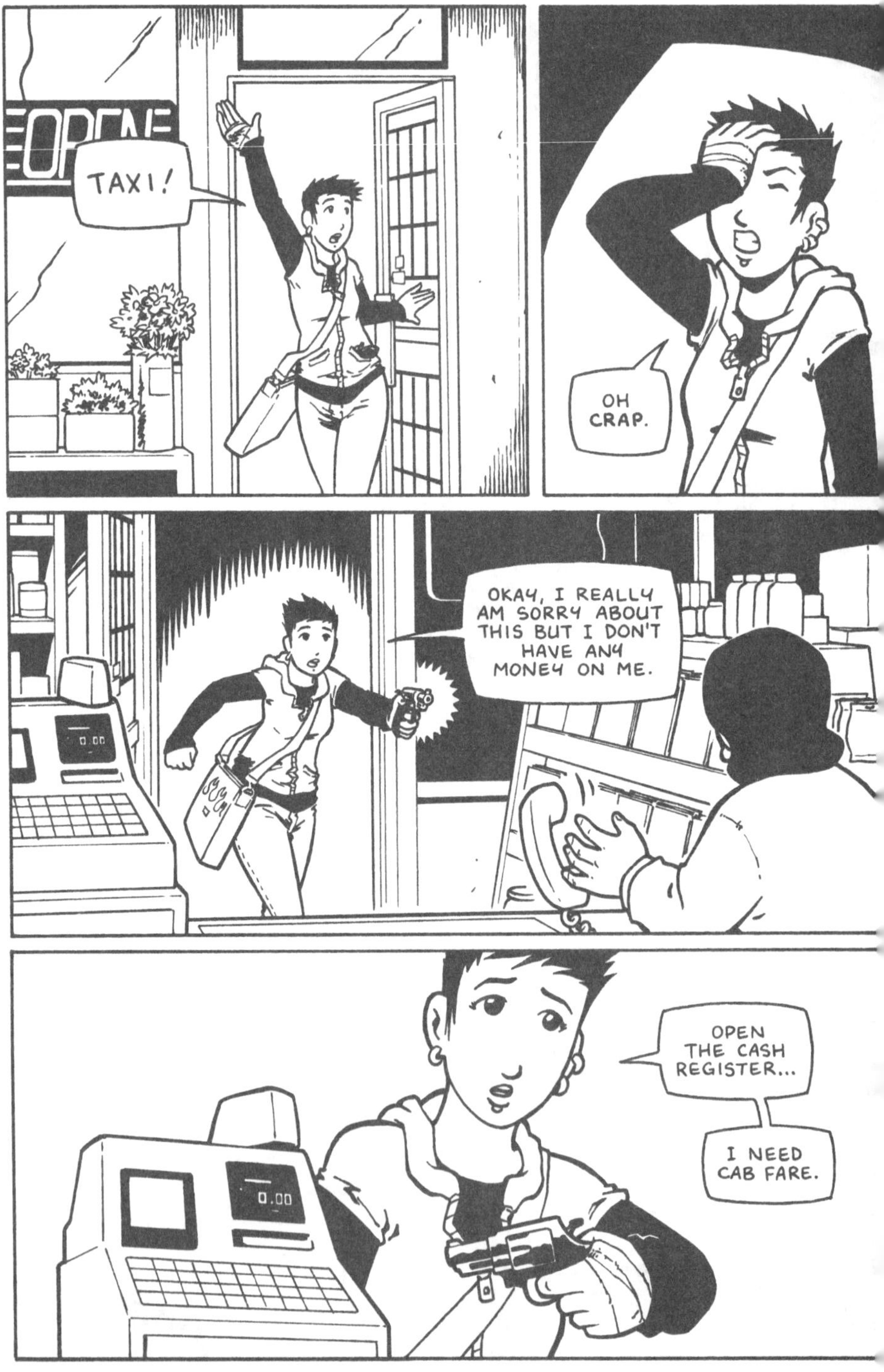
TAXI!
OH CRAP.
OKAY, I REALLY AM SORRY ABOUT THIS BUT I DON'T HAVE ANY MONEY ON ME.
OPEN THE CASH REGISTER...
I NEED CAB FARE.

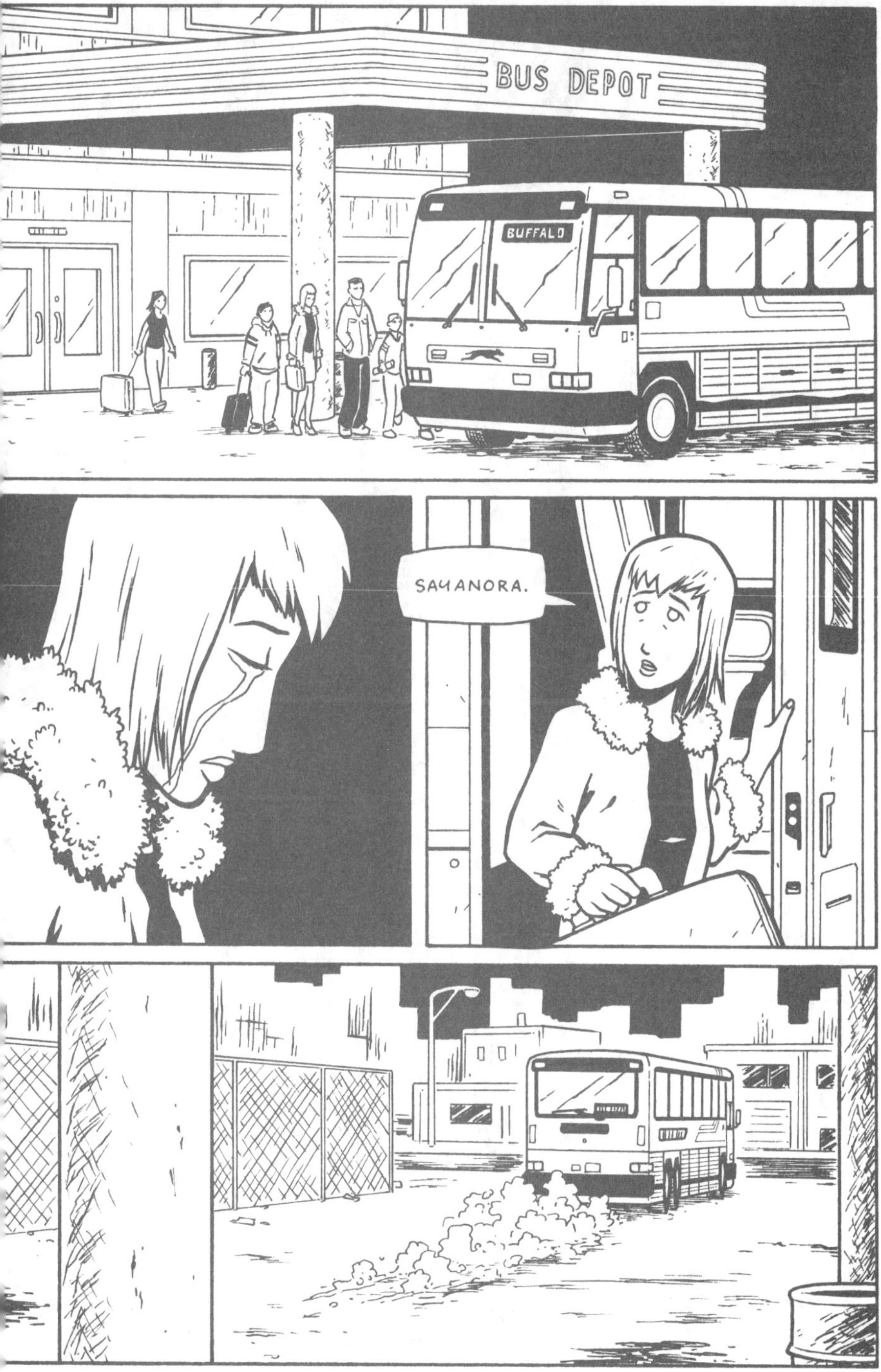
BUS DEPOT
BUFFALO
SAYANORA.

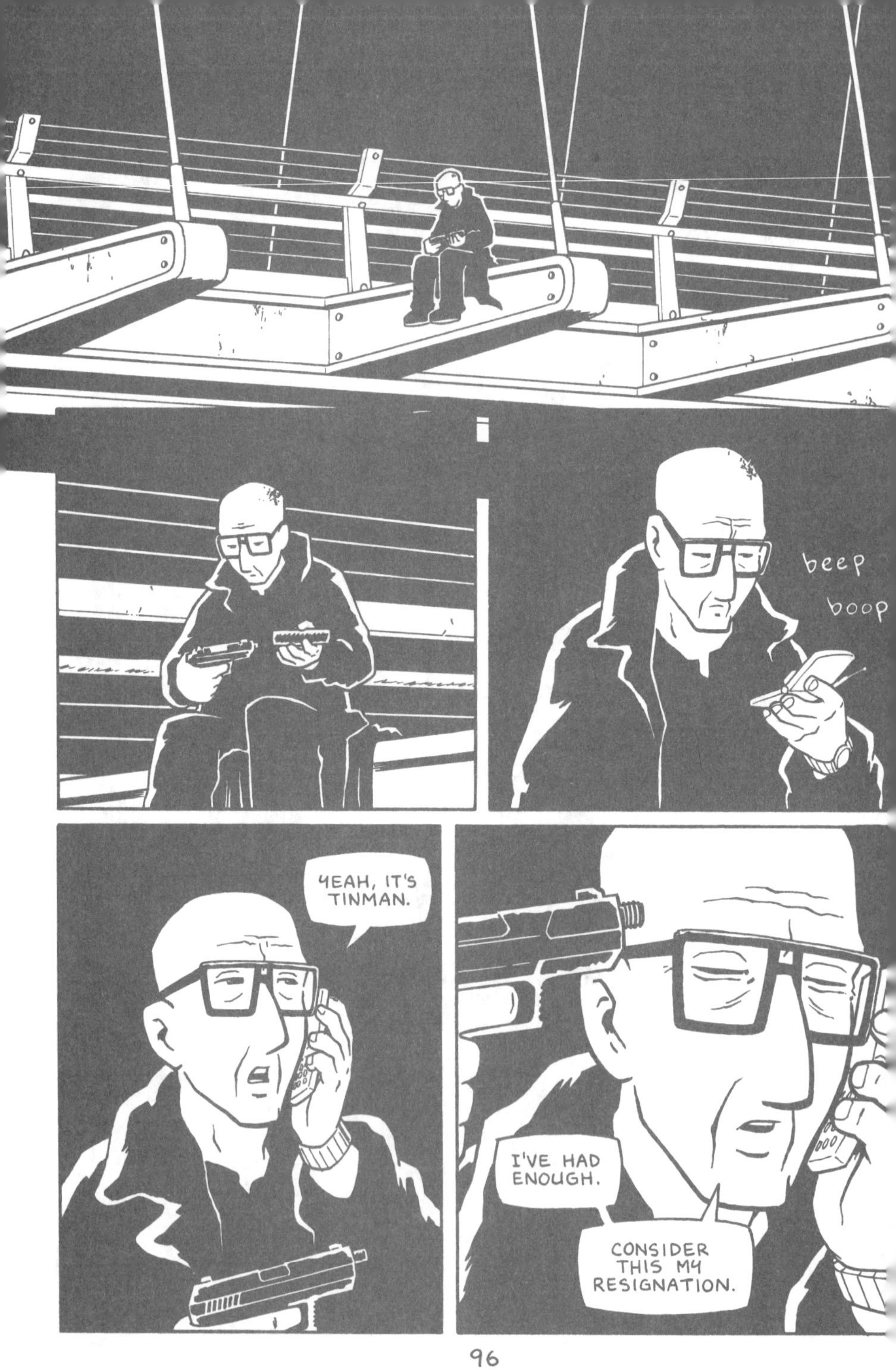
beep
boop
YEAH, IT'S TINMAN.
I'VE HAD ENOUGH.
CONSIDER THIS MY RESIGNATION.

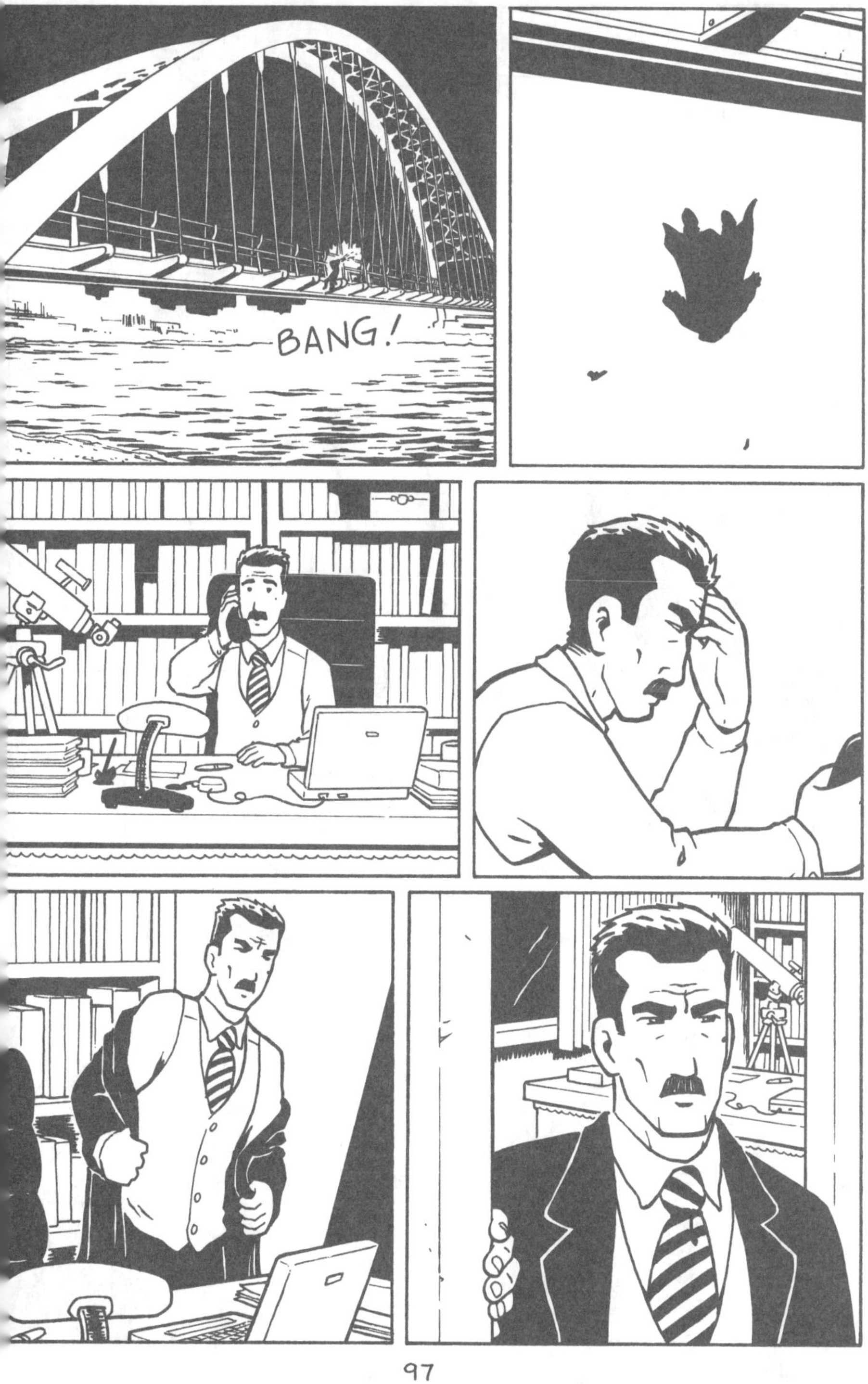
BANG!

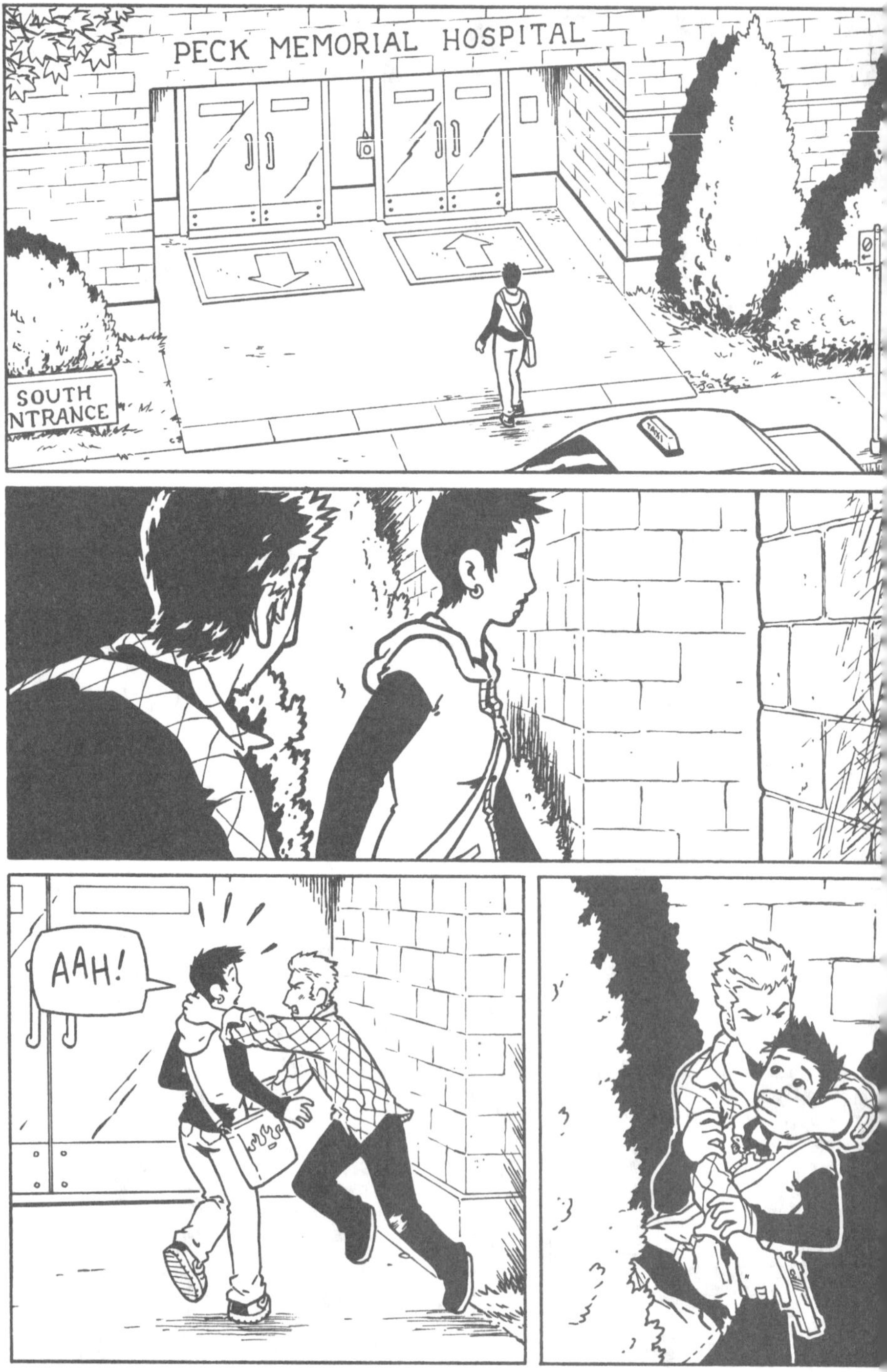
PECK MEMORIAL HOSPITAL
SOUTH
NTRANCE
AAH!

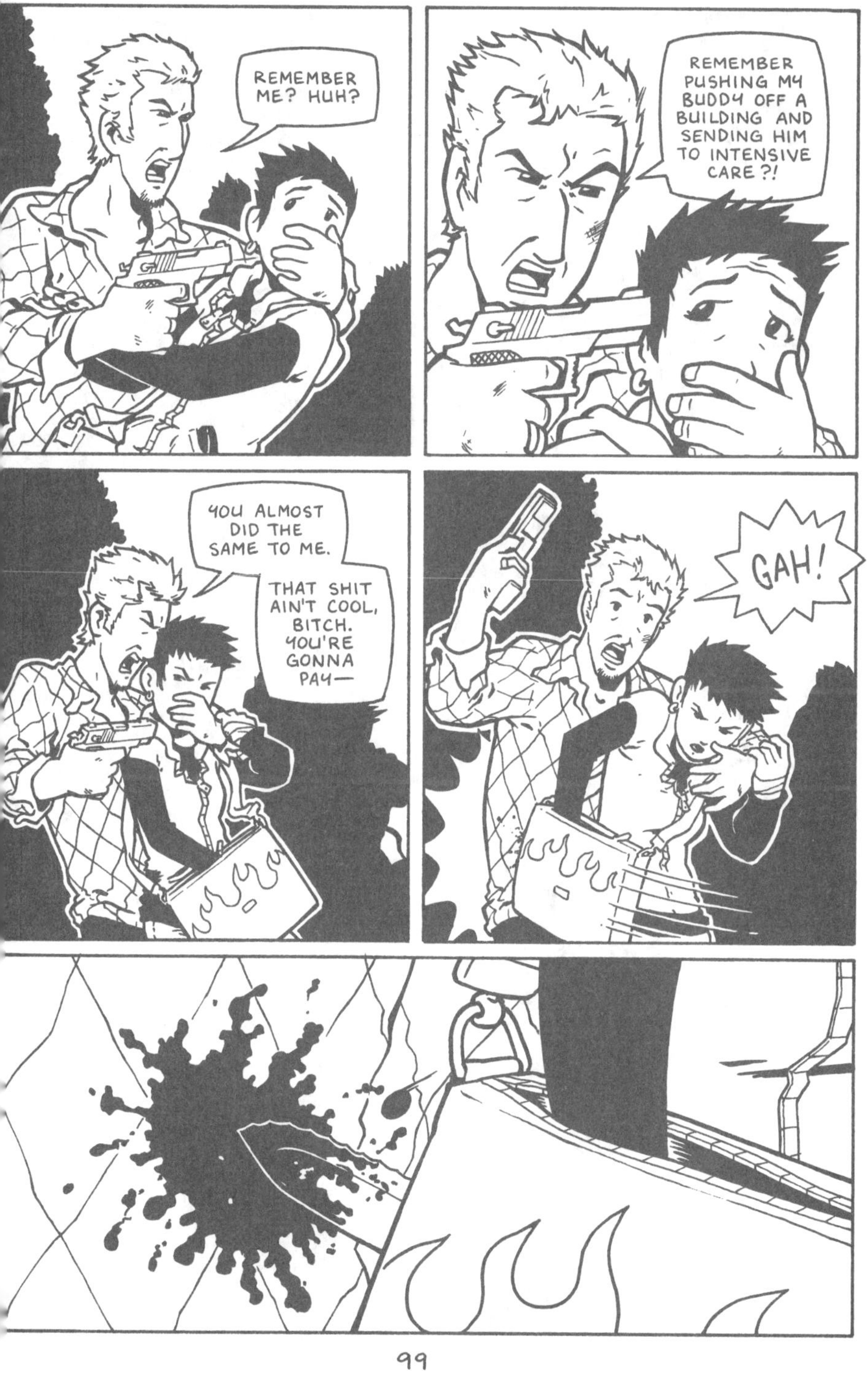
REMEMBER ME? HUH?
REMEMBER PUSHING MY BUDDY OFF A BUILDING AND SENDING HIM TO INTENSIVE CARE?!
YOU ALMOST DID THE SAME TO ME.
THAT SHIT AIN'T COOL, BITCH. YOU'RE GONNA PAY—
GAH!

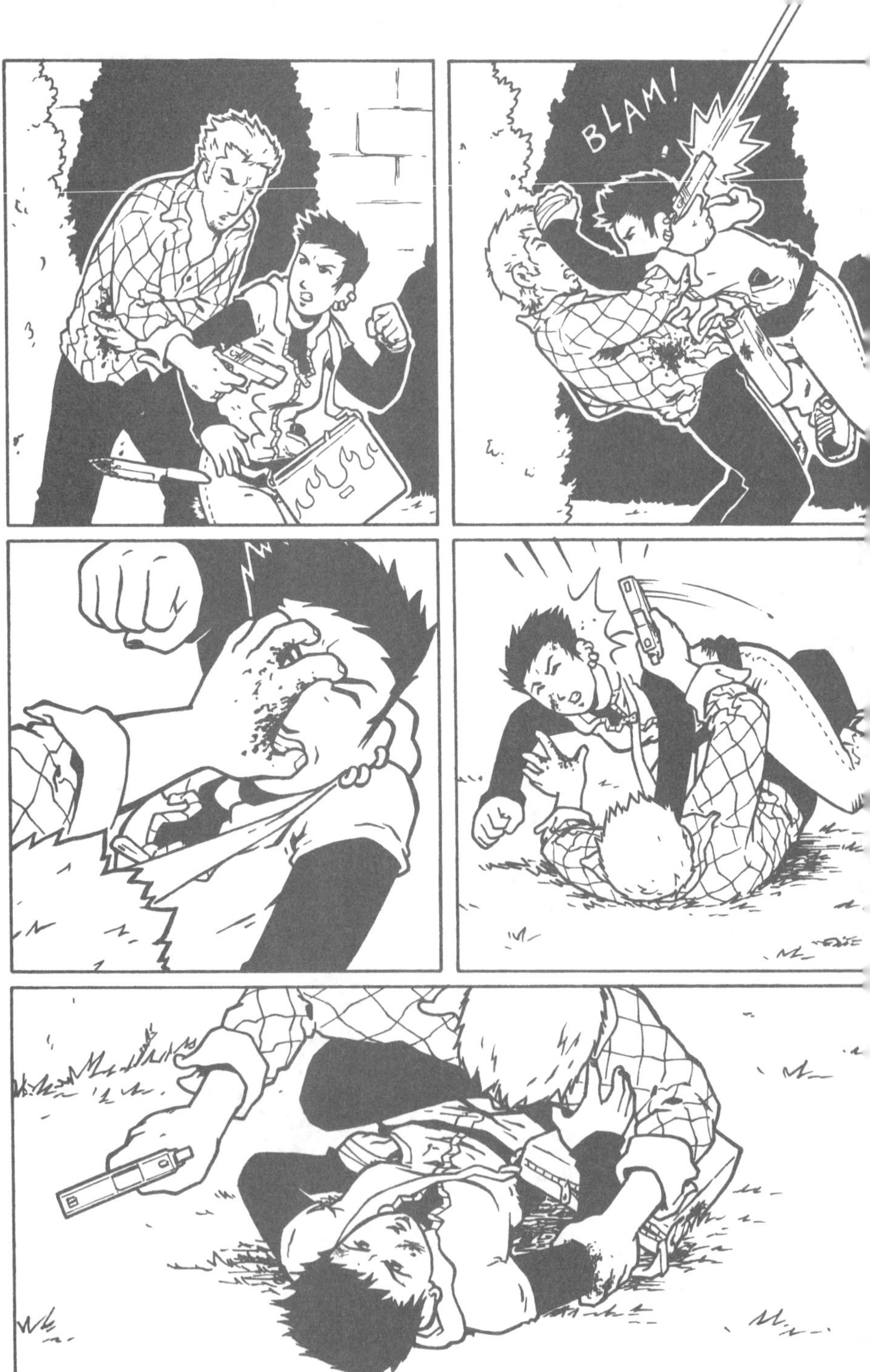
BLAM!

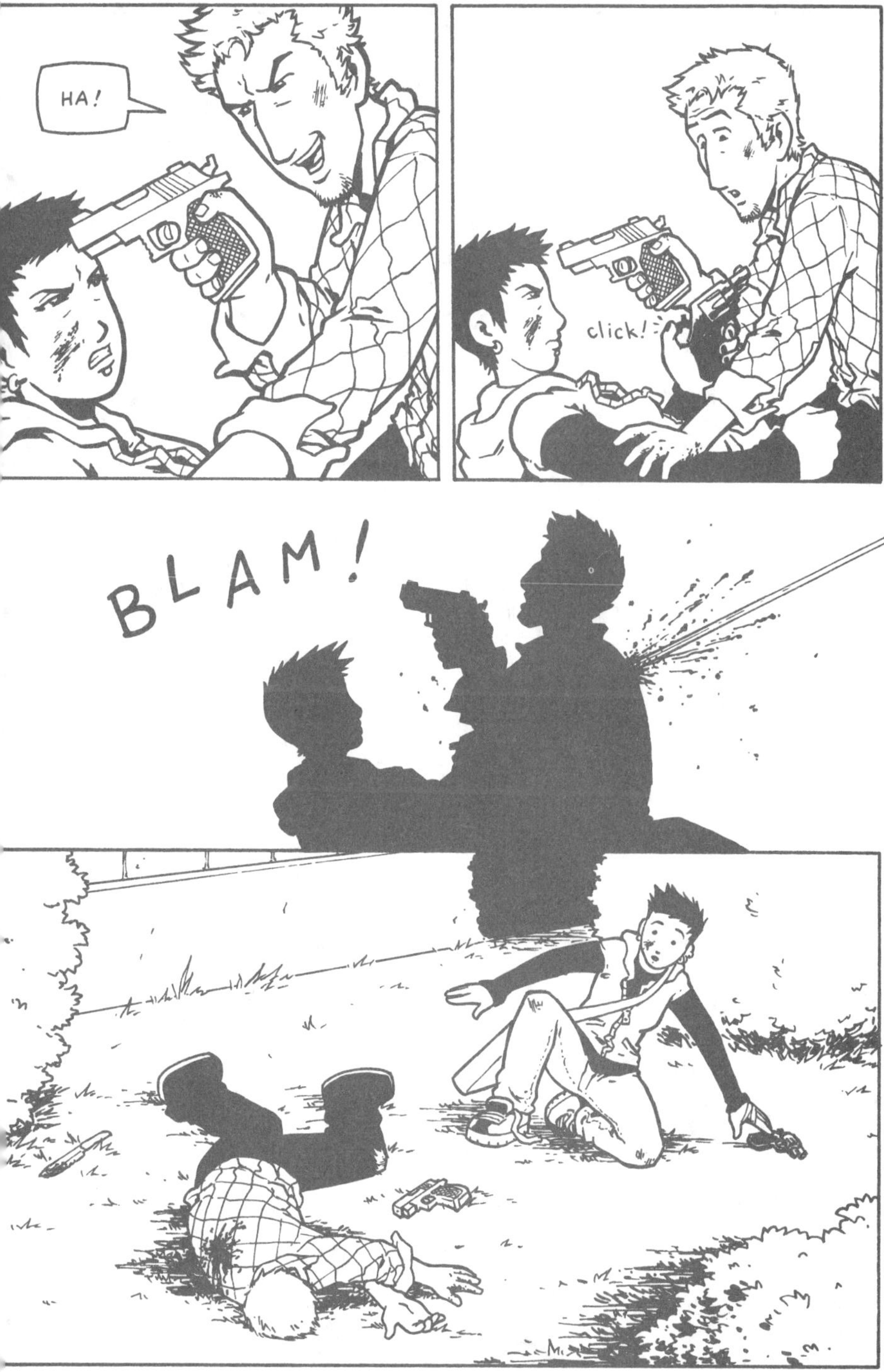
HA!
click!
BLAM!

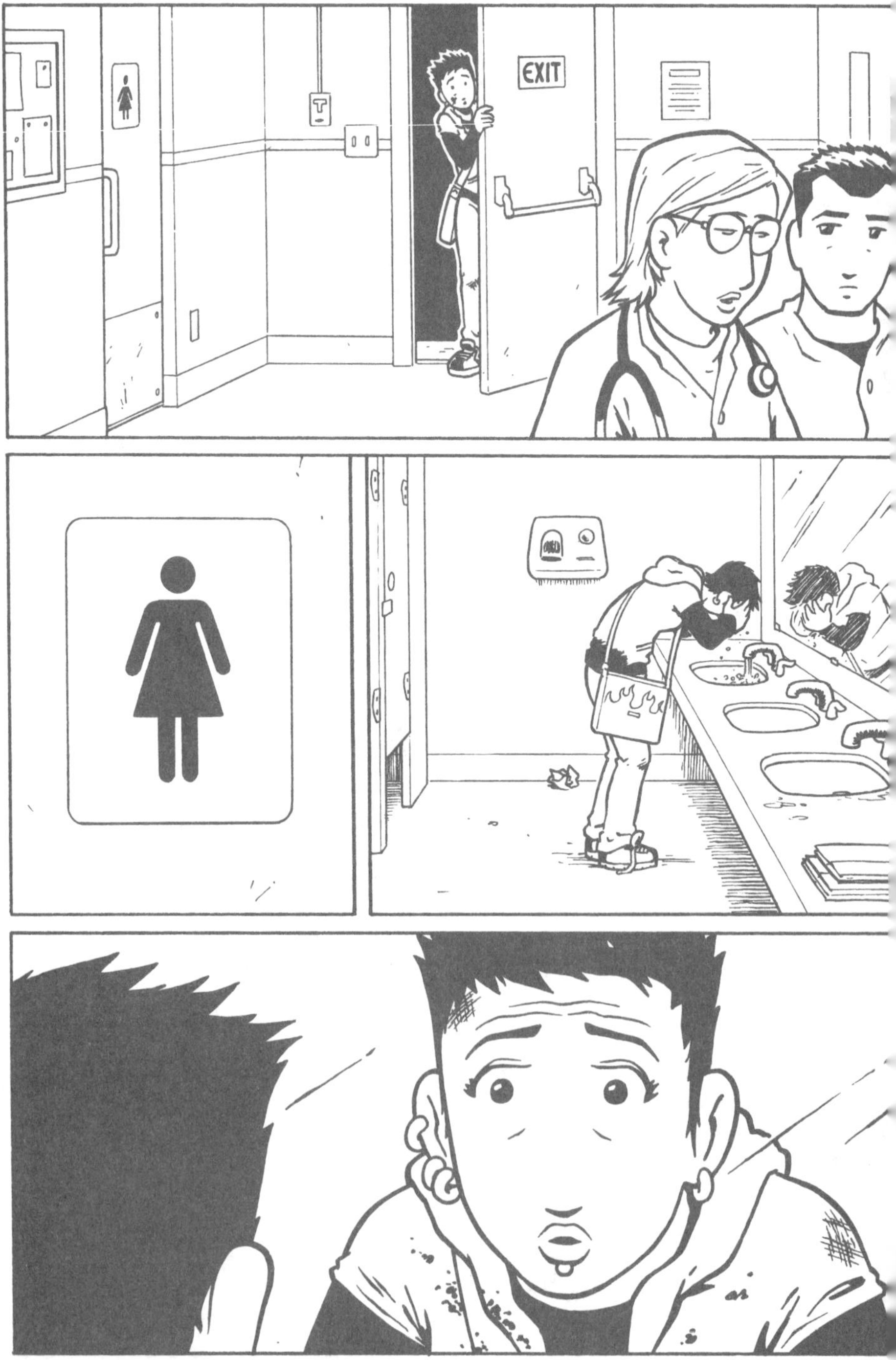
EXIT

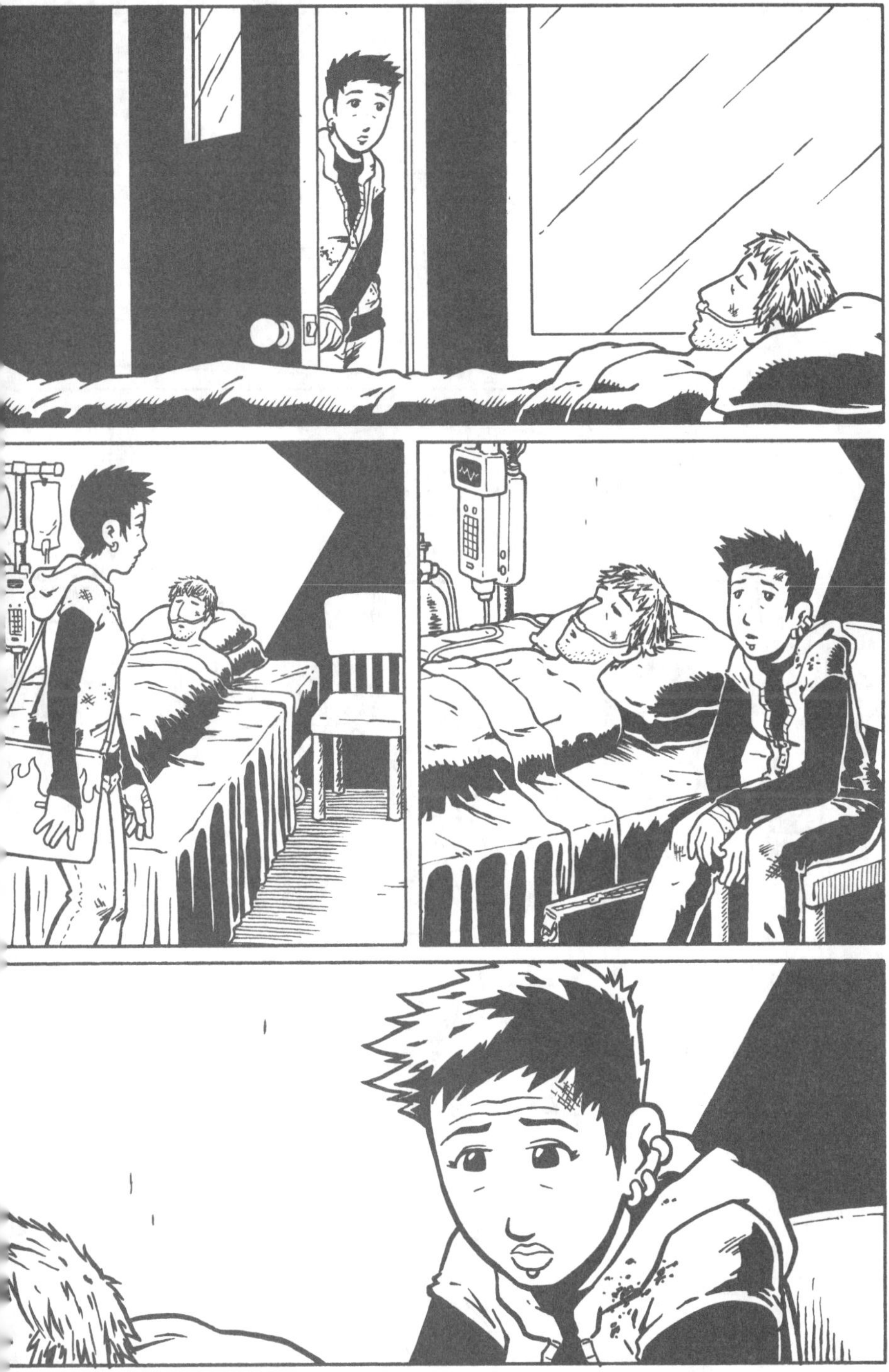

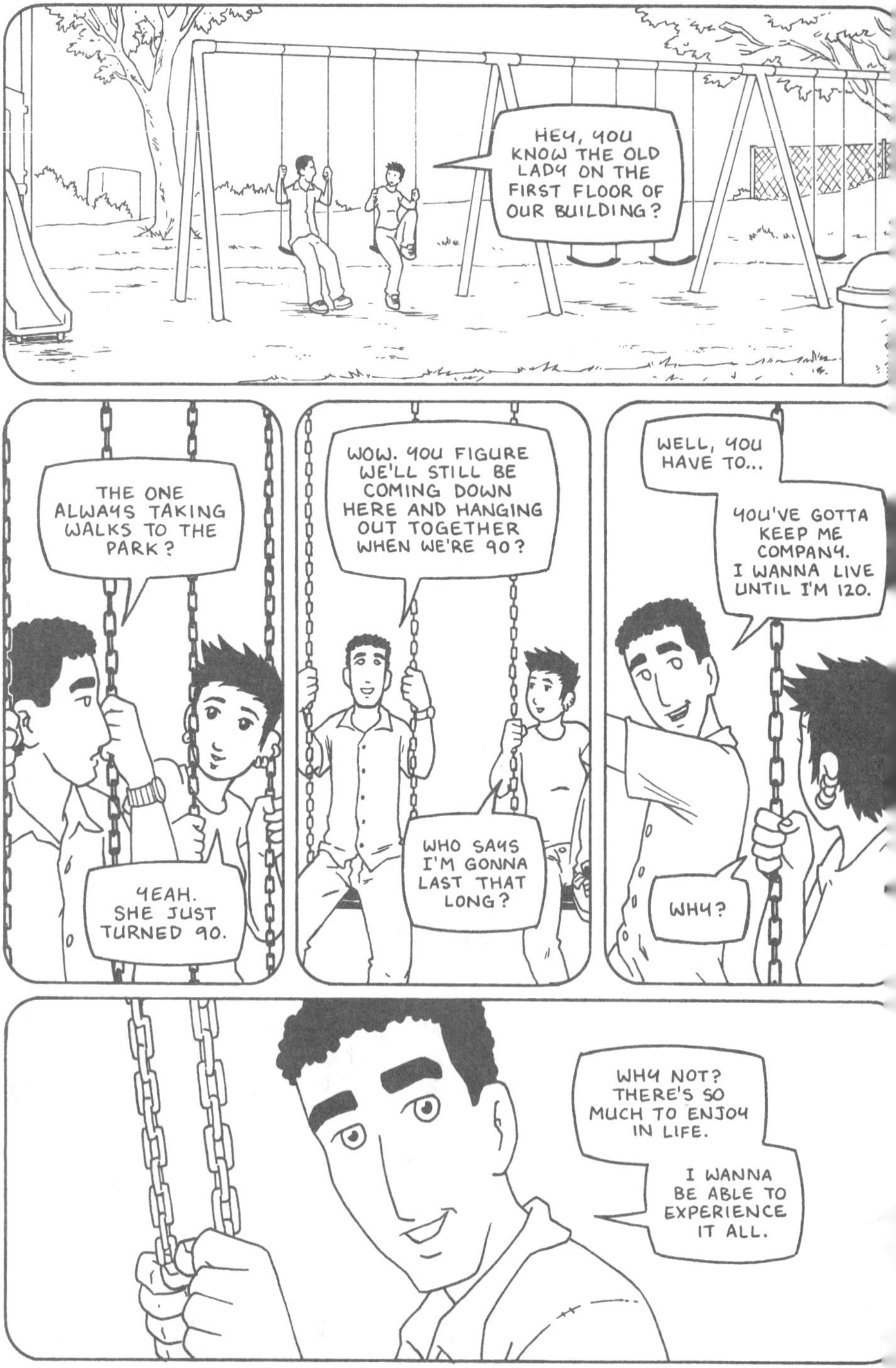
HEY, YOU KNOW THE OLD LADY ON THE FIRST FLOOR OF OUR BUILDING?
THE ONE ALWAYS TAKING WALKS TO THE PARK?
YEAH. SHE JUST TURNED 90.
WOW. YOU FIGURE WE'LL STILL BE COMING DOWN HERE AND HANGING OUT TOGETHER WHEN WE'RE 90?
WHO SAYS I'M GONNA LAST THAT LONG?
WELL, YOU HAVE TO...
YOU'VE GOTTA KEEP ME COMPANY. I WANNA LIVE UNTIL I'M 120.
WHY?
WHY NOT? THERE'S SO MUCH TO ENJOY IN LIFE.
I WANNA BE ABLE TO EXPERIENCE IT ALL.

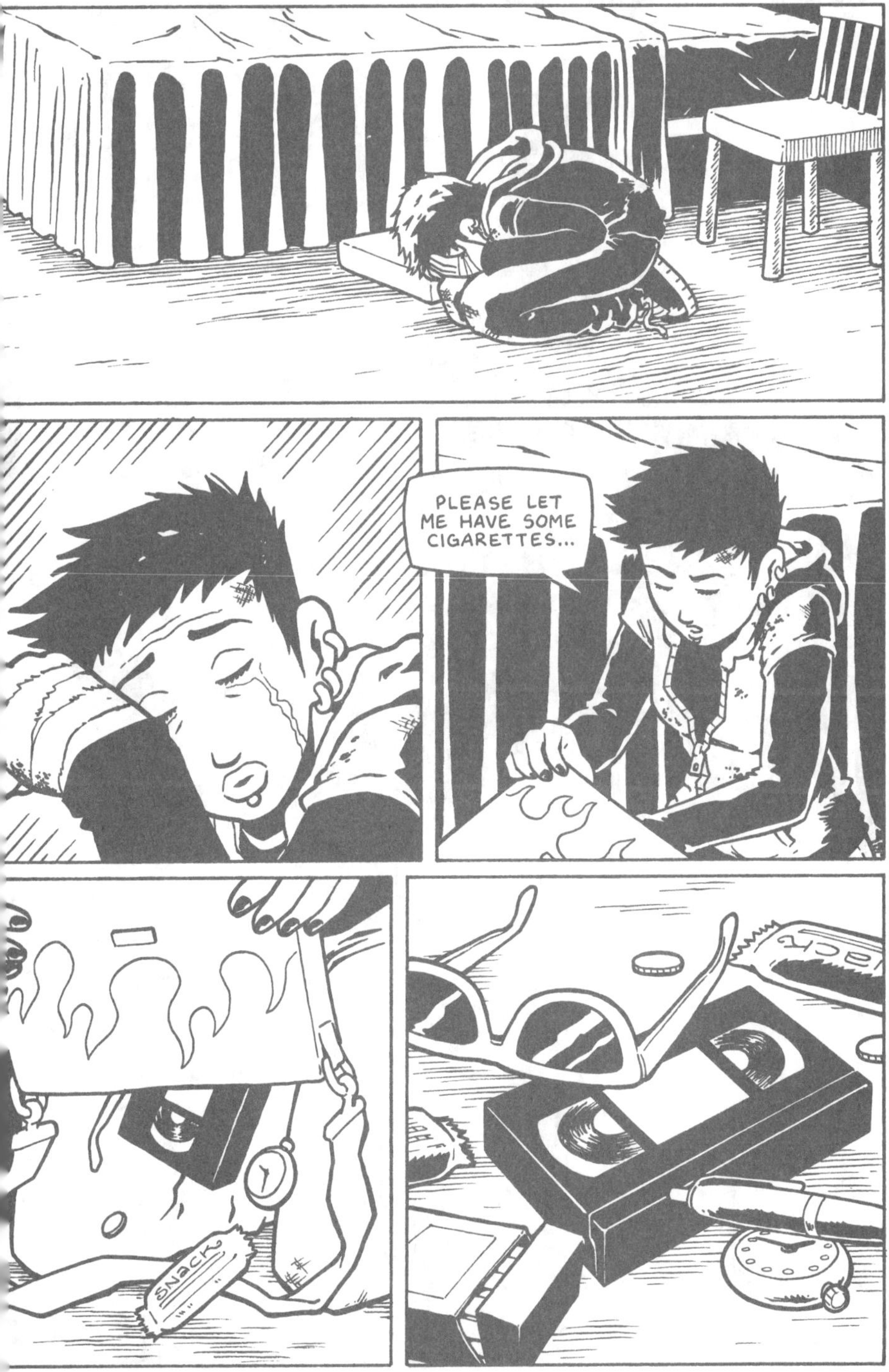
PLEASE LET ME HAVE SOME CIGARETTES...
SNACK

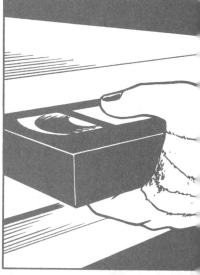

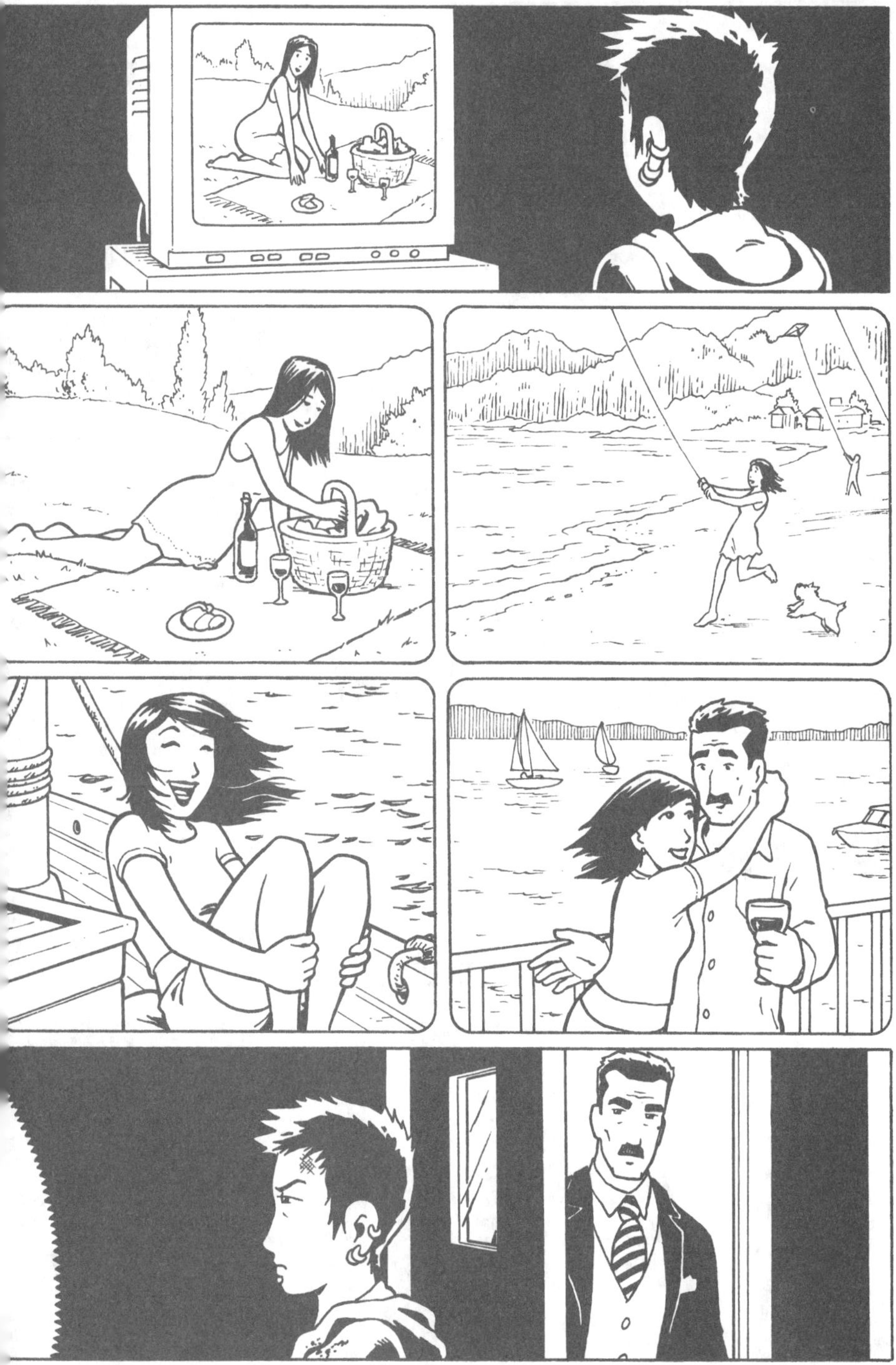

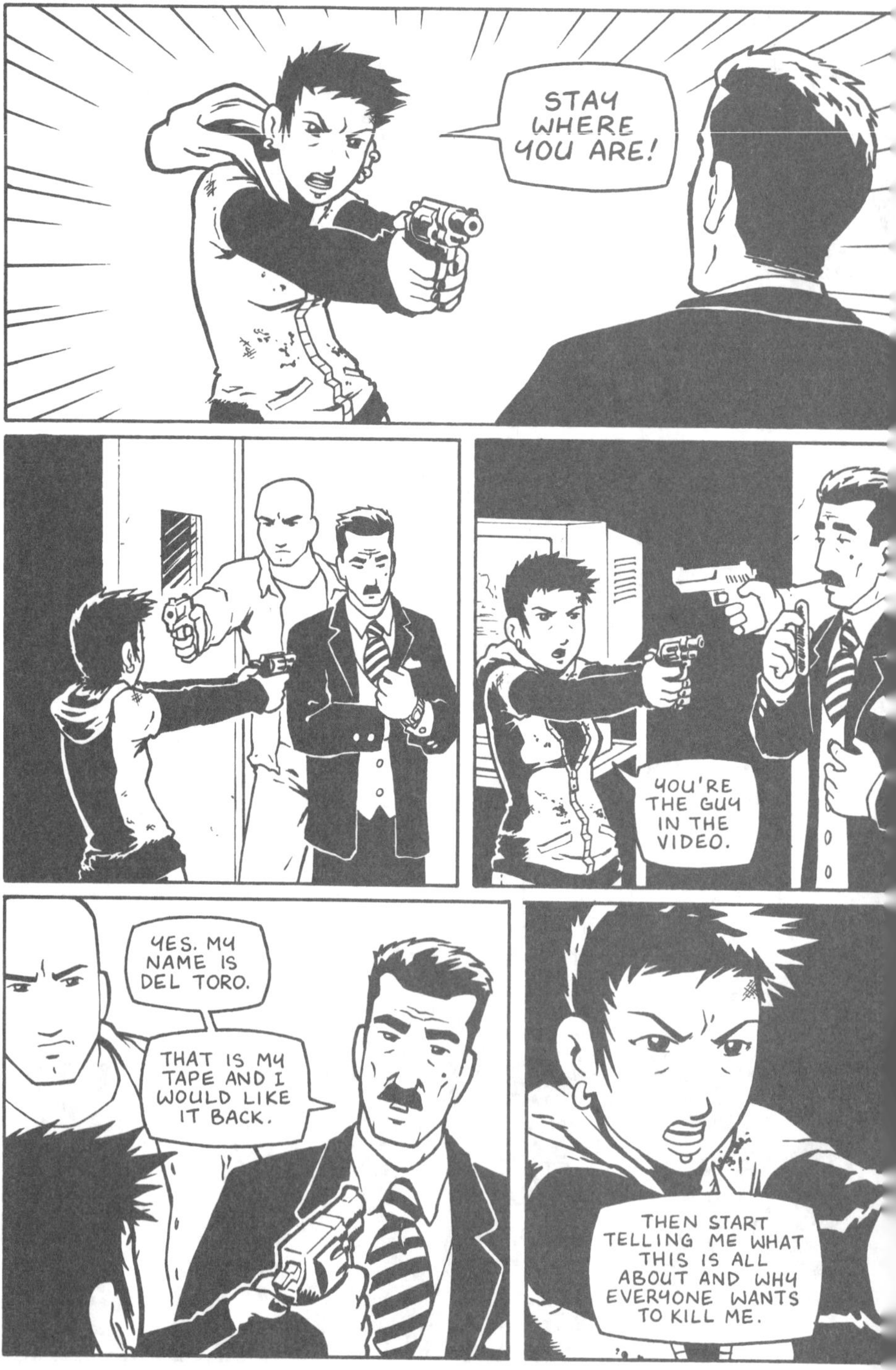
STAY WHERE YOU ARE!
YOU'RE THE GUY IN THE VIDEO.
YES. MY NAME IS DEL TORO.
THAT IS MY TAPE AND I WOULD LIKE IT BACK.
THEN START TELLING ME WHAT THIS IS ALL ABOUT AND WHY EVERYONE WANTS TO KILL ME.

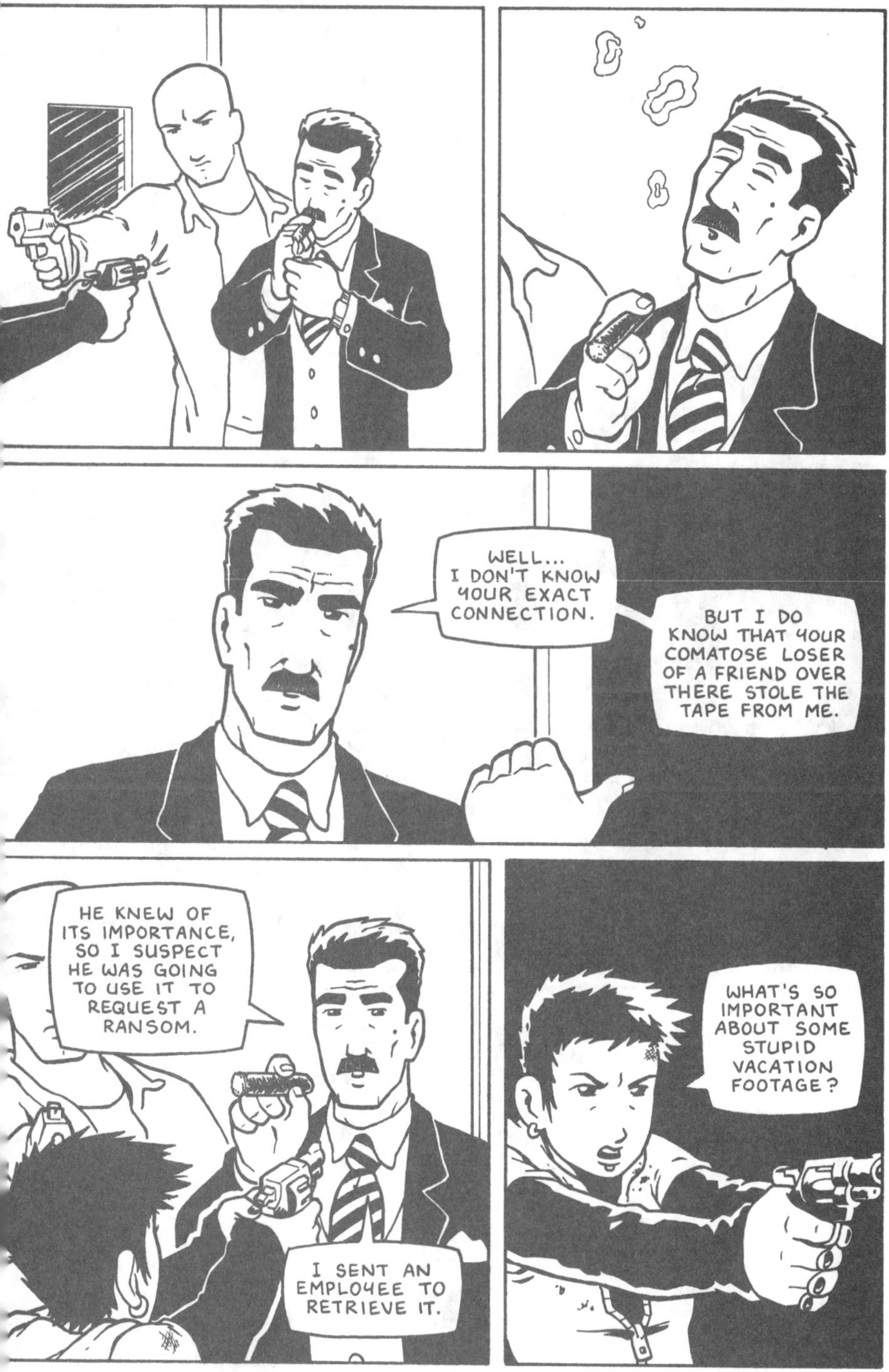
WELL... I DON'T KNOW YOUR EXACT CONNECTION.
BUT I DO KNOW THAT YOUR COMATOSE LOSER OF A FRIEND OVER THERE STOLE THE TAPE FROM ME.
HE KNEW OF ITS IMPORTANCE, SO I SUSPECT HE WAS GOING TO USE IT TO REQUEST A RANSOM.
I SENT AN EMPLOYEE TO RETRIEVE IT.
WHAT'S SO IMPORTANT ABOUT SOME STUPID VACATION FOOTAGE?

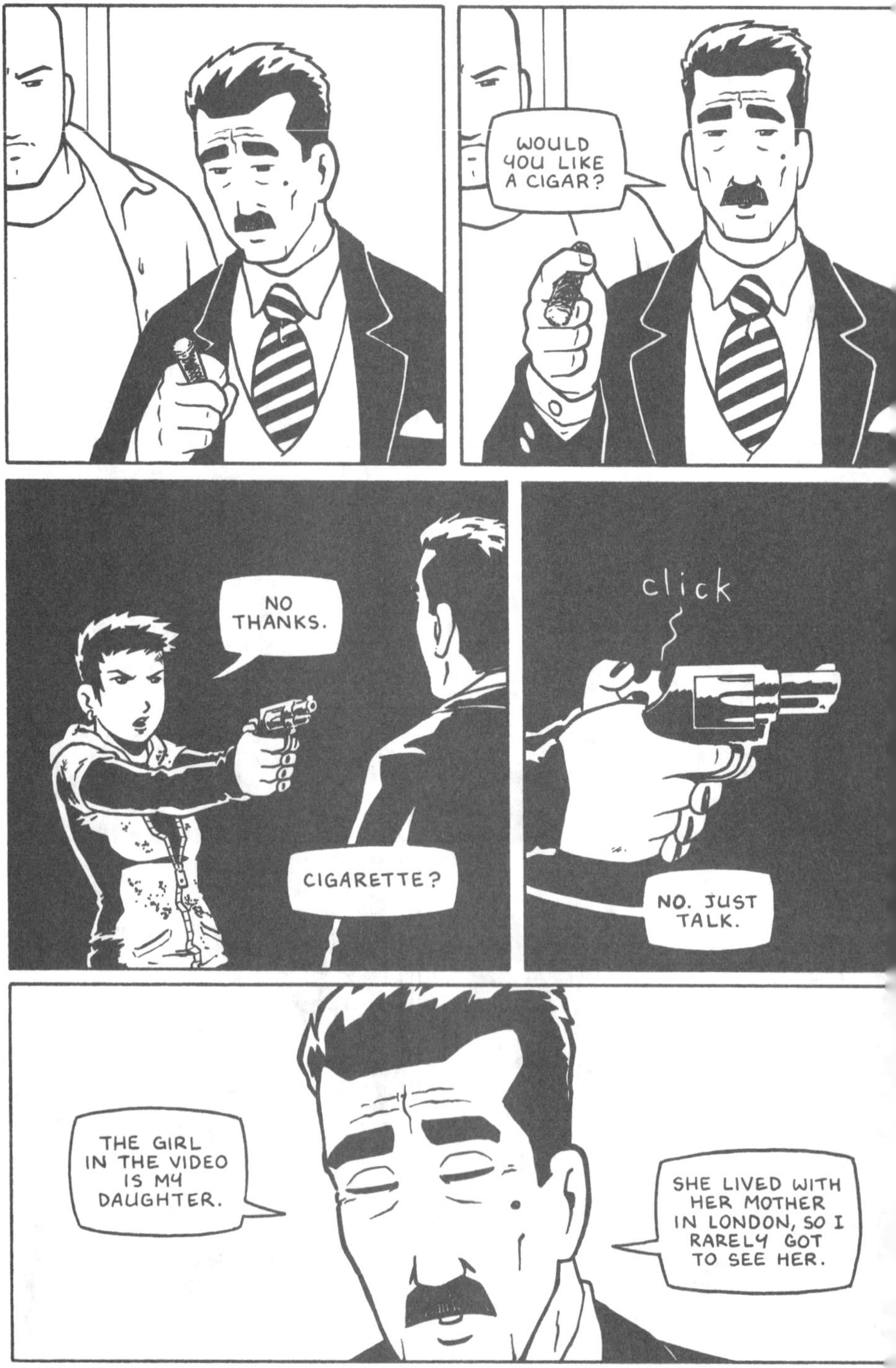
WOULD YOU LIKE A CIGAR?
NO THANKS.
CIGARETTE?
click
NO. JUST TALK.
THE GIRL IN THE VIDEO IS MY DAUGHTER.
SHE LIVED WITH HER MOTHER IN LONDON, SO I RARELY GOT TO SEE HER.

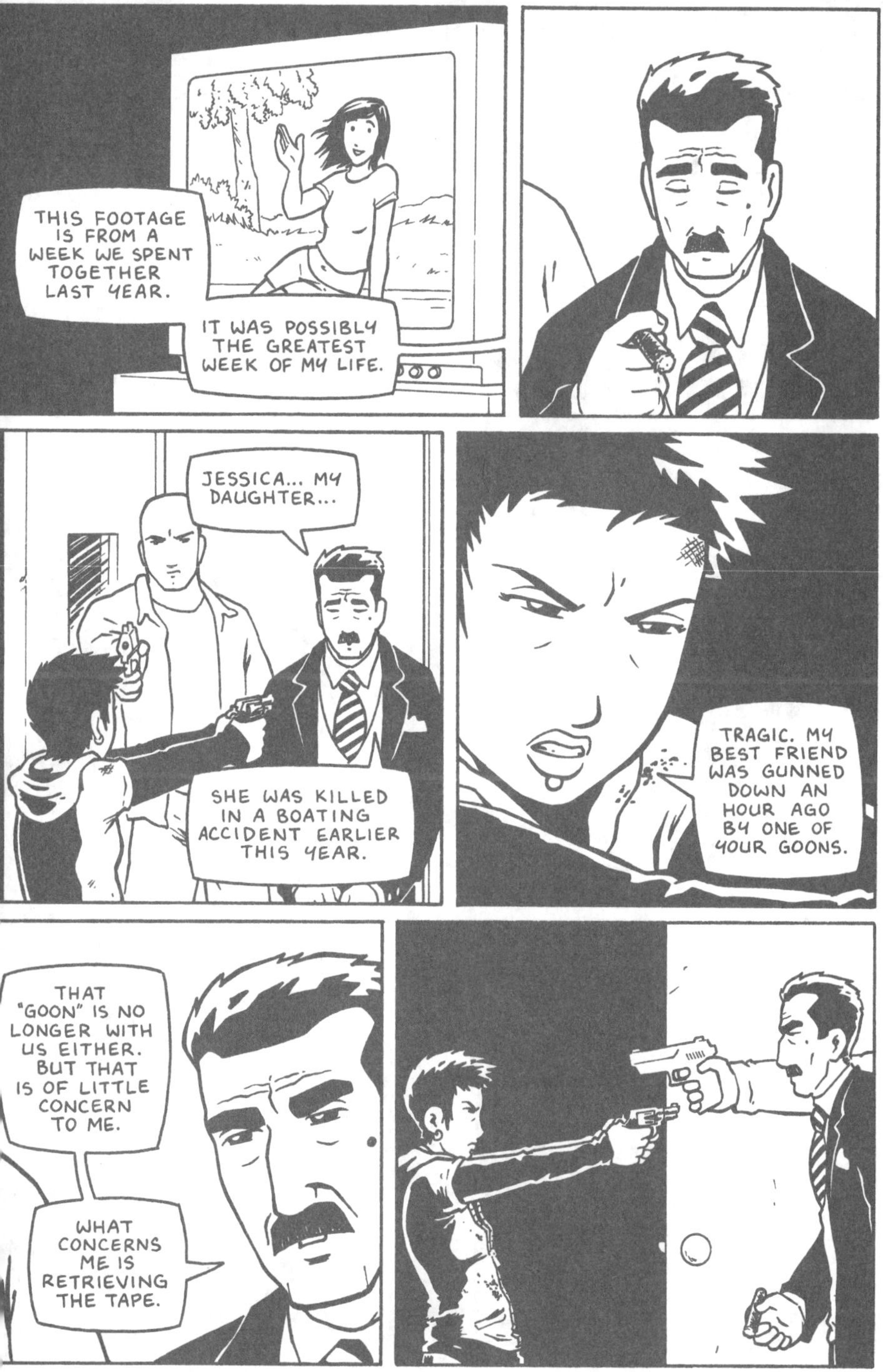
THIS FOOTAGE IS FROM A WEEK WE SPENT TOGETHER LAST YEAR.
IT WAS POSSIBLY THE GREATEST WEEK OF MY LIFE.
JESSICA... MY DAUGHTER...
SHE WAS KILLED IN A BOATING ACCIDENT EARLIER THIS YEAR.
TRAGIC. MY BEST FRIEND WAS GUNNED DOWN AN HOUR AGO BY ONE OF YOUR GOONS.
THAT "GOON" IS NO LONGER WITH US EITHER. BUT THAT IS OF LITTLE CONCERN TO ME.
WHAT CONCERNS ME IS RETRIEVING THE TAPE.

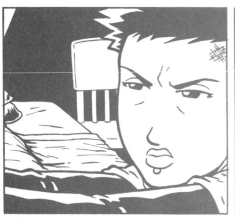

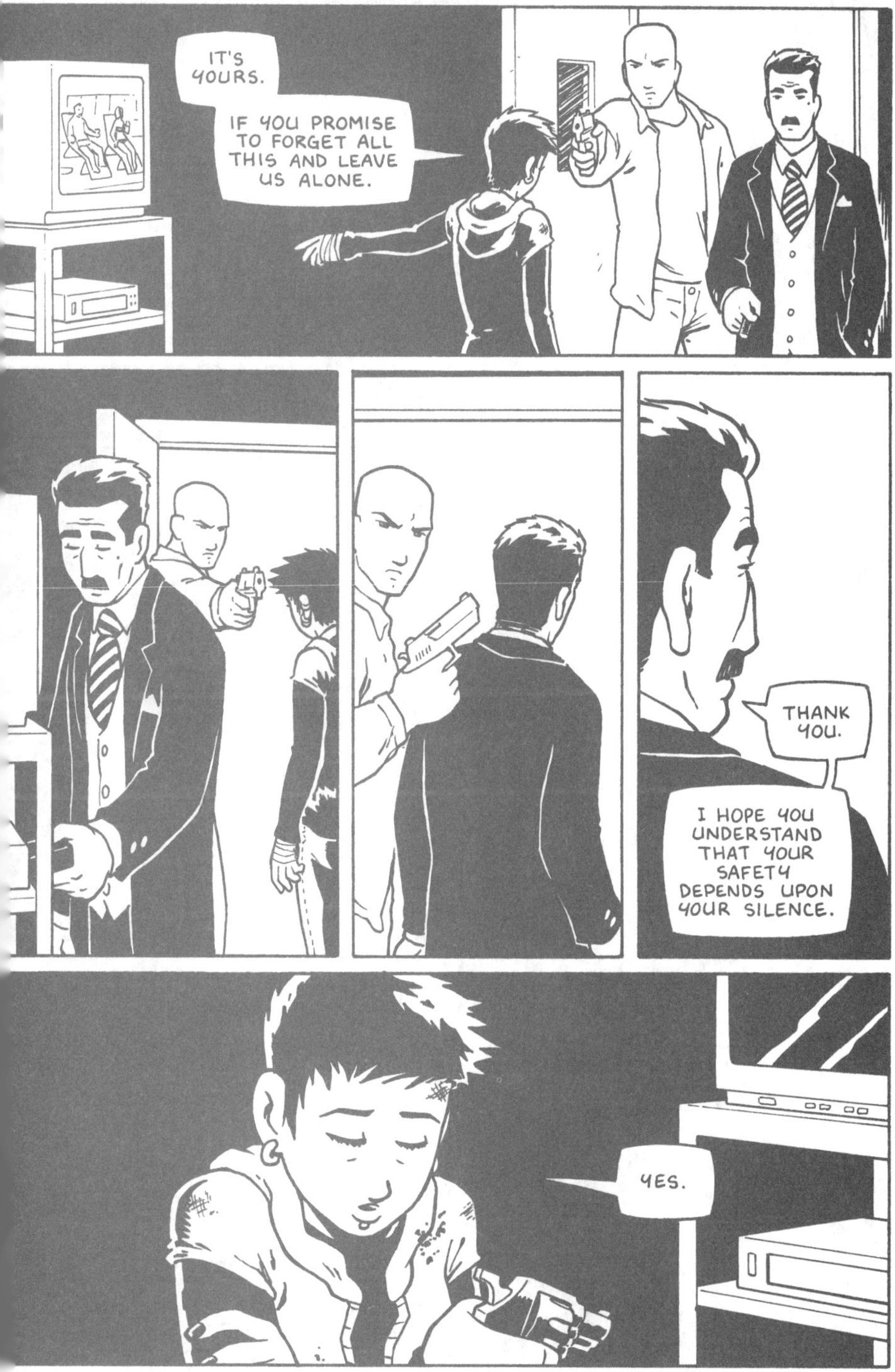
IT'S YOURS.
IF YOU PROMISE TO FORGET ALL THIS AND LEAVE US ALONE.
THANK YOU.
I HOPE YOU UNDERSTAND THAT YOUR SAFETY DEPENDS UPON YOUR SILENCE.
YES.

AND IF YOUR FRIEND THE THIEF RECOVERS, YOU SHOULD RECOMMEND THAT HE LEAVE TOWN AND NOT COME BACK.

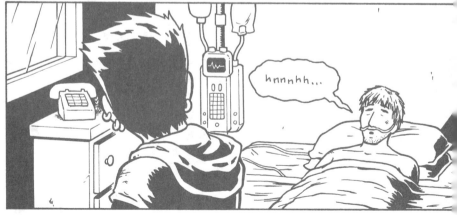

hnnnhh...

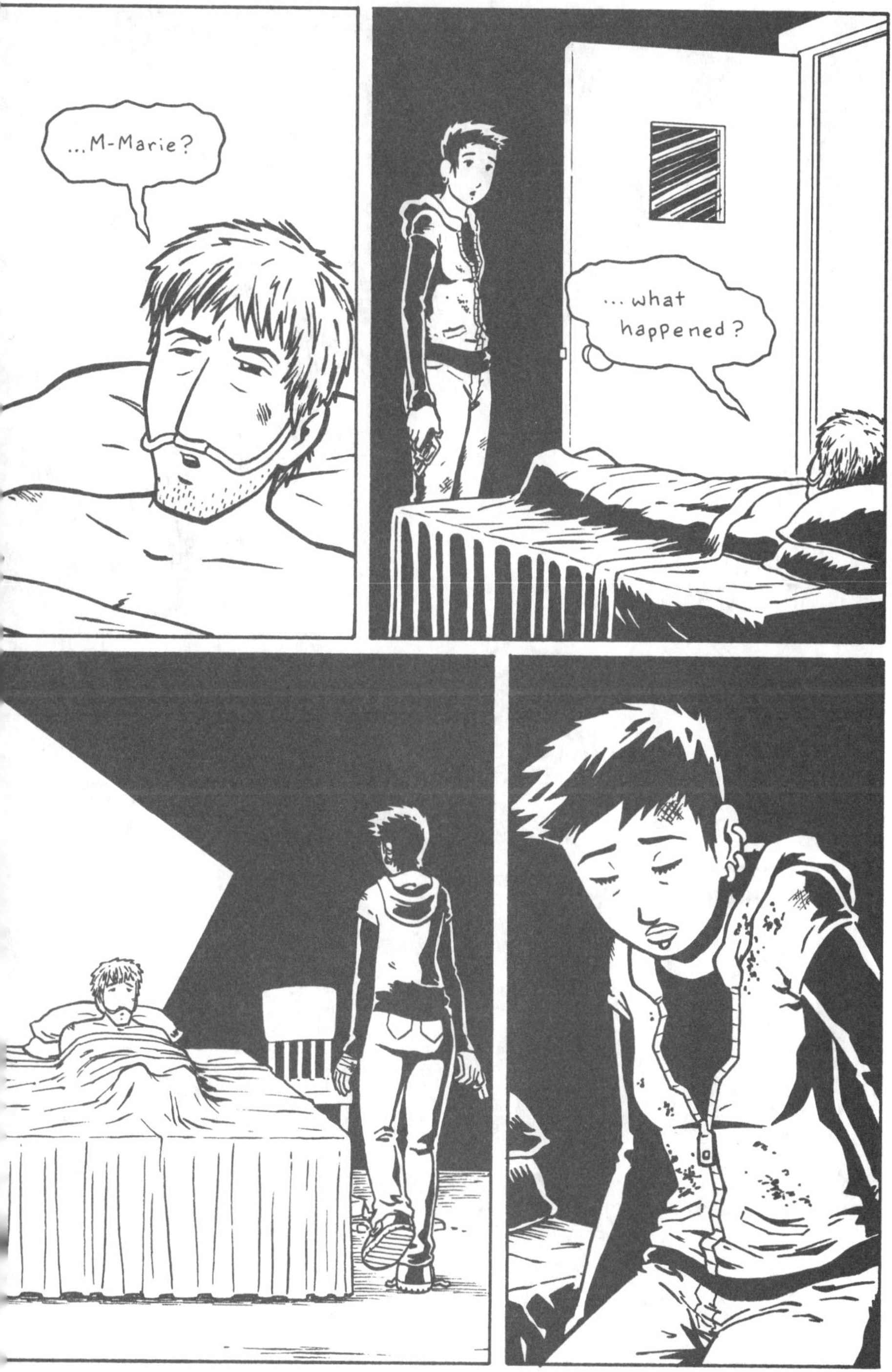
...M-Marie?
... what happened?

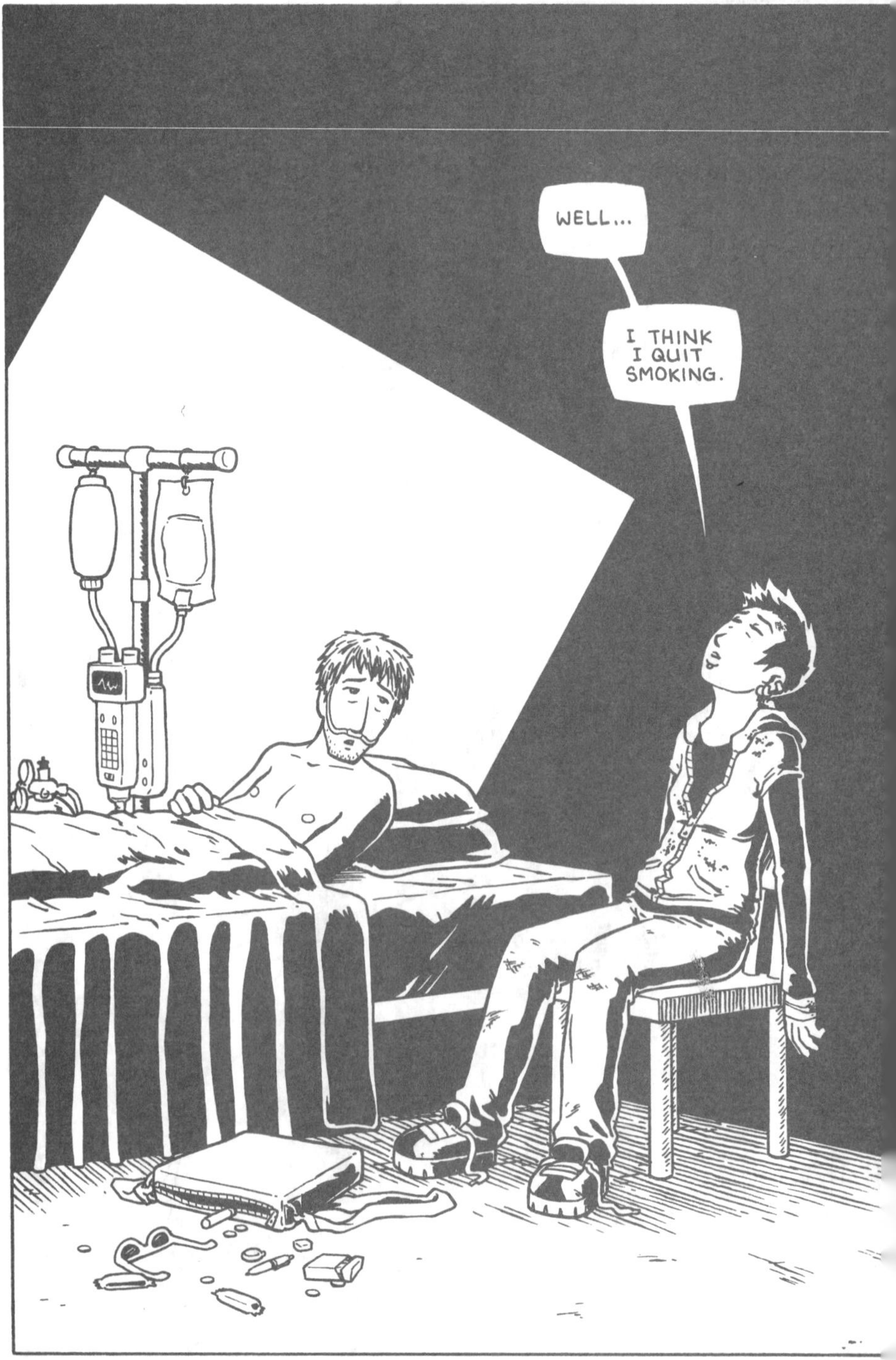
WELL...
I THINK I QUIT SMOKING.

the end

OTHER BOOKS FROM STEVE ROLSTON & ONI PRESS...

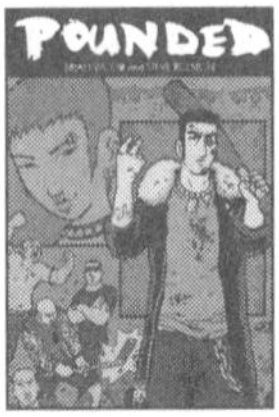
POUNDED

POUNDED™
by Brian Wood & Steve Rolston
96 pages,
black-and-white interiors
$8.95 US
ISBN 1929998-37-6

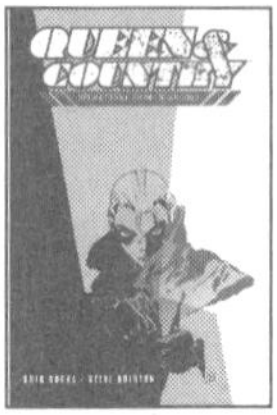
QUEEN & COUNTRY

QUEEN & COUNTRY™, VOL 1: OPERATION: BROKEN GROUND
by Greg Rucka & Steve Rolston
128 pages,
black-and-white interiors
$11.95 US
ISBN 1929998-21-X

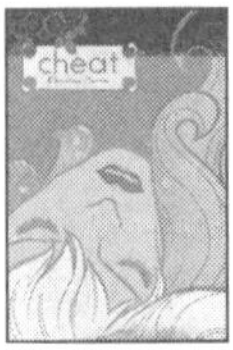
cheat

CHEAT™
by Christine Norrie
72 pages,
black-and-white interiors
$5.95 US
ISBN 1929998-47-3

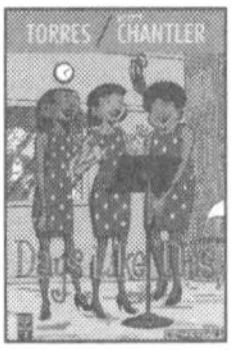
TORRES
CHANTLER

DAYS LIKE THIS™
by J. Torres & Scott Chantler
88 pages,
black-and-white interiors
$8.95 US
ISBN 1-929998-48-1

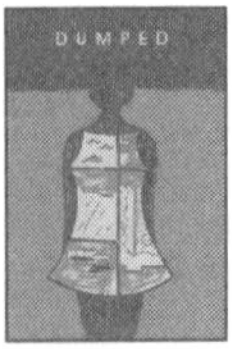
DUMPED

DUMPED™
by Andi Watson
56 pages,
black-and-white interiors
$5.95 US
ISBN 1929998-41-4

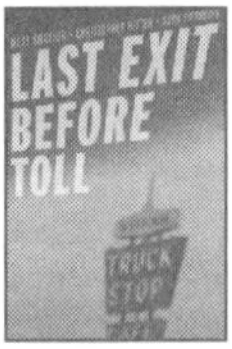
LAST EXIT BEFORE TOLL

LAST EXIT BEFORE TOLL™
by Neal Shaffer, Christopher Mitten, & Dawn Pietrusko
96 pages,
black-and-white interiors
$9.95 US
1-929998-70-8

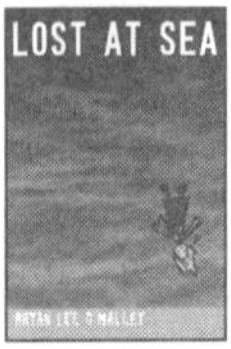
LOST AT SEA

LOST AT SEA™
by Bryan Lee O'Malley
160 pages,
black-and-white interiors
$11.95 US
ISBN 1929998-71-6
Available October 2003!

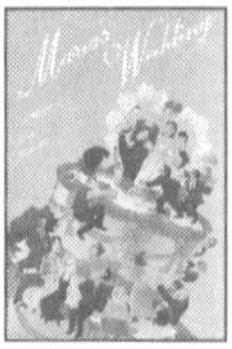

MARIA'S WEDDING™
by Nunzio DeFilippis, Christina Weir, & Jose Garibaldi
88 pages,
black-and-white interiors
$10.95 US
ISBN 1929998-57-0

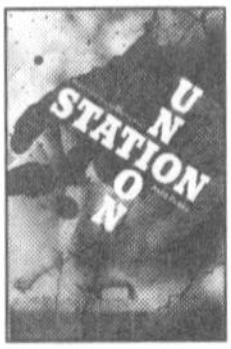
UNION STATION

UNION STATION™
by Ande Parks & Eduardo Barretto
112 pages,
black-and-white interiors
$11.95 US
ISBN 1929998-69-4

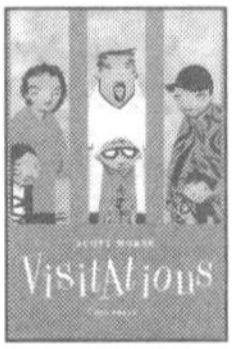
Visitations

VISITATIONS™
by Scott Morse
88 pages,
black-and-white interiors
$8.95 US
ISBN 1-929998-34-1

Available at finer comics shops everywhere.
For a comics store near you, call 1-888-COMIC-BOOK.
For more information on more Oni Press titles go to: www.onipress.com